KIERANTIMBERLAKE

FULLNESS

VOLUME 1
ALL IN

KIERANTIMBERLAKE

FULLNESS

The Monacelli Press

For those who have given us the opportunity to make architecture.

A Note on Structure
All In

KieranTimberlake: Fullness outlines seventeen projects completed over a decade. The projects traverse a range of scales and programs, from houses, to small and large campus buildings, to a park and transit hub and an embassy.

The book is split into two volumes. This volume—*All In*—presents photographs of each project, depicting the visual whole of the architecture as a fully resolved work. The second volume—*In All*—reveals the sum of its parts—the pivotal junctures that give rise to final form, including both moments of discovery and our pragmatic tools of analysis, prototyping, and communication.

The projects presented in this book live in the contemporary gap between the conventionally separated cultures of art and science to produce what English novelist and physicist C.P Snow called "creative chances." We believe these works become moving as architecture precisely because they dare to work in the seams between the two cultures, all in all, refusing to choose between them.

Contents

ALL IN

The Art of the Whole
Stephen Kieran and James Timberlake

Across much of the long arc of history, architecture was understood and conceived as a fully humanistic medium that fused diverse disciplines drawn from across the arts and sciences into a singular whole.

It was simultaneously aspirational and pragmatic, artistic and technological. The sciences underpinned the pragmatism of sheltering human activity that is at the origin of all architecture. The arts in turn gave aspirational shape and form to human shelter. At its best, the whole of an architecture of humanism was so integrated and unified that the origins and forms of its constituent parts could not be conceptually separated.

The same, of course, holds true today. Architecture is neither art nor science. It springs from both. It should not begin with science that adds art to form, nor should it begin with form that adds science to art. The two must evolve simultaneously, in unison, each giving form to and shaping the other. Roles in this unified world devolve into shape shifters, where art becomes science and science art. Form is not derived solely from the embodiment of physical forces, nor is it the product of singularly willful form shaping. Architecture becomes beautiful in large measure because its origins are no longer readily decipherable. It is whole: the physical embodiment of a worldview and process of making that thoroughly integrates art and science, rather than segregating the two.

However, in the polarities of contemporary life, art and science are today rarely seen as a unified field. English novelist and physicist C.P. Snow articulated this segregation in his 1959 Rede Lecture at Cambridge University, "The Two Cultures and the Scientific Revolution."

He pinpoints the moment of change at the inception of the Industrial Revolution of the eighteenth and nineteenth centuries. This is when thinking and making began to diverge, when conception and craft separated, with the machine increasingly assuming much of the role of maker. The import of the intellectual and factual rupture that was the Industrial Revolution cannot be overstated. While we have possessed tools to make objects of use at least since Neolithic times, the earliest tools were applied directly by individual human craft to form, shape, and join materials. The machines that powered the Industrial Revolution were conceptually just new tools, but their capacity to repeat motions and mass-produce artifacts altered the direct physical and emotional connection people had to making. New economies and industries arose to manage growing access to material products. In turn, scientific and engineering disciplines expanded and continued to form themselves about ever-evolving prospects for new and improved processes and products. Post-secondary education simultaneously evolved in ways that largely mirrored and reinforced the wedge between art and science. While Liberal Arts education in the United States offered students entryways into both cultures, the disciplines themselves seemed to fold inward, identifying themselves in contrast to the other.

Little has changed in the ensuing generations since Snow's talk, except the intellectual gap between the arts and the sciences continues to widen. Snow observed, "The clashing point of two subjects, two disciplines, two cultures—of two galaxies, so far as that goes—ought to produce creative chances. In the history of mental activity that has been where some of the break-throughs came."[i] In our current epoch, the two rarely meet, let alone "clash" together in a productive way. While significant transdisciplinary threads are beginning to be woven, these are most often between allied disciplines. Only occasionally do they cross the great divide between the arts and sciences. The increasing breadth and depth of training, knowledge, experience, and skill that are at the core of scientific understanding and advancement today contribute to, and perhaps even accelerate, this growing segregation between artistic and scientific ways of knowing. The sophistication of the tools we use to peer into the underlying form and behavior of our world have increased in unison with the depth of our understanding. These same tools, however—such as the Atomic Force Microscope used in nanotechnology or the Super Proton Synchrotron of particle physics—are often so specialized that they are beyond the capacities of all but the most sophisticated full-time users. As such, they deepen rather than unite artistic and scientific dialogue.

In architecture, the divide between science and art parallels that which Snow describes across the broader intellectual and cultural landscape since the Industrial Revolution began in the eighteenth century. However, the timetable and specific causes differ. While building products began to evolve with the Industrial Revolution, the methods of architectural assembly on individual sites, element by element, have remained stubbornly similar. The great difference-maker for architecture remains the uniqueness of site circumstance from building to building. As such, the moment of significant inflection, the epoch when the art and science of building began moving into separate disciplines, started significantly later, toward the end of the nineteenth century. There are three factors that gave rise to this gap. First, building systems increased from one or two more than a century ago to dozens today. In that time frame, we have moved from buildings of one system, such as fireplaces for heating, to dozens of systems: central heating, air conditioning,

i C.P. Snow, *The Two Cultures* (London: Cambridge University Press, 1959).

mechanical ventilation, hot water, cold water, waste water, sewage, electrical power outlets, lighting, fire protection, fire detection, lightning protection, security, telephone, data, and digital controls. Each system adds quality, convenience and control to our architecture. Each is designed, engineered, and inserted into architecture, with system and architectural enclosure each forming itself about the other. Second, each system requires energy, water, and other resources to operate. Not surprisingly, across the past century vast energy and environmental resources have been incrementally added to operate our architecture. Though they were once seen as unlimited, at least since the 1970s we are increasingly experiencing these resources as limited and not renewable. This realization has in turn spurred further specialized architectural initiatives dedicated to resource conservation and the integration of renewable energy resources into architecture. Third, since the 1990s an expanding array of digital interfaces that manage the entire contemporary enterprise of designing and making architecture has evolved. At their best, these tools provide deep insight into design and performance. We use them to form and visualize our architecture wholly and simultaneously across innumerable quantitative and qualitative dimensions. While the capacity to willfully and endlessly develop new shapes and forms receives much of the visual attention, the most important use of digital tools in present architectural realms is the design and management of the dozens of systems that now course through our buildings. Architecture now draws heavily upon computation, moving architects to a different skillset than their predecessors. Parametric modeling, visualization, systems integration, and the development of new algorithmic tools require constant upgrading, specialized knowledge, and skill to develop and use.

All these circumstances contribute to and reinforce the sense that architecture can no longer be whole. That it must choose: art or science, not both. One can begin with willful form making and bring science to bear to support and enable preconceived form. Or one can begin with science as the giver of form and add the art. At KieranTimberlake, we refuse to accept either of these contemporary poles. We embrace, explore, and seek out the full humanistic integration of architecture as an artistic science in search of a deeply resonant beauty.

ARCHITECTURE IS A JOURNEY OF DISCOVERY

As young architects drawn to the University of Pennsylvania, we were initiated to architecture within the aspirational spheres of Louis Kahn and Robert Venturi and Denise Scott Brown. Louis Kahn died soon after we arrived in Philadelphia, but his legacy loomed over and mentored us then, as it does now. Toward the end of his life, he moved backward to take us forward. He titled his seminal 1967 talk at the Aspen Institute, "I Like Beginnings." His fountain of youth was in the primal origin of things. His programs were not quantifiable tables and lists. He sought the nature and soul of our relationships to each other as the basis for forming rooms and structuring the planning relationships between those rooms into buildings, institutions, and cities. He committed to and gave agency to the most ancient and elemental materials. Brick, concrete, and wood—taken back to what they want to be, not what we wish them to do—become the material presence of his architecture. These materials give shelter to the institutions they house, bathed in the orchestrated light of day. It is this visible energy that he saw as the substance of space, the materials creating a worldly vessel to give shape and form to light and use.

Robert Venturi and Denise Scott Brown, our earliest direct mentors and employers, saw the prospects for a future architecture through a more formal, historicist lens that sought simultaneous histories and forms collated across time into single structures. Like Kahn, they too looked back to take us forward. However, their lens did not seek origins but instead an architecture that fused historic vestiges and references into contemporary construction. Architecture for Venturi and Scott Brown was fundamentally contemporary and modern at its core. At the same time, it was imbued with simultaneous histories, allowing the past and present to merge in a sort of canny dialogue across time. Yet in their work each history also remains distinct, pointing at and rhetorically illuminating the simultaneous difference of the other within the frame of the whole. We were enthralled with the brilliance and inclusion of this prospect. The present did not need to kill the past. Modernism did not need to engage in wholesale replacement. It could instead exist within and in conversation with the past. Given the pervasive disappointment and disillusionment at the core of American life in the 1960s and early 1970s, driven by the Kennedy and King assassinations and the Vietnam War, this was a compelling vision—in urban and architectural terms—for a way out.

Where one begins always impacts where one goes. It does so in two ways for the reflective young architect. First, our mentors provide an early, formative encounter with the relationship between underlying belief and architectural form. Second, they represent a touchstone to work not only with but also against as we forge our own ethic. The culture within which one first learns how to be an architect varies from school to school and practice to practice. Underlying each such culture, however, is a set of beliefs that guides the making of architecture, including the lenses that the architect chooses to frame and limit the work. These lenses—whether related to history, or materials, or environment, or physical form—become the core ethic of the architect. We believe that the design of the culture within which we make architecture is the most important act of design. The culture of our practice has been and continues to be our guide through the tens of thousands of decisions that go into any work.

As we set out on our own passage in 1984, we framed and bounded our beliefs both within and beyond these Philadelphia legacies. For us, *Complexity and Contradiction in Architecture* (1966) and *Learning from Las Vegas* (1973) were brilliant and insightful texts. They energized many of our generation, including ourselves. But the architecture that evolved from these texts had begun to seem limited, even repetitive and formulaic. This was an admittedly vague but increasingly discomforting observation for us as we set out on our own. Each work in this vein begat a similar work, not a new or thoroughly evolved work. Perhaps the problem lay in part in what Harold Bloom called the "anxiety of influence,"[ii] a generational need to distinguish oneself from what came before and set a different course. However, even at that time we sensed it was more than just a generational urge to be different. The problem for us lay in limiting the lenses, deciding what to look at and what to give agency to, what we desired to assume within the ethical boundaries of our work. Our instinct here was first that the lenses were being applied too narrowly, and second that the resolution allowed—even celebrated—the independence of form rather than the interdependence and union of all that should ethically underpin architecture. In short, the Venturi and Scott Brown texts and work were brilliant in theory, but they gave rise to an intellectual rather than a deeply emotive architecture. It was an inaccessible and academic approach that required deep knowledge of the history

ii Harold Bloom, *The Anxiety of Influence: A Theory of Poetry* (New York: Oxford University Press, 1973).

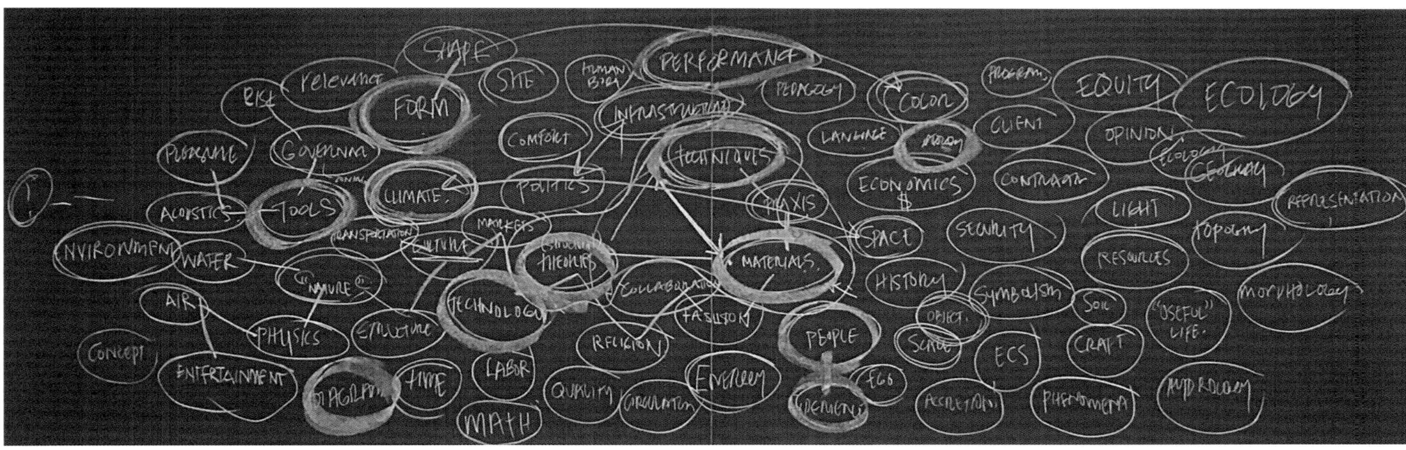

A mind map drawn by Billie Faircloth explores the varied, competing lenses that influence the creation of architecture.

of architecture and culture to comprehend the meaning of contemporary form.

It is our belief that architecture is most resonant, beautiful, and artful when it connects deeply across levels and dimensions in ways that resolve into a new whole—a whole that is expansive, unified, and far greater than the sum of its parts. As we began our own practice, we saw more promise in extending ourselves and our architecture by going back to the love of beginnings, the place where Kahn focused his reverie over the last several years of his life. We sought an architecture that begins at the beginning, with the materials and the assemblies of those materials that we use to give form to program and purpose. This requires a culture of inquiry, a culture that asks us to treat each work of architecture with something like the wonder of a child, to go back to origins and ask why. We had to become penetrating observers of the world as we found it. Unlike Kahn, however, who focused on a few elemental materials, we set out to give agency to and explore a wide range of contemporary materials, structures, and building systems. The latter focus on architecture as an assemblage of not just materials, but also of all the systems that course through all contemporary building, was a defining addition for us at the outset. It was our way of beginning a quest to reunify art and science as the inseparable soul of architecture.

As we observed it, the world of architecture we were entering had evolved from Kahn's architecture of silent, static rooms and walls, organized hierarchically as served and servant spaces and systems, to an architecture of materials with systems as the equally important life blood coursing through it all. This was a necessary and new prospect for the art of architecture. We set out to embrace this reality and to integrate material and system into a unified, compelling, and artful whole. We began at the beginning with each material and system, giving agency to each through research and asking what form it wanted to become rather than what shape we wished it to assume. Rather than assuming form and fitting materials and systems to this preconceived assumption, we sought deep understanding of inherent limits and possibility, then developed architecture from and about material and building prospects. We sensed immediately that the prospects for art ironically expand when we forget about art as a goal and immerse ourselves into the nature and composition of the materials and systems themselves. We deliberately set out to explore and expand our lenses, embracing several different structures and materials.

We developed a school with transverse block bearing walls, each pair supporting precast concrete planks and defining a classroom. Slate shingle infill walls enclosed the perimeter. Artfully profiled zinc flashings at windows and edges of the slate shingle walls provided constructive and visual boundaries. We developed a freestanding steel frame laboratory building with a self-bearing brick wall wrapping its perimeter. Windows were set back deeply within the brick walls at the plane of the interior steel frame, revealing the full depth of the masonry and its independence from the internal frame. We expanded a student center with a concrete frame and clad the perimeter in granite, employing an early example of open-joint rainscreen wall. The large granite panels lapped over the window frames beyond, reveling in the fact of the newfound independence between the external skin of a building and its window openings. We researched materials and improved upon assemblies. We did not bury systems. Instead we accepted them into the whole of the work, composing and integrating them holistically with program, structure, and enclosure. Each detail became a crafted embodiment of the whole.

The occasion of the publication of our first monograph, entitled *Manual* (2002), was for us an important moment, a summary, but also an impetus to forge an ambitious path forward. In the ensuing years around the millennium, we added significant further aspirations, tools, capacities, and processes. These in turn expanded the lenses through which we conceive our architecture. We began to see architecture as an enterprise that could no longer be segregated. We had to breach the cultural, legal, and ethical firewalls that divided us from building, from science and engineering, from product design, and from an environmental ethic that assumed responsibility for every ounce of material and joule of energy embodied within our architecture. We had to find a way to become whole again, to unify the science and art within our buildings. With these dramatically wider lenses, our architecture evolved rapidly. We expanded our agency, taking on the very structure of architectural production. With fifteen years of making behind us, we had come to believe that the soul and beauty of architecture was intimately bound to and threatened by the failure of the building arts to confront the full systematic complexity of design, fabrication, and construction in the twenty-first century. The science, systems, and engineering now inherent in architecture were overwhelming the quality and control of the art. The response for architects and clients to ever-escalating complexity was often to separate and choose between the two worlds: art or science, design or construction, but not both. A culture arose of the artist architect, a giver of form first, who only after establishing form then asks the scientist engineer to make it stand, to shed water, manage energy, and move air, energy, and systems. These are both worlds of limited lenses that premiate visual or constructed form above all else and relegate the hundreds of other ways we can form our architecture to supporting roles. The design-build model does the opposite, premiating the constructor as the agent of control and marginalizing the architect. Yet the result is the same. We needed rapid evolution, perhaps even a revolution, in the processes we were using to reassert control over the artistic and scientific whole of architecture.

We began by doubling down on the depth, breadth, and quality of our research during the first decade of the new century. We revamped the structure of our practice, infusing a research-based process of inquiry into our office, with commitments to full-time researchers drawn not only from architecture, but from engineering, environmental science, building physics, anthropology, and computation. Our aim was and is to bring architecture forward as a science and art by integrating disciplines and intelligences across the whole of the contemporary spectrum.

In 2003, we published *Refabricating Architecture* as a manifesto, a not-so-gentle call to transform the soul of design and construction with forward-looking processes that integrate rather than segregate art and science in the service of architecture. Models of collective intelligence and design, fabrication, and construction are at its core. While these integrative models did not exist in architecture and construction, they had evolved in the prior two decades across the aircraft, automotive, and ship-building industries. These enterprises recognize the vast extent and specialization of modern knowledge. Like the rapid technological progress of the Industrial Revolution, it is this exponential growth in the depth and breadth of knowledge that is at the core of the present separation of art and science. At the same time, it is ironic that the technologies that initially separated us can today instigate integration. While no individual can singly embody this expanse of skill and knowledge, emerging digital design and communication tools have offered us a new prospect for reunification. Parametric modeling tools drawn from other industries became for us the enabling systems that supported integrated conception and construction. Design, fabrication, and construction could be unified once again through the agency of the parametric building information model. This model would become the tool that offered the means to reconnect design and craft, thought and artistry, art and science. We also foresaw the prospect that BIM would become the enabling mechanism to relocate large portions of integrated component fabrication off site, to controlled factory production facilities, as a central strategy for improvement in the quality, cost, and artistry of architecture.

Based on our manifesto, we designed a small house on the Chesapeake Bay, building it virtually, part by part, as a solid parametric model, just the way Boeing was conceiving and building its aircraft. This model allowed us to conceive the house in our studio in Philadelphia, fabricate it in a factory in New Hampshire—panel-by-panel, module-by-module, integrating heating, air conditioning, and electrical systems off-site—and later assemble the dwelling within an aluminum scaffold over six weeks on site in Maryland. The artistry of the dwelling is all the more elemental and moving because it embraces and expresses the methods and systems of fabrication and assembly. Again, it became clear that thinking about everything but art yields art. We went even further with an experimental five-story house for exhibition at a museum in New York City. We modularized most of the structure in a factory in New Jersey, slashing the field assembly time to less than three weeks. We wrapped it with a double skin of PET plastic layered with printed circuitry and thin-film photovoltaics. The floors and stairs were translucent plastic with integrated LED lighting. The whole of the dwelling glowed, a lantern in the city. We disassembled it in a single week after the exhibition, each part bar coded for re-assembly, demonstrating complete recovery of all the carbon embodied in the materials of the home.

Over the decade that followed, we probed ever more deeply, beyond assemblies into worlds of new and evolving materials and methods. We did so in search of an ever broader and deeper ethical basis for our architecture. The environmental consequences of inhabitation have escalated. The crisis of access and affordability has widened. We recognize that art without science may move the soul but only acts as salve for the wound while ignoring broadly based ethical implications. Meanwhile, science without art lacks the soul to move us to action. We matured our research ethos, adding capacity and new knowledge bases that gave rise to ever more provocative questions. We rooted a culture of inquiry in the daily fabric of our studio. We sought not to force solutions, but rather to give them space to evolve, to come to us across time, through inquiry. No preconceptions. Every new undertaking began with questions. These questions provoked research, experimentation, prototyping, testing, revising, and improving. Some initiatives failed. Others succeeded and infused themselves into our architecture, forging a new alliance. We developed software tools to model the environmental impacts of our building material selections at the speed of design. Prior tools assessed the damage after the design was complete. That wasn't good enough. We sought ethical comprehension of impacts that extended beyond the surface of things. These new tools informed, guided, and pushed us while we evolved architectural form.

The data we unearthed became the provocation for action as we molded the art and science of our architecture about a deepening environmental ethic and understanding.

THE ART OF THE WHOLE

Architecture is the art of a thousand lenses—site, history, geology, materials, codes, time, cost, program, environment, to name but a few—coming together into singular focus. Each lens is a way of looking deeply into the circumstances about which the whole of architecture forms itself. Each lens connects us to the evolving ethical compacts that exist between architect, client, society, and place. Each allows us to see into and probe the boundaries of building. To the extent that we recognize and accept these lenses as agents, we broaden and enrich architecture, imbuing it with meaning and beauty.

What are these lenses, these looking glasses? Where do they come from? Who makes them? Who gets to decide which ones we must look through to see? Which are more important, which less? With each project, we begin anew. A mind map that makes visible their intersecting strands and competing urges is an initial exercise in bounding the art of architecture. We use geographical maps to guide us through unknown terrain to places of desire, but a mind map guides a different sort of journey—through awareness, to cognition, and on to understanding. Client aspirations, program, historical context, energy use, structure, systems; these are among the dozens of realms to be explored and probed for meaning and limit. We go deep here. The origin of all art and science is exquisite, penetrating observation of our world as it is. We research. We observe. We scan observed patterns for insights that inform the design problem. We seek relevant and compelling limits, boundaries to work against, as these give rise to possibility.

Scientists and artists intuitively understand that without defined and observed boundaries, there can be no creative thought. This is creativity's eternal irony— t cannot be unleashed freely without the presence of limits and constraints. Yet the second irony is that without the dissolution of boundaries between specific lenses and problems, there can ultimately be no art, no solution that goes beyond elements to a previously unseen whole. We will not find the art of the whole by seeking it at the outset within the bounds of an individual lens. Instead we find artistry by first giving agency to and immersing ourselves in the many lenses we use to realize all that architecture must assume and resolve within its form.

When these thousand lenses dissolve, the architecture becomes whole, a unified gestalt that is not the sum of its parts but something altogether new, unseen at the start, an amalgam of art and science. This is what we seek. While instinct and experience matter, it is impossible to know at the outset which lenses will give rise to compelling form. That becomes clear only in the forging of the work of architecture as it evolves from observation to discovery and insight.

A campus laboratory in Houston, Texas, offers a recent example of a work that gathers together dozens of threads drawn from the realms of art and science and weaves them together into a whole that renders the original threads indecipherable. The laboratory is a vessel that embraces in pragmatic and aspirational terms the passage of people and the elements that course through the site. In the hot southern environment, welcome wind accelerates through narrow slots and openings in the volumes, detailed and tuned through predictive software. Volumes arrange themselves in concert with the broadest definitions of program and context, from the originating campus master plan, to the use of mass to shade other volumes and outdoor spaces, to the arrangements of laboratories and offices that encourage encounter. Other software helps give form to the various façades as they are tuned to manage the sun, barring wavelengths that let too much heat in, and inviting wavelengths that provide glare-free daylight and view. The whole is here crafted as both art and science. It is formed about a deep sense of place that unfolds layer by layer, lens by lens.

This is the ethical responsibility of the architect: to engage the whole of the physical and social worlds we inhabit. No matter how enticing, we cannot allow ourselves to bow to the easy allure of any singular altar, be it art or science, visual form or environmental performance. We must commit to the hard work of embracing and forging new wholes through each work of architecture. Architecture becomes beautiful because of what it chooses to include, not because of what it excludes. When beauty and purpose are one, neither can be taken away. This is the urgent terrain of "creative chances" that C.P. Snow suggested will take us into new worlds.

It is our work to go deeper still, layer by layer, lens by lens, integrating what we cannot yet see, through the insights and tools of science, as we seek an even more expansive soul for architecture—one that moves us through waves of resonance with our most deeply felt aspirations for shelter and beauty.

A neon sign of repurposed letters from a defunct car dealership hang in our studio lobby and daylight shines through skylights stretching the full length our open work space.

KT

20

2

08-018

THE MUSEUM OF MODERN ART New York, New York

Cellophane House™

In 2008, The Museum of Modern Art held an exhibition on factory-made housing. In the tradition of the museum's "House in the Garden" series begun in the 1950s, the show would present full-scale designs for prefabricated homes. Our scheme was one of five selected for display on a site adjacent to the museum in Midtown Manhattan. We seized the moment to explore rapid assembly and disassembly methods, calculate the carbon embodied in materials, and prototype SmartWrap™, a lightweight, high-performance, energy gathering building envelope. The house stood for four months and was visited by nearly 750,000 people before it was systematically deconstructed for redeployment elsewhere.

MoMA
MoMA The Museum of Modern Art
Please enter on 54th Street for
HOME DELIVERY
FABRICATING THE MODERN DWELLING

HOME
DELIVERY
SHOP

PAGE

26 Opening night of the *Home Delivery: Fabricating the Modern Dwelling* exhibit.

28 At all floor levels the rooms open fully to the outside.

29 The aluminum frame is both structure and frame to join floors, walls, and ceilings.

30 The translucent stair is held together with mortise and tenon joints rather than adhesives.

31 Structural plastic floors and ceilings diffuse light throughout the house, and stairs are lit by LED lights in each tread.

32 Photovoltaics are adhered to the facade and connected with thin-film circuitry.

33 For the site on West 53rd Street, we extended the scaffold framework to a height of five stories.

34 While the building was designed to adapt to any site, it sat well with its now demolished neighbor, the American Folk Art Museum.

RICE UNIVERSITY Houston, Texas

Brockman Hall for Physics

Laboratories are usually relegated to large plots on campus edges, not slipped into intricate precincts. At Rice University, we test-fit the program for a new Physics building on ten sites before settling on a thin strip of green in the school's Science Quad. On this narrow site, we tucked 110,000 square feet of space into a new split-mass building of two thin bars—while extending Rice's dialect of rectilinear forms, covered passages, outdoor rooms, and intimate landscapes into the twenty-first century.

PAGE

36 Glass block, bricks, and terra-cotta baguettes extend the language of Rice's historic campus with contemporary materials and forms.

38 An axial campus passage extends the originating Ralph Adams Cram master plan through the center of the Hall of Physics.

40 Brockman Hall seen from an adjacent portal.

41 Campus passages slip beneath and through the lab, revealing a lecture hall.

42 The building is split into two parallel bars with an open passage that admits natural light and breezes.

43 One of the bars is elevated on columns to provide shaded outdoor space in the Science Quad.

44 The site is energized with open passages, covered outdoor rooms, and luminous interiors.

46 Water, wind, and people move through the slype between the two buildings.

47 Tapered, vertical board-formed columns sit lightly in the landscape among live oaks.

48 Landscape reveals itself layer by layer across a main campus axis.

50 Patterns drawn from physics mingle across the facade with reflections from nature.

51 Dichroic glass in the lobby fragments light in ceaselessly changing patterns.

52 Passages through, within, and up intersect at the main portal.

53 The laboratories are a vessel for unending experimentation.

54 A Penrose-patterned window provides long views to the north.

55 The architecture frames a canyon with axial campus walks below.

56 Columns line a temple-like space below the offices.

58 Bridges shelter events in an open court below.

YALE UNIVERSITY New Haven, Connecticut

Morse and Ezra Stiles Colleges

Our renovations at Morse and Stiles represent a conversation with a respected predecessor, architect Eero Saarinen, who designed the buildings in the late 1950s. Our work here was subtle and surgical, addressing student dissatisfaction with the housing dynamic composed largely of stand-alone single rooms, and the lack of activity space and green landscape. We transformed single rooms into suites and added below-ground student life space, made inviting and light-filled through skylights. We wove landscape through the architecture, bringing water and greenery to sunken courtyards and a waterfall and terrace that extends the dining hall into the courtyard.

EXIT

PAGE

60 The convergence of new landscapes, walkways, and underground rooms weaves new life into Eero Saarinen's Morse and Stiles Colleges.

62 The addition and alterations to Morse and Stiles Colleges brought Saarinen's midcentury modern buildings into the future with new programs and reimagined architecture.

64 A new sunken courtyard and bridge heighten the drama of the passage between Saarinen's two colleges.

65 New board-formed concrete moat walls became a plinth for molded concrete sculptures by Costantino Nivola.

66 Saarinen's remarkable dining hall was extended to the outside with new doors and openings.

67 The passage of water and people slope down to the dining hall.

68 A terraced fountain cascades down the courtyard, beneath a new wooden dining deck.

70 A new loading dock takes a sculptural approach to the pragmatics of service.

71 Sections of Saarinen's moat walls were joined to new walls to provide light below.

72 An addition underground created a unique dialogue between new and old.

73 Underpinning and exposing existing foundations generated an artful assembly of wood, steel, and concrete.

74 Tucked beneath a pedestrian bridge, the sunken court is a welcome outdoor lobby for the adjoining theater.

75 A glass wall wraps the sunken court, admitting daylight and view in subterranean spaces.

76 A large vault provides space for a tree's roots to grow down and through the addition.

77 Walls lean back, and ceilings lean up and out toward the sky.

78 The old concrete has stone cast within. The new concrete bears the imprint of wood formwork.

UNIVERSITY OF CALIFORNIA SAN DIEGO La Jolla, California

Charles David Keeling Apartments

Climate, landscape, and views gave shape to these sustainable residences in La Jolla, California. Standing among eucalyptus trees overlooking the coastal cliffs, the three buildings of the Keeling Apartments reference classic campus buildings, including their use of cast-in-place white concrete, while updating the aesthetic for the twenty-first century. The arrangement of rooms along single-loaded corridors invites daylight and breezes inside, enabling a passive ventilation strategy to replace mechanical cooling, while offering each student views to the ocean or mountains.

Keeling Apartments

1
2
3

2

GREEN • ENVIRONMENT • SUSTAINABLE
ECOLOGY • RENEWABLE • ECOSYSTEMS
NATURE • GREEN • ENVIRONMENT
SUSTAINABLE • ECOLOGY • RENEWABLE
ECOSYSTEMS • NATURE • GREEN
ENVIRONMENT • SUSTAINABLE
ECOLOGY • RENEWABLE • ECOSYSTEMS
NATURE • GREEN • ENVIRONMENT
SUSTAINABLE • ECOLOGY
ECOSYSTEMS • NATURE • GREEN
ENVIRONMENT • SUSTAINABLE
ECOLOGY
ECOSYSTEMS

4-2305

PAGE

80 In homage to environmental scientist Charles David Keeling, new campus apartments fuse the daily life of students with the natural world.

82 The whole of Keeling is an instrument that tunes the passage of sun, air, and people into, around, and through.

84 Water is both a precious resource and an occasional threat. Here, the landscape infiltrates and moves water as part of the daily experience.

85 The heart of Keeling is an open courtyard to rest, reflect, and commune with friends and the outdoors.

86 Structure, panels, and windows play across the facade in an ever-changing composition of light and shadow.

87 Seen from balconies between buildings, intersecting masses frame surprising streetscapes.

88 Three buildings create varied landscape ecologies at the edge of the campus.

90 Wayfinding is human-scale and sited to become furniture.

91 Stair landings between two buildings become balcony overlooks.

92 Flat and finned pre-cast concrete panels overlap a rectilinear frame.

93 What is background during the day becomes foreground at night.

94 Industrial fiberglass gratings transform a balcony into an ever-shifting display of light and shadow.

96 A green roof and walkway are an aerial analog to the lawns, bioswales, and paths to the courtyard below.

97 Double-height study rooms and lounges open to each other and are flooded with light and view.

98 Light rakes across the balcony and into an apartment.

99 Polished concrete floors, cast concrete walls, and 14-foot window walls enclose a student common room.

100 Exterior balconies and vertical fiberglass grates shade the south facade.

101 Pure concrete frame and precast stairs materialize in the light of the western sun.

102 At dusk, the balconies and walls glow in the soft light.

SIDWELL FRIENDS SCHOOL Washington, DC

Quaker Meeting House and Arts Center

The Quaker Meeting House forms itself about the ideals of silence and light, protected by multiple layers of structure and space that buffer the noise and activity of the campus beyond. Housed in a former gymnasium, the worship space embodies Quaker values of stewardship and simplicity informed by responsibility, reuse, and respect for the environment. The muted square space creates a tranquil, light-filled environment for the students, teachers, and staff who gather at Sidwell Friends each week for meeting for worship. A new art center adjacent to and below the meeting room provides enhanced creative and practice space, and the reimagined garden and loggia now serve as the school's main entryway.

PAGE

104 Suspended planes and walls in the Quaker meeting modulate light and sound. Absorptive and reflective surfaces amplify the smallest voice.

106 Elegantly thin canopies hover over building entries, transforming disjointed and nondescript earlier structures into an urban plaza at the heart of the campus.

108 Canopy, pocket garden, and gallery are thresholds that transport one from the busy campus to the quiet of the Quaker meeting.

109 The view through the entry doors reveals layers of space from the lobby, to the garden, the canopy, and the plaza.

110 Overlapping planes of the ceiling hollow out a mysterious light from above that projects a void at the center of the room.

111 Thin vertical slots allow light and fleeting views of fragments of nature into the meeting.

112 Silence and light are the architectural mediums that foster introspection as the meeting seeks the light from within. One of the great triumphs was hiding the systems of contemporary life—lights, wires—in order to make way for inner light.

114 Locker rooms in the old gymnasium improbably become loft-like art studios flooded with northern light.

115 A modest stair between worship and art spaces is a major connector for the entire campus.

116 Once called “Pigeon Alley,” this informal circulation route was enclosed with a glass and wood addition, formalizing an important link between the upper and lower campus.

117 The new wood facade, profiled in metal, expands music practice facilities above a new plinth.

118 Wood planes fold back to reverse bay windows at the corners within the metal frame of the addition.

120 The cantilevered addition is clad with black locust set at different depths to create shade and texture across the facade.

UNIVERSITY OF NORTH CAROLINA AT CHARLOTTE Charlotte, North Carolina

Center City Building

A new mid-rise building brings a suburban university into the city center, creating a distinctive presence in downtown Charlotte. Three masses rotate off the central axis of the tower, creating a sense of movement as well as a visible spatial differentiation between academic programs. Each of the three volumes houses a different academic community, with dedicated classroom, office, and meeting spaces. The building's aluminum and glass curtainwall and its unique form set it apart from the surrounding commercial high-rises, creating a vibrant new identity for UNC Charlotte's urban campus.

Club Car

1003
OFFICE

CENTER CITY BUILDING
320
UNIVERSITY of NORTH CAROLINA at
CHARLOTTE

ONE WAY
CENTER CITY BUILDING
CHARLOTTE

PAGE

122 A central obligation was to anchor development in this neighborhood at the edge of Charlotte's central business district.

124 The building is segregated into three-story neighborhoods to provide intimate environments for learning.

126 The tower enhances the skyline, with rotated masses that shade the floors below.

127 The architecture frames horizontal views to the park beyond and vertical views to the stair within.

128 A corner café brings the life of the street and park into the building.

129 The gallery frames both art and movement in public spaces.

130 Work environments are infused with light and view both in and out.

131 Rooms are nestled within larger volumes, connecting spaces to each other.

132 A continuous glazed stair pins the rotated blocks together.

133 A glass-walled student lounge and auditorium reveal the activity of the university at the main street entry.

134 The form gives the university an identity of vertical campus neighborhoods, distinguishing it from Charlotte's corporate skyline.

Edgar N. Putman Event Pavilion

JAMES A. MICHENER ART MUSEUM Doylestown, Pennsylvania

Edgar N. Putman Pavilion

The James A. Michener Art Museum desired a new pavilion to host lectures and events as part of a planned expansion. Built among the ruins of a historic prison in Doylestown, the museum engages with towering stone walls that create its exterior courtyard. We encouraged the client to place the event pavilion adjacent to the wall, in the center of the courtyard space, and to build it of seamless structural glass custom-made in Germany. Constructed of glass walls among the largest and tallest of their kind in North America, the pavilion stands as a crystalline jewel box—thin, delicate, and utterly transparent—before the massive stone wall of the historic prison.

Edgar H. Putnam Event Pavilion

PAGE

136 The 23-foot-high glass pavilion divides the sculpture garden into two outdoor rooms.

138 The glass pavilion has an ephemeral presence within the walls of a nineteenth-century prison.

139 A thin pivot door sits elegantly within a glass panel, free of hardware.

140 The glass pavilion is an object of wonder in direct conversation with the massive stone wall.

142 At dusk, the glass walls dissolve and the sheltering plane of the ceiling comes into focus.

143 Two slender columns allow the ceiling to float within the sculpture garden.

144 The space between the two walls dissolves into light, shadows, reflections, textures, and views between and beyond.

CENTER CITY DISTRICT Philadelphia, Pennsylvania

Dilworth Park

The land on which Philadelphia's City Hall now stands began its civic life as one of five squares plotted by William Penn in his 1683 plan for the city. By the late 1970s, the space next to City Hall had become a sunken concrete plaza—dark, dank, and difficult to navigate. We transformed it into an open park, accessible and inviting for daily use as a meeting place and transportation hub. Monumental new entryways of structural glass frame the historic masonry building and usher light and passengers into the transit networks below ground, while a lawn, splash fountain, and café enliven the civic space at street level.

Concourse access
Market Frankford Line
Broad Street Line

BOOTHBAY HARBOR

1401

Concourse access

PARK
Market Frankford Line

FedEx

Street

SIPS
PNC

SIPS

PAGE

PRIVATE RESIDENCE Pound Ridge, New York

Pound Ridge House

The site for this home is a boulder-strewn granite escarpment that rises over a hundred feet above a wetland. Its owners were drawn to the magical sense of tranquility they felt upon their first visit to this heavily forested land, much of which is striped with loose-laid fieldstone farm walls from the nineteenth century. When the time came for them to build a home on this pristine property, their mandate to us was simple but not simplistic: they wanted to live in a "house in the woods, of the woods," a home where they could feel the presence of the forest and rock ridges indoors and commune quietly with nature within naturally lit, open, airy, and warm rooms.

PAGE

168 The ascent to the house through a field of glacial boulders.

170 A ravine passes beneath a bridge.

171 A corner dissolves into the autumn landscape.

172 The living room nestles between rock ridges.

174 A wood ceiling extends from inside to outside.

175 A glass bridge spanning the ravine connects social and private spaces.

176 Stone sentinels anchor the house at both ends.

177 Organic and man-made forms engage across the day.

178 A brass stair rail twists upward from the ground.

179 Wood and stone treads float above a concrete base.

180 Glancing view to the ravine above from the ascending stair.

181 Skylights project illuminated portals down the hall.

182 The house is intertwined in a geological passage along the ridge.

184 A media room is an enclosed volume within the larger living quarters.

185 Kitchen, living, and dining flow together within the landscape.

186 Windows frame compositions in their own right.

188 The living room extends to an outdoor terrace.

189 The rock escarpment bounds the living room.

190 The dwelling dramatizes nature, sometimes disappearing into the landscape.

192 Polished and brushed stainless steel, coated copper, and glass magnify the presence of the forest and terrain.

PENN STATE UNIVERSITY Philadelphia, Pennsylvania

Consortium for Building Energy Innovation

These two buildings in the Philadelphia Navy Yard—one a retrofit of a former naval facility, the other a new classroom building—embody and demonstrate best practices for building energy efficiency. A lofty, sky-lit atrium formed within the skeleton of a decommissioned rec center is a highlight of the retrofit, helping to fulfill its role as a living laboratory of energy innovation where new technologies can be showcased. Meanwhile, the classroom building exemplifies a holistic approach to sustainability for new construction. This work was governed by an integrative process, including collaborative teams of architects, engineers, and builders.

PAGE

194 A 1930s Navy Yard recreation hall is a programmatic companion to the new classroom building.

196 The new building is long and low, stretching the full length of the block, providing an edge for the adjacent park.

198 The corner site opens to gather water, light, and view. The auditorium lobby cantilevers above a rock garden.

199 Steel beams and columns frame openings and windows.

200 Structure, circulation, and system intertwine across the length of the classroom building.

201 The rock garden forms a welcoming urban corner.

202 Open-weave brick shades southern light within a steel frame.

204 New stairs and bleacher seats lead to skylit mezzanines. Triangulated steel braces replaced the demolished brick walls separating the gym and pool.

205 Research labs and offices open to the great hall.

206 Glulam arches of a former pool and gymnasium provide dramatic structure for the new research center.

HARVARD UNIVERSITY Cambridge, Massachusetts

River House Renewal

Intensive site studies across the River House district at Harvard allowed us to understand the assets and challenges of these residences built in the 1920s and 30s. Our work to renew the Houses offers a way forward for these historic residences, bringing them up to date with the culture of contemporary student life while maintaining their architectural character. We upgraded the performance and sustainability of the buildings and made improvements to circulation, life safety, and accessibility, while adding smart classrooms and student activity spaces to under-utilized lower levels. State-of-the-art building systems were added to the historic dining halls and other rooms above as we carefully restored them to their original character.

McKINLOCK HAL

McKINLOCK HALL

FITNESS
001

HARVARD
2015

QUINCY
HOUSE

STONE
HALL

KT

KIERANTIMBERLAKE Philadelphia, Pennsylvania

Ortlieb's Bottling House

During the second half of the twentieth century, the industrial building that now houses our firm's design and research studio served an important role as the bottling house of the Ortlieb's Brewery complex, with a daily capacity of one million bottles and cans. We saw the potential to reimagine this National Register building as an office, workspace, and shop that highlights the "makers" still present in the historic manufacturing neighborhood of the Northern Liberties. An open floor plan, lofty ceiling, restored light monitor, and operable windows afford us ample daylight and fresh air and allow us to experiment with passive cooling strategies to reduce energy consumption.

1869
HOUSE
SPEED 25 LIMIT

DEWALT

AUTHORIZED
PERSONNEL
ONLY

PAGE

232 A new one-piece stair lands on a platform in the lobby of a former beer bottling plant.

234 The 1948 International Style industrial building is on the National Register of Historic Places, and is one of the few remaining industrial buildings in a rapidly evolving neighborhood.

236 The facade enclosing the old loading dock opens fully to the street.

237 The former loading docks make for a wonderful street-front shop and fabrication lab.

238 The original walls have been modified over time with concrete masonry, steel guards, lighting, and fire protection systems.

239 The loft-like interior serves a wide array of needs.

240 Mock-up panels adorn the walls of the former beer cooler.

242 The zippered stair risers descend from the studio above through a new floor opening.

243 The rollers of the creased steel stair meet the platform like a ship's gangplank.

244 The roof monitor and double row of side windows infuse the interior with light.

246 Meetings can and do occur everywhere and anywhere in the studio.

248 Artificial lighting is rarely needed in the studio.

CONGREGATION RODEPH SHALOM Philadelphia, Pennsylvania

Renovation and Addition

This historic synagogue is an icon of Philadelphia's Broad Street artery, brought to new life through insertions that include a four-story addition and a street-level community room clad in channel glass that acts as a beacon of light. Our renovation of the building preserves its most beloved characteristics—paying respect to the limestone-clad exterior, stained glass windows, and mosaics—while enhancing its functionality and circulation to serve an ever-growing congregation, the oldest Ashkenazic assembly in the Western hemisphere.

CONGREGA ON RODEPH SHALOM
LOVE PEACE AND PURSUE IT
RODEPH
SHALOM
ONE WAY
NO TURN

שויתי

CONGREGATION RODEPH SHALOM

CONGREGATION RODEPH SHALOM
LOVE PEACE AND PURSUE IT

PAGE

250 The exterior walls of the synagogue continue within the addition. The conversation between new and old is ever-present.

252 A former used car lot is now an urbane and welcoming corner streetscape.

254 An art gallery mediates between the synagogue and the addition.

255 Light-filled hallways, stairs, and galleries connect new community rooms to the synagogue.

256 Built in 1928, the synagogue is listed on the National Register of Historic Places.

258 A luminous new meeting hall converses with the limestone-clad mass of the historic synagogue.

259 Glowing channel glass walls of the addition are a welcoming presence on Broad Street.

260 The new meeting hall and walled garden form indoor and outdoor meeting spaces along the flank of the historic building.

262 A new loggia opens the synagogue community to the city.

PRIVATE RESIDENCE Willits, California

High Horse Ranch

Site is the primary driver in the design of this home high in the mountains of Mendocino County. Our goal was to preserve the wilderness and enhance the experience of climbing the sloping site to its pinnacle and taking in views of the valley below. Using a material palette of wood, steel, and glass, we designed a main house and two tethered satellite cabins. During the assembly and construction process, preconstructed modules were craned into place and set upon their foundations, barely touching the site.

The Art of Richard Diebenkorn

PAGE

264 Materials and architecture frame and extend the landscape of this Northern California site.

266 The home touches the landscape lightly and embraces the forces of nature.

267 Corner windows separate wall planes and open glancing views out to the landscape.

268 The canyon-facing wall opens completely, drawing the landscape up, into, and through the home.

270 The kitchen anchors the great room between living and dining.

271 A wood ceiling floats above glass walls and paintings by Joan Moment.

272 Corner windows frame views and a moveable tile artwork by Brendan Lott.

273 An outdoor fireplace mirrors the glow of the interior at dusk.

274 Natural light floods the gallery through a hidden clerestory.

275 Rooms are defined by tree lines and views, instead of walls and windows.

276 The wood ceiling extends the interior and shelters outdoor living at the canyon edge.

278 Guest cabins are nestled into pocket clearings with unique views.

279 Sliding glass blurs the boundaries of nature and shelter.

280 Roof, Corten steel, firewood, and porch are the simple elements of this retreat.

281 Walls and overhang shelter and expand the porch entry.

282 The cabins sit on platforms above the steep terrain.

WELLESLEY COLLEGE Wellesley, Massachusetts

Pendleton West

With this project, Pendleton Hall was reenvisioned as an arts loft with open-plan studios, while a three-story addition was designed to unite it with the adjacent Jewett Arts Center. Giving new life to the tradition of making at the college, the renovations and addition here lend coherence to the art and music programs and create a new entryway to the Academic Quadrangle. Materials and textures echo the natural landscape on this campus of hills and valleys, with cast-in-place concrete bearing the imprint and texture of wood.

#80
#100
#120
#180
FF

PAGE

284 An elevated courtyard between new and old space frames moments of pause and passage.

286 A new art and music center defines a crossroad between Paul Rudolph's 1956 Jewett Arts Center to the left and Charles Klauder's 1934 Pendleton Hall.

288 A campus walkway wraps around and under the building as it ascends to the Academic Quadrangle.

289 Ceiling, window, wall, and historic fragment converge at the front door.

290 Red fabric acoustic ceilings trace passage through the addition.

291 A garden bridge traverses a green roof.

292 A slice of open space between buildings reveals unexpected light, foliage, and views.

294 Board-formed concrete and white oak interiors originate in the wooded surrounding.

295 Light and views beyond inspire the performance of music within.

296 Reflective wood and absorptive gaps between tune the hall like the sounding board of a piano.

298 A new green roof meets a worktable in the printmaking studio.

299 The flexible loft-like interior accommodates a range of art-making and teaching.

300 The outside is brought in through slivers of light.

301 Materials mirror the site, reflecting and accepting nature and light.

302 Board-formed concrete walls receive and amplify light and shadow throughout the day.

BROWN UNIVERSITY Providence, Rhode Island

Engineering Research Center

This project defines a new Engineering Quadrangle at Brown, joining together three disparate structures. The transparent, light-filled research center brings greater visibility to the inquiry and experimentation being performed on campus while inviting students and faculty from other disciplines to its welcoming commons. Loft-like, flexible lab spaces with open plans and accessible systems foster dialogue between researchers across disciplines. Throughout the building, a series of imaginative installations by artist Spencer Finch asks occupants to consider the beauty of tessellated patterns and their underlying mathematics.

BROWN
UNIVERSITY
BROWN

PAGE

304 Spencer Finch's work *The Garden in the Brain* fuses the underlying structures of art and engineering.

306 The architecture gives the School of Engineering an urban presence within the city of Providence.

308 A new quad anchors the central campus axis.

309 The walk to the front door parallels a portal into nanotechnology.

310 Portico, stair, and entry passages intersect at the hinge between wings.

311 A stair landing perches above the double-height passage along the nanotechnology lab to the street.

312 All campus walks converge in an Engineering Commons, the heart of the new school.

313 Spencer Finch's pattern design in glass provides a veil between a teaching lab at the front door and the Engineering Commons.

314 Teaching is front and center at the main entry, visible to and from the Commons and the quad beyond.

316 A lightwell brings view and greenery into the joint between existing and new.

317 Flexible collaborative workspaces adjoin and open to the laboratories.

318 Exterior shading systems manage glare indoors and project ever-changing shadows on walls and floors.

319 A terraced bench navigates the grade change between the new building and existing structures.

320 Students ascend the terraced quad to the front portico with the nanotech suite beyond.

321 Lawn, porch, bay window, and stone bench create a welcoming and urbane front yard along Brook Street.

322 Three elements intersect at the front door: expanded metal screening, vertical shading fin, and woven metal strands.

323 Fins are wide against the facade to enhance insulation and curve out to a thin blade to shield the sun and permit expansive views from within.

324 The combination of horizontal and vertical shading to the south manages solar gain and glare, allowing a largely transparent envelope.

326 Approached from the west, the facade appears almost solid as it shields late-day sun.

US DEPARTMENT OF STATE London, United Kingdom

US Embassy in London

The program brief for the new US Embassy in London was so detailed that when we printed it out, the stack of pages stood more than one meter tall. Our challenge was to encompass principles of transparency, openness, and equality, creating a strong sense of welcome, while also meeting requirements for security, diplomatic work, and environmental sustainability. We responded with a crystalline glass cube atop a monumental colonnade set within a park—a holistic fusion of urbanism, building, and landscape.

UNITED STATES OF
James Monroe
William Pinkney
Jonathan Russell
Aaron Vail
Andrew Stevenson
Reverdy Johnson
J. Lothrop Motley
Robert C. Schenck
Joseph H. Choate
Whitelaw Reid
John G. Winant
W. Averell Harriman
Anne Legendre Armstrong
Kingman Brewster, Jr.
Matthew W. Barzun

ITATIVES OF THE UNITED STATES OF AMERICA TO THE COURT OF

ED STATES, IN
PROVIDE FOR TH
TO OURSELVE
OF AMERICA. ART
TION. 2. THE HOUSE OF
THE PEOPLE OF THE SEVERA
UISITE FOR ELECTORS OF THE
RHODE-ISLAND AND PROVIDENCE
ENNSYLVANIA EIGHT, DELAWARE
AND GEORGIA THREE
AUTHORITY THEREOF SHALL
B SHALL CHUSE THEIR SPEAKER
REOF SHALL HAVE BEEN
ED STATES, SHALL BE
RAISING REVENUE SHAL
EXECUTIVE
PEACHMENT
UNDER THE
7. ALL BILLS
PROPOSE OR CONCUR WITH AMENDMENTS
OF REPRESENTATIVES AND THE SENATE
THE UNITED STATES
THAT HOUSE IN WHICH IT SHALL HAVE ORIGINATED
AND PROCEED TO RECONSIDER IT
AGREE TO PASS THE
ECONSIDERED AND IF APPROVED
IN A TENDER IN PAYMENT OF DEBTS
CONSENT

SHALL HAVE THE
BE PRESENTED TO THE
TWO THIRDS OF THAT
TO THE OTHER
IT SHALL
EX POST
CONGRESS.
OR SHIPS OF WAR
DELAY.

PAGE

328 The consular entry welcomes visitors through an open 30-foot-high colonnade.

330 The new embassy in Nine Elms has generated a vibrant new urban district along London's South Bank.

332 Formed glass panels create a rhythmic pattern across the whole of the north riverfront facade.

333 Glass pavilions provide a graceful threshold to the embassy and infrastructure for photovoltaic panels.

334 A tile mosaic by American artist Sean Scully titled *Golden Frieze* lines the walkway to the Consular entry.

336 Following the tradition started at Grosvenor Square, the names of the ambassadors to the Court of St. James's are engraved into the wall beneath the Great Seal of the United States.

337 Dignitaries and staff enter through the main lobby.

338 A monumental artwork by Rachel Whiteread titled *US Embassy (Flat pack house; 2013-2015)* adorns the lobby.

340 The ceiling is pulled back from windows to increase natural light in consular waiting areas.

341 Translucent materials and natural light provide serenity in the consular waiting room.

342 A double-height gallery features a glass stair and bridge, bringing daylight to exhibit and event spaces.

344 The gallery stair is constructed with glass treads and risers.

345 Mark Bradford's commissioned artwork, *We the People*, is visible from Nine Elms Lane.

346 Six two-story gardens spiral up through the building, providing social and conference spaces and alternative routes between floors.

348 Regional plantings specific to United States ecosystems populate the interior gardens.

349 The Pacific Forest garden features a variety of ferns and perforated metal "trees."

350 The outer envelope is ever-changing across days and seasons.

352 A massive shaped column rises from the lower gallery to the main lobby above.

353 The view from Nine Elms Lane along the bank of the River Thames.

354 The embassy glows golden in the late day sun.

356 A curved path draws walkers from the traffic of Nine Elms Lane into the quiet of the embassy landscape.

Acknowledgments

The thousands upon thousands of acts of design that align to project the wholeness of our architecture are beyond the capacity of any individual. They are the product of a carefully curated culture. That culture has been forged across time, both within and beyond the cauldron of each of the eighteen projects that are the subject of this book. We are grateful to all who have given themselves to the creation of this culture, and to the architecture that reflects its presence in our lives.

COLLABORATORS 2008 - 2018

Alex Aftuck
Joanne Aitken
Abigail Allen
Eli Allen
Margo Angelopoulos
Perry Ashenfelter
Michael Awalt
Bradley Baer
Tatiana Baglioni
Alexander Bahr
Carlo Bailey
Amanda Baker
Saarinen Balagengatharadilak
Jacob Balfour
Lawrence Baraldi
Collin Barlage
Roderick Bates
Grace Bertolino
Michael Bianchi
Christopher Boskey
Casey Boss
Emily Bower
Isaac Bracher
Dimitri Brand
Amanda Brandt
Karen Branick
Derek Brown
Kenneth Burkhalter
Carmen Bushong
Andrea Calabretta
Vincent Calabro
Stephen Cantando
Stephanie Carlisle
Mary Carroll-Coelho
Camille Cazon
Britt Chapman
Zhengneng Chen
Merlin Cherian
Christy Choi
Jason Ciotti-Niebish
Laura Clark
Melissa Clark
Richard Clark
John Cline
Alex Cohn
Jared Cole
James Coleman
Christopher Connock
Connor Cook
Fookling Cooper
Adrian Corbey
Aracely Coronado
Daniel Cox
Andrew Cronin
Erin Crowe
Joshua Cruz
Brandon Cuffy
Jeff Cumpson
Peter Curry
Andrew Curtis
Kate Czembor
Yang Dai
Nathalie Dalziel
Mark Davis
Jonah Detofsky
Neonta DeVose
Emily Dodson
Angie Door
Chadwick Dotson-Jones
Abraham Drechsler
Jacob Dugopolski
Adrienne Dunsing
Claire Edelen
Erica Ehrenbard
Eric Eisele
Christopher Elsworth
Elizabeth Escott
Andrew Evans
Billie Faircloth
Charles Falone
Jessa Farkas
Danielle Farmer
David Feaster
Georgeanna Foley
Jose Galarza
David Gale
Amanda Gann
Sara Gatti
Yves Gauthier
Bradley Gay
Ben Gidaro
Haley Gilbert
Paul Golisz
Anamika Goyal
Michael Grauer
Jazz Graves
John Greenwood
Benjamin Gregory
Evan Greulich
Brad Groff
Wade Hart
Zuoda He
Laurent Hedquist
Daina Higgins
David Hincher
Ashley Hobart
Richard Hodge
Andrew Hoffmann
John Holden
Tyler Holdren
William Hood
Trevor Horst

Cheryl Hu
James Huemoeller
Scott Jenkins
Aurora Jensen
Steven Johns
Whitney Joslin
Uk Jung
Elizabeth Kahley
Kevin Kaminski
Bradley Kaye
Brian Kerr
Elizabeth Keshet
Stephen Kieran
Kyuhun Kim
Yunoh Kim
Darby Kline
Randall Knight
Alexander Knipe
Aaron Knorr
Caleb Knutson
Christian Kraft
Matthew Krissel
Lorraine Liu Kung
Nora Kusaka Herrero
Lily Lauben
Lawrence Lazarides
Blake Lehmann
Jeremy Leman
Vincent Leung
Emily Levy
Jacky Liang
Kai Liao
Adria Longenderfer
Rolando Lopez
Rebecca Zhenyuan Lou
Adam Loughry
Lingzhe Lu
Sofia Lundeholm
Daniel Luster
Nathan Lutz
Christopher Macneal
Suzanne Mahoney
Richard Maimon
Kevin Malawski
Jacob Mans
Elliot Manuel
Jessica Mathews
Kristi Maulding
Joseph Maylie
Alexander McBride
Andrew McBride
Peter McBride
Jon McCandlish
Sean McKay
Brian McVeigh
Taylor Medlin
Kiana Memarandadgar
Ryan Meuller
Joshua Meyer
Brendan Miller
Kate Milligan
Petar Mitev
Anthony Monica
Johann Mordhorst
Patrick Morgan
Iain Morris
Benjamin Muller
Ollie Nieuwland-Zlotnicki
Shelly Noga
Fatima Olivieri
Brayton Orchard
Justin Oscilowski
Lea Oxenhandler
Amanda Palasik
Edward Palka
Misook Park
Shaun Patchell
Sydell Paul
Crystal Peebles
Yuye Peng
Jeannette Penniman
Christian Pepper
Timothy Peters
Chris Peterson
Sara Pettit
Max Piana
Lana Press
Daniel Preston
Matthew Price
Dominic Primerano
Shawn Protz
Bella Purdy
Cesar Querales
Benjamin Quint-Glick
Murali Ramaswami
David Rariden
Joyce Raybuck
Carly Regn
Sarah Richendollar
Lisa Rigby
George Ristow
David Riz
Marilia Rodrigues
Alexander Roscoe
Sam Rosen
Lane Rubin
Marina Rubina
Peter Salim
Nora Salzman
Sarah Savage
Bessie Saylee
Thomas Schaperkotter
Cooper Schilling
Andrew Schlatter
Nathaniel Schlundt
Emily Scrimger
Jonathan Seagull
Paul Seletsky
Nicholas Sillies
Dunja Simunovic
Luke Sinopoli
William Smarzewski
Jason Smith
Keri Smotrich
Charles Sparkman
Theresa Starrs
Rachel Stoudt
Leah Strenger
Neil Stroup
Bailey Stultz
Megan Suau
Asarin Tandanand
Kevin Tayah
Jordan Teitelbaum
Maria Tiliakos
James Timberlake
Daniel Toretsky
Sebastian Torres
Sarah Totora
Bunny Tucker
Ian Utz
Saeran Vasanthakumar
Rachel Vassar
Neena Verma
Clifford Vickrey
Kathryn Viechnicki
Janki Vyas
Matthew Wagar
Ryan Wall
Kristine Wander
Patricia Ward
Ryan Welch
Michael Westrate
Lauren Whitehurst
Carin Whitney
Laura Willwerth Dunbar
Thomas Wilson
Janice Woodcock
Paul Worrell
Alison Worthington
Laura Wu
Sean Yang
Evan Yassky
Jae Pil Yoo
Hale Youngblood
Loren Yu
Zinat Yusufzai
Paul Zamorano
Lingfeng Zhang

Project Data

CELLOPHANE HOUSE

2008

Client: The Museum of Modern Art, *Home Delivery: Fabricating the Modern Dwelling Exhibition*

New York, New York

1,800 square feet

Single-family home with roof deck and carport

Fabrication and Assembly: Kullman Buildings Corporation; Construction Manager: F.J. Sciame Construction Co., Inc.; Structural Engineer: CVM; Exterior Wall Panel Fabricator: Universal Services Associates, Inc.; Lighting Consultant: Arup

Photographs by Peter Aaron/OTTO: pages 26, 28–34

BROCKMAN HALL FOR PHYSICS

2011

Client: Rice University

Houston, Texas

110,000 square feet

Laboratories, lecture hall, seminar rooms, offices, collaborative spaces, outdoor gathering space, astronomy observatory

Construction Manager: Gilbane Building Company; Construction Administration Consulting Architect: Jackson & Ryan Architects; Structural Engineer: Haynes Whaley Associates; MEP Engineer: CCRD Partners; Lab Consultant: Innovate Lab Systems Design; Landscape Architect: The Office of James Burnett; Civil Engineer: Walter P Moore; Acoustics: JE Acoustics; Lighting Consultant: Arup; Concrete Design Consultant: Fred Langford Architect

Photographs by Peter Aaron/OTTO: pages 36, 40, 42, 46, 47, 50, 51, 56–57; Paul Hester: pages 53–55, 58; Michael Moran/OTTO: pages 38–39, 41, 43–45, 48–49, 52

MORSE AND EZRA STILES COLLEGES

2011

Client: Yale University

New Haven, Connecticut

285,000 square feet (260,000 renovated; 25,000 additional)

Residential space, dining halls, libraries, lounges, fitness and dance rooms, art and music studios, theater, outdoor gathering spaces

Construction Managers: Turner Construction Co. and The Whiting-Turner Contracting Company; Structural Engineer: CVM; MEP Engineer: Altieri Sebor Wieber; Landscape Architect: OLIN; Civil Engineer: URS Corporation; Environmental Consultant: Atelier Ten; Lighting Consultant: Arup; Acoustics: Metropolitan Acoustics; Theater Consultant: Theatre Projects Consultants; Food Service Consultant: Ricca Newmark Design; Interior Design: Marguerite Rodgers Interior Design

Photographs by Peter Aaron/OTTO: pages 60, 62–63, 65, 67, 68–78; Richard Barnes/OTTO: 64, 66

CHARLES DAVID KEELING APARTMENTS

2011

Client: University of California San Diego

La Jolla, California

147,000 square feet

Six-person apartments, lounges, green roof terrace, courtyard with multiple use areas

Construction Manager: Swinerton Builders; Structural Engineer: Inertia Engineers; MEP Engineer: IBE Consulting Engineers; Electrical Engineer: Sparling; Civil Engineer: Nasland Engineering; Landscape Architect: Spurlock Poirier; Environmental Consultant: Atelier Ten;

Lighting Consultant: Candela

Photographs by Tim Griffith: pages 80, 82–87, 90–102; Lenska Aerials: pages 88–89

QUAKER MEETING HOUSE AND ARTS CENTER

2011

Client: Sidwell Friends School

Washington, District of Columbia

22,940 square feet

Worship space, art studios, music rehearsal rooms, gallery space in circulation areas, campus entry

General Contractor: The Whiting Turner Contracting Company; Structural Engineer: CVM; MEP Engineer: Bruce E. Brooks & Associates; Civil Engineer: VIKA, Inc.; Landscape Architect: Studio Bryan Hanes; Lighting Consultant: Arup; Acoustics: K2 Audio

Photographs by Michael Moran/OTTO: pages 104, 106–120

CENTER CITY BUILDING

2011

Client: University of North Carolina at Charlotte

Charlotte, North Carolina

143,000 square feet

Classrooms, offices, auditorium, bookstore, gallery, café, plaza

General Contractor: Rodgers Builders; Architect of Record: Gantt Huberman Architects; Structural Engineer: King Guinn Associates; MEP Engineer: McCracken & Lopez, PA; Civil Engineer: Bulla Smith Design Engineering; Landscape Architects: Shadley Associates, PC; Lighting Consultant: Arup; Acoustics: Metropolitan Acoustics

Photographs by Peter Aaron/OTTO: pages 122, 124–134

EDGAR N. PUTMAN PAVILION

2012

Client: James A. Michener Art Museum

Doylestown, Pennsylvania

3,400 square feet

Event and exhibition space within a sculpture garden

Construction Manager: Adams-Bickel Associates, Inc.; Structural Engineer: CVM; MEP Engineer: Bruce Brooks & Associates; Civil Engineer: Carroll Engineering Corporation; Landscape Architect: OLIN; Lighting Consultant: Sean O'Connor Lighting, Inc.; A/V and Acoustics: Metropolitan Acoustics; Curtainwall Consultant: Dewhurst Macfarlane & Partners

Photographs by Michael Moran/OTTO: pages 136, 138–144

DILWORTH PARK

2014

Client: Center City District

Philadelphia, Pennsylvania

4-acre park and transit hub

Underground transit hub, public park and plaza, café

Project Manager/Civil Engineer: Urban Engineers, Inc.; Landscape Architect: OLIN; General Contractor: Daniel J. Keating; Structural Engineer: CVM; MEP Engineer: Urban Engineers, Inc.; Glass Engineer: Dewhurst MacFarlane and Eckersley O'Callaghan; Lighting Consultant: Arup; Food Service Consultant: Ricca Newmark; Fountain Design: CMS Fountain Consultants; Public Art: Janet Echelman

Photographs by James Ewing/OTTO: pages 148–157, 159–161, 163–166; Christopher Leaman: pages 146, 158, 162

POUND RIDGE HOUSE

2014

Private Residence

Pound Ridge, New York

5,250 square feet

Single-family home

General Contractor: Prutting & Company; Structural Engineer: CVM; Civil Engineer: Kellard Sessions Consulting, P.C.; Landscape Architect: Reed Hilderbrand; Lighting Consultant: Filament 33

Photographs by Peter Aaron/OTTO: pages 168, 170–192

CONSORTIUM FOR BUILDING ENERGY INNOVATION

2014

Client: Penn State University

Philadelphia, Pennsylvania

The Center for Building Energy Science & Engineering

35,000 square feet

Atrium event space, Immersive Construction Lab, symposium, workrooms, telepresence room, meeting rooms, and offices

The Center for Building Energy Education & Innovation

25,000 square feet

Lecture hall, equipment gallery, classrooms, training centers, offices, and administrative space

General Trades Contractor: Ernest Bock & Sons, Inc.; Construction Manager as Agent: Balfour Beatty; Structural Engineer: CVM; MEP Engineer: Bruce E Brooks Associates; Civil Engineer: Hunt Engineering; Landscape Architect: Studio Bryan Hanes; Environmental and Lighting Design: Atelier Ten; A/V and Acoustics: Metropolitan Acoustics

Photographs by Michael Moran/OTTO: pages 194, 196–206

RIVER HOUSE RENEWAL

2015

Client: Harvard University

Cambridge, Massachusetts

340,000 square feet (three houses combined)

Student rooms, common rooms, classrooms and study spaces, dining halls, music and art rooms, library, gallery, fitness center, theater

Stone Hall: Construction Manager: Dimeo Construction; Structural Engineer: CVM; MEP Engineer: BVH; Landscape Architect: Stephen Stimson Associates; Civil Engineer: Nitsch Engineering; Environmental and Lighting Design: Atelier Ten; Acoustics: Metropolitan Acoustics

McKinlock Hall: Construction Manager: Dimeo Construction Company; Structural/Envelope Engineer: CVM; MEP: BVH; Civil Engineer: Vanasse Hangen Brustlin, Inc.; Landscape Architect: Stephen Stimson Associates Landscape Architects, Inc.; Environmental and Lighting Design: Atelier Ten; Acoustics: Metropolitan Acoustics

Dunster House: Construction Manager: Turner Construction; Structural/Envelope Engineer: CVM; MEP: vanZelm Heywood & Shadford, Inc.; Civil Engineer: Vanasse Hangen Brustlin, Inc.; Landscape Architect: Stephen Stimson Associates Landscape Architects, Inc.; Environmental and Lighting Design: Atelier Ten; Acoustics: Metropolitan Acoustics

Photographs by Michael Moran/OTTO: pages 208, 210–230

ORTLIEB'S BOTTLING HOUSE

2015

Client: KTRE, LLP

Philadelphia, Pennsylvania

60,000 square feet

Open plan office, flexible conference rooms, fabrication labs, lobby, below-grade parking, and gym

Contractor: AJ Lewis; MEP Engineer: Elliott-Lewis; Lighting Consultant: Fisher Marantz Stone; Historic Preservation Consultants: Jon Milner, Architectural Historian; Surveyor: SSM Group

Photographs by Jason Fulford: pages 246–247; Michael Moran/OTTO: pages 232, 234–245, 248

RODEPH SHALOM RENOVATION AND ADDITION

2016

Client: Congregation Rodeph Shalom

Philadelphia, Pennsylvania

75,000 square feet, existing (7,000 renovation; 18,000 addition)

Accessible lobby, gallery, multipurpose community room, courtyard, offices, and classrooms

General Contractor: INTECH; Structural Engineer: CVM; MEP: Bruce Brooks & Associates; Civil Engineer: Stantec; Landscape Architect: Studio Bryan Hanes; Lighting Consultant: Sean O'Connor Lighting; Acoustics: Metropolitan Acoustics; Interior Design: Marguerite Rodgers Interior Design

Photographs by James Ewing/OTTO: pages 250, 252–262

HIGH HORSE RANCH

2016

Private Residence

Willits, California

2,580 square feet (main house); 290 square feet each (guest cabins)

Main House: Master suite, open kitchen/dining/living area, gallery, study, terrace, and porch; Guest Cabins: Porch, bedroom, bathroom

General Contractor: Buckeye Construction, Moderna Homes (Modular); Structural Engineer: CVM; MEPF: Engineering 350; Civil Engineer: Adobe Associates, Inc.

Photographs by Tim Griffith: pages 264, 266–282; Featured artworks by Joan Moment: page 267, Brandon Lott: page 268

PENDLETON WEST

2017

Client: Wellesley College

Wellesley, Massachusetts

58,000 square feet (48,000 renovation; 10,000 addition)

Art studios, music rehearsal hall, salon, classrooms

General Contractor: Consigli; Structural Engineer: LeMessurier; MEP Engineer: Altieri Sebor Wieber; Civil Engineer: Nitsch Engineering; Landscape Architect: Michael Van Valkenburgh Associates; Acoustical: Acentech; Lighting Consultant: Fisher Marantz Stone; Environmental Health and Safety: OEHS2; Environmental Consultant: Atelier 10

Photographs by Michael Moran/OTTO: pages 284, 286–295, 298, 300 301; Bob O'Connor: pages 296–297, 299, 302

ENGINEERING RESEARCH CENTER

2017

Client: Brown University

Providence, Rhode Island

80,000 square feet

Laboratories, microelectronics and bio cleanrooms, seminar rooms, collaborative spaces, offices

Construction Manager: Shawmut Design and Construction; Structural and MEP Engineer: BuroHappold; Civil Engineer: Vanasse Hangen Brustlin; Laboratory and Cleanroom Design: Research Facilities Design; Landscape Architect: Gustafson Guthrie Nichol; Sustainability: Vidaris; Facade Consultant: BuroHappold

Photographs by Peter Aaron/OTTO: pages 308, 319–325; Warren Jagger: pages 304, 306–307, 309–318, 326

US EMBASSY IN LONDON

2018

Client: US Department of State

London, United Kingdom

600,000 square feet

Public and work spaces, ceremonial and symbolic spaces, dining, recreation and support spaces within a landscaped precinct

U.S. Lead Contractor BL Harbert International; U.K. Lead Subcontractor Sir Robert McAlpine; Structural and Physical Security Engineer: Thornton Tomasetti; MEP, Civil, Facade and Sustainability Engineer: Arup; Landscape: OLIN; Interior Workplace: Gensler; Technical Security Design: Sako & Associates; Lighting Design: Fisher Marantz Stone; Acoustical and Audiovisual: Shen Milsom Wilke; Fountain Design: CMS Collaborative; Graphics and signage: C+G Partners; Roofing and Waterproofing: Wiss Janney Elstner Associates; Elevator, Façade Access: Lerch Bates; Glass Engineering: Heintges & Associates; London Real Estate: Cushman & Wakefield; London Planning: DP9

Photographs by Richard Bryant: pages 328, 330–353, 356; Jason Hawkes: pages 354–355

KIERANTIMBERLAKE

FULLNESS

VOLUME 2
IN ALL

KIERANTIMBERLAKE

FULLNESS

The Monacelli Press

A Note on Structure
In All

KieranTimberlake: Fullness outlines seventeen projects completed over a decade. The projects traverse a range of scales and programs, from houses, to small and large campus buildings, to a park and transit hub, and an embassy.

The book is split into two volumes. The first volume—*All In*—presents photographs of each project, depicting the visual whole of the architecture as a fully resolved work. This volume—*In All*—reveals the sum of its parts—the pivotal junctures that give rise to final form, including both moments of discovery and our pragmatic tools of analysis, prototyping, and communication.

The projects presented in this book live in the contemporary gap between the conventionally separated cultures of art and science to produce what English novelist and physicist C.P Snow called "creative chances." We believe these works become moving as architecture precisely because they dare to work in the seams between the two cultures, all in all, refusing to choose between them.

Contents

IN
ALL

ONE WAY
BUILDINGS
323

Cellophane House™

The Museum of Modern Art

New York, New York

We designed Cellophane House for an exhibition at The Museum of Modern Art titled *Home Delivery: Fabricating the Modern Dwelling.* The exhibit explored the ongoing modernist experiment with the off-site fabricated dwelling. "Home delivery"—coupled together, those two simple and familiar words have a compelling ring of not just hope but expectation. Almost anything today can be ordered online and delivered to our homes. Why not the house itself?

The MoMA exhibition had two components. First, drawings, photographs, films, models, archival materials, and fragments of historic dwellings were assembled within MoMA's exhibition halls to reveal the pervasiveness of this aspiration from the nineteenth century to the present. Second, an adjoining lot on West 53rd Street was made available for the construction of five competitively commissioned, off-site fabricated dwellings, including Cellophane House.

There is a certain beauty inherent in a well-crafted question. Cellophane House is our response to the question of how an artful dwelling can be home delivered. Great experiments often have long lineages, marked by both successes and useful failures. The lineage of Cellophane House began with an earlier experiment that explored the radical idea of a printed building skin made of flexible polymer that we trademarked as SmartWrap.

While we were able to make a small functioning prototype of SmartWrap for exhibition, we needed to suggest that this sample could be much more—that it could be scaled to enclose architecture. To convey this potential, we wrapped printed representations of SmartWrap around an aluminum scaffold system in the garden of the Cooper-Hewitt National Design Museum in 2003.

We recall standing in that garden and thinking to ourselves that this small, spiraling scaffold and its skin could indeed become a building. A subsequent experiment involved the use of this same aluminum scaffold system as the structure for our two-story Loblolly House on Taylors Island, Maryland. This success emboldened us at Cellophane House to go higher, to five stories, and to wrap the entirety of the dwelling in a double-skin development of SmartWrap.

Limitations often generate beautiful and creative solutions. We were afforded only fourteen days on site to erect Cellophane House. This required substantial pre-assembly into structural modules at an off-site building factory in New Jersey. The strategy we developed divided each floor into three sections: front, back, and middle. The back U-shaped section included not only the aluminum frame structure but the stair. The front U-shaped section housed a folding-door system. When set by riggers, these structures were linked at the center with beams and floor panels.

The visual and pragmatic elegance here is in the marriage of spatial and structural typologies appropriate to the circumstance. The fully off-site fabricated spatial modules at the front and back not only provide self-stabilizing structure during building, but they also integrate off-site the most complex portions of the dwelling: the stairs and the fully operable front wall. The central portion between the modules is open space, spanned simply by flat floor panels dropped into position between the front and back modules. This allowed us to decrease the volume of the space to be shipped by one-third. The last thing you want to ship is air.

Joints are everything at Cellophane House. The materials and methods of assembly and disassembly require that all joints be exposed and accessible. The impact of gravity and wind forces are everywhere revealed and legible. The eye inevitability makes its way along these lines of force to the joints between members. The members and the methods of attachment trace the invisible lines of force between joints as they move across and down the dwelling. The simple joint between columns and beams is the central player here. Lateral gravity loads are transferred through a pair of plugs that slip into drill holes in columns. The L-shaped joints between columns and beams are in turn held in position by proprietary hardware that slips into the scaffold channels. Diagonal struts transfer lateral loads from joint to joint, stabilizing the whole. There is a richness and an elegance to the artistry of revelation in this joinery. Circumstances of assembly and disassembly give rise to the art of the joint.

The aluminum scaffold is the matrix to which all other materials attach. Cellophane House pushes the luminous world of contemporary and evolving materials to new extremes. The aesthetic effect is one in which nearly every surface within the dwelling becomes a lamp. We are accustomed to reflected light in space. But here nearly every surface is translucent or transparent, and light transfer is through materials. Not only are the walls sheathed in PET polymer with photovoltaic tracery, but even the floors, ceilings and stairs are translucent acrylic. The result in the evening is an inviting, lantern-like glow from within.

The stair treads are acrylic panels joined through simple mortise and tenon construction with no adhesives or further structure. The stair walls with which the treads interlock are acrylic. The floors are translucent cellular plastic.

The assembly of architecture is engrained with direction. Its construction almost always proceeds from parts to the whole. It is rarely designed to reverse itself through disassembly from the whole back to the parts. Cellophane House asks the dwelling to go both ways: from parts to whole and back again to parts.

This demand was in part pragmatic. Cellophane House had to come apart at the end of the exhibition even more swiftly than it came together. To enable compact shipping and storage of the house, the aluminum scaffold frame modules that were delivered to the site were disassembled after the exhibition into individual members: columns, beams, joints, and diagonal struts. Wall panels were disassembled whole as flat panels with structure and skin intact. Each part was tagged with a barcode linked to the Building Information Model used to design and assemble the dwelling. In this way the parametric model becomes the repository of instructions for reassembly in another location.

Heating, cooling, ventilating, lighting, and powering architecture uses as much as 40 percent of the total energy our culture consumes. The consequence of this has been a decades-long focus on operational energy. A lesser-known fact is that the equivalent of as much as forty years of operational energy is already embodied in a building upon completion of construction. Embodied energy is the new frontier of conservation. The most compelling way to conserve is to reuse what already exists. Through design for disassembly, Cellophane House takes reclamation and re-use to a closed loop that offers nearly complete recovery of embodied energy.

SMART FACADE

The facades build upon prior work exploring two ideas. The first is the use of print technology to develop active multi-functioning facade performance, proposed in our 2003 SmartWrap exhibition at the Cooper Hewitt, Smithsonian Design Museum. At Cellophane House, we extended this idea to an actual dwelling. Printed ink circuitry and solar collectors, here represented by copper tape circuitry and thin film photovoltaics, are adhered to the PET plastic facades. The second idea is the deployment as an active wall with two layers of PET to either side of a large air cavity. The cavity can be sealed or opened at the top to retain or evacuate heat depending upon environmental circumstance.

DIS/CONNECT

The joint is a key detail in off-site fabrication of architecture. To erect most of the dwelling in a week, we developed factory-fabricated front and back modules with a floor plate linking the two at each level. Modules stacked one atop the other. Structural sleeves within each lower aluminum frame receive the frame above, which are then pinned together. The floor plates connecting front and back modules are bolted to ledgers. Diagonal cables attached to bolted brackets stabilize the five-story dwelling. All joints are rapidly assembled and disassembled with rachets.

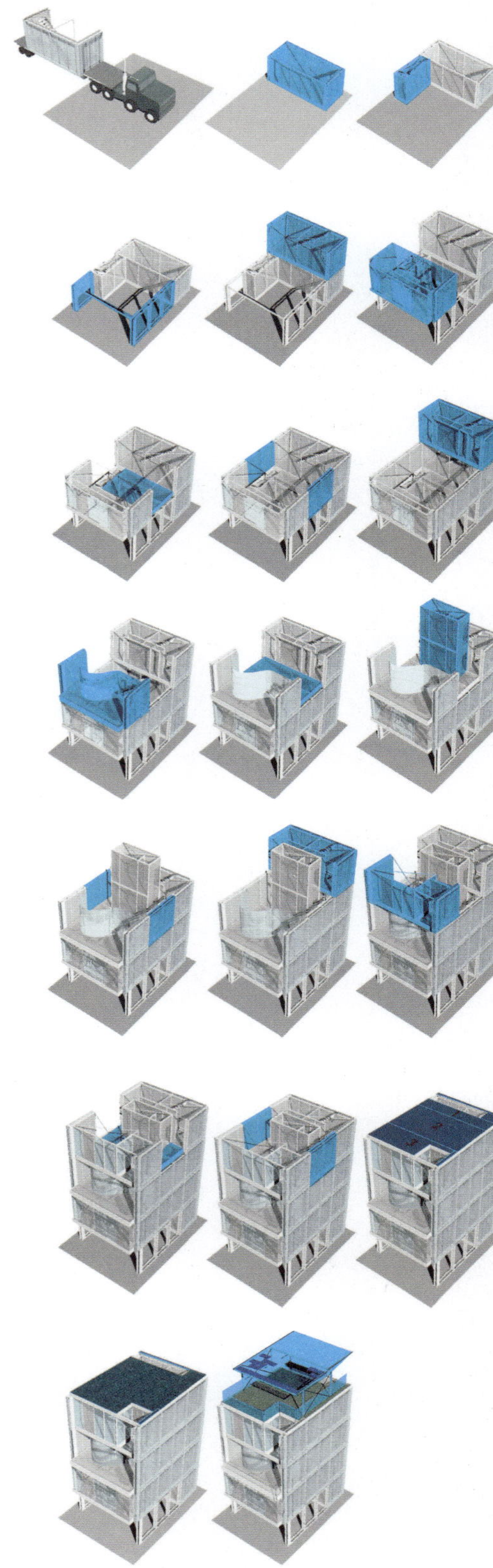

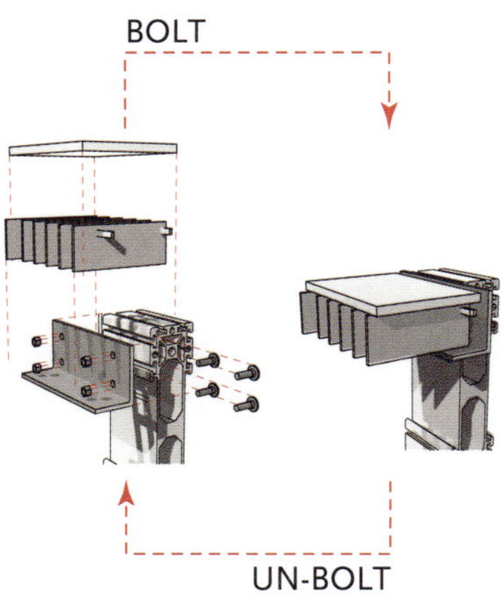

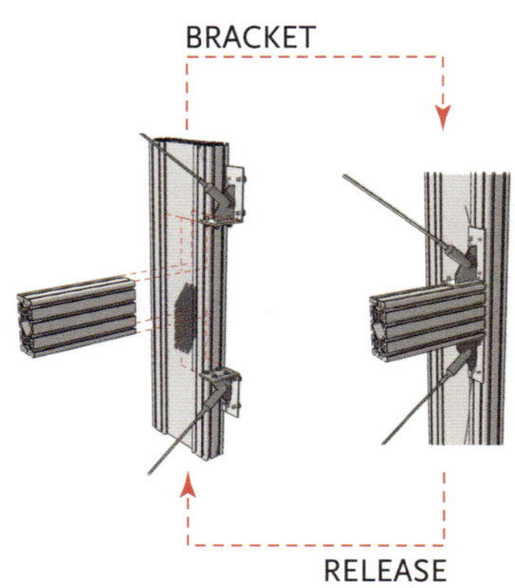

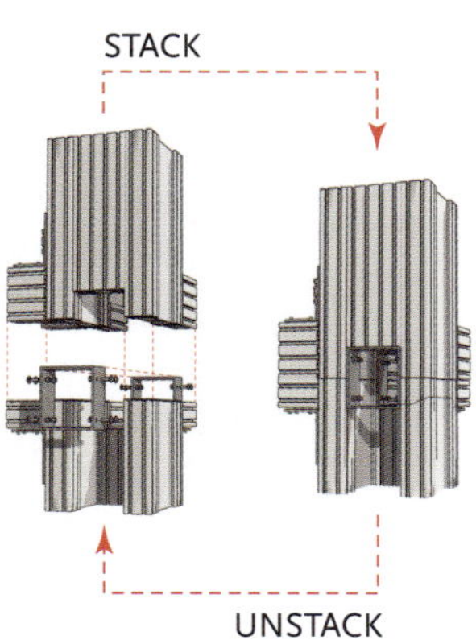

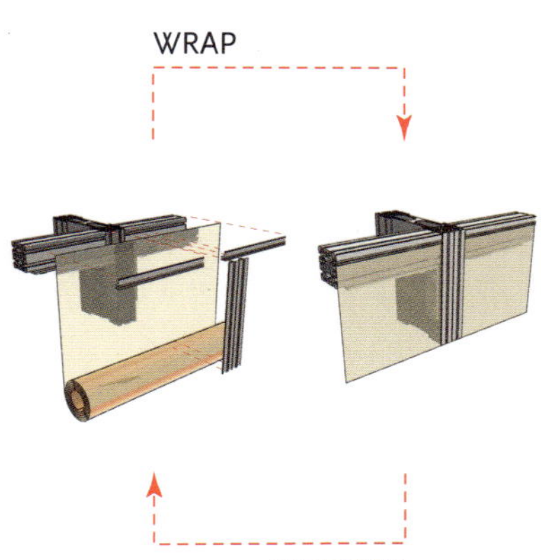

DIS/ASSEMBLY

Design and construction could not be separated here. They are one and the same. The whole of the dwelling is both more artful (delightful) and well-built (firm) as a result. Special cradles were designed and fabricated to lift the aluminum modules from flatbed trucks to the dwelling. The same cradles raised off-site fabricated bathroom modules, fixed to floor plates at the factory, into the frame. Lifts gave access to the perimeter for installation of the active facade panels.

While fully assembled module frames arrived at the site to speed erection, after the exhibition units were offloaded from the frame to the ground, then labeled and disassembled for compact shipping and storage.

KULLMAN

PARK

McCollister's

McCollister's

	 **Frame**	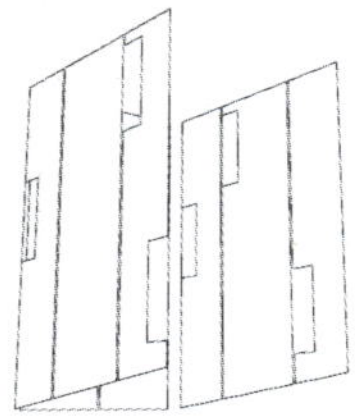 **Skin**	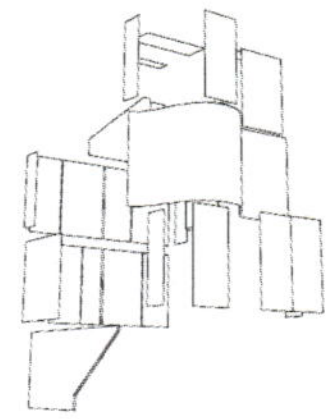 **Glazing**	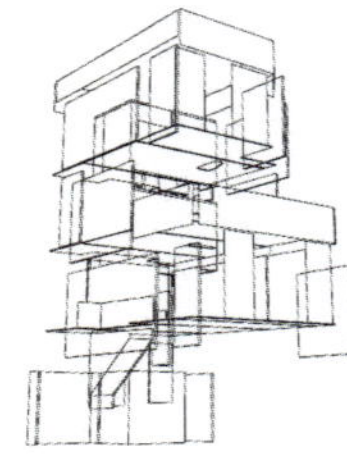 **Wall Panels**	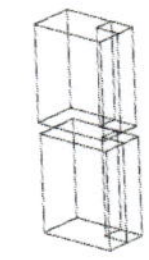 **Bathroom Pods**
MATERIAL	Bosch Aluminum Framing Steel Connector Steel Bolts	SmartW (PET) Aluminum Louvers	Schüco Glass Schüco Aluminum Frame	3form Varia (PETG)	Fiberglass
TOTAL EMBODIED ENERGY	955,631 kWh	22,224 kWh	71,423 kWh	22,577 kWh	71,448 kWh
% RECOVERED	99.99%	100%	100%	100%	100%
RECOVERED EMBODIED ENERGY	954,675 kWh	22,224 kWh	71,423 kWh	22,577 kWh	71,448 kWh

	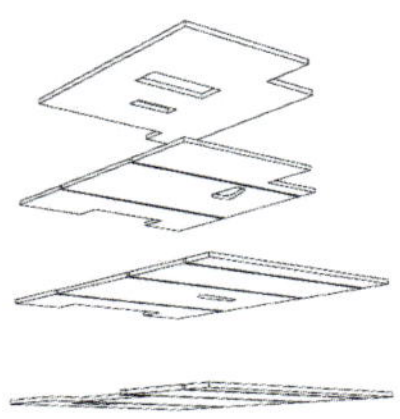 **Floors**	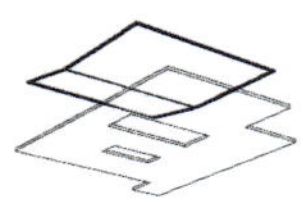 **Roof**	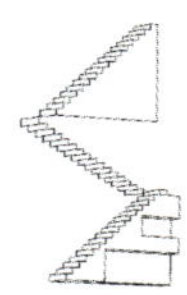 **Stairs**	 **Foundation**
MATERIAL	Aluminum Grate 3form Stage (PC)	PVC Downspouts Steel Gutters Danpalon (PC)	Acrylic	Concrete Steel Rebar
TOTAL EMBODIED ENERGY	146,008 kWh	8,214 kWh	235,001 kWh	15,264 kWh
% RECOVERED	100%	100%	100%	0%
RECOVERED EMBODIED ENERGY	146,008 kWh	8,214 kWh	235,001 kWh	0 kWh

TOTALS FOR 1,800 SF

TOTAL EMBODIED ENERGY
1,547,790 kWh
860kWh/sf

% RECOVERED
98.95%

RECOVERED EMBODIED ENERGY
1,531,570 kWh
851kWh/sf

EMBODIED ENERGY

The energy embodied in the fabrication and construction of architecture is already vast the day it opens for use. This is not something that architects, engineers, owners, and builders normally measure today. During the design of Cellophane House, we measured the energy in kilowatt hours of all building components. The total for even this small dwelling approaches 1,550,000 kWh. Design for disassembly allows for nearly full recovery of that energy.

Fragments of the house are now deployed in our office. Our Tally® software product grew out of this early effort. It measures impacts, including embodied energy, throughout the design process so we can make informed and ethical judgments.

Brockman Hall for Physics
Rice University
Houston, Texas

Despite their importance to the educational missions of colleges and universities, it is tempting to relegate new science teaching and research facilities to the periphery of our campuses. This happens because it is easy to do so, not because it is right. The buildings are often large, sites are scarce, control and separation from the elements are paramount, and service access is constant. It is also easy because a sense of otherness continues to exist between the arts and the sciences. They are often seen as worlds apart, opposing intellectual poles rather than aspects of a singular enterprise.

Rice University did not take the easy path of segregating disciplines. The site chosen for Brockman Hall is located close in, opposite Hamman Hall, a performing arts building, and amidst several existing science laboratories from earlier eras. Together with Brockman Hall, the whole of this assemblage is deeply integrated, not only to the original campus, but to the entirety of Rice. This sense of wholeness derives from the legacy of the first Rice University campus plan, developed by Cram, Goodhue & Ferguson in 1910. It is a brilliant work of planning that continues to organize and guide the physical university more than a century later.

Most new university plans, then and now, are set pieces. They rely largely on two tools to organize a campus: building mass and open space. The Cram plan instead deploys a unified and extensible field of lineation—not a fixed form but a network that focuses on the framework for movement, connection, and views. Even as the campus has expanded from a handful of buildings to hundreds, that unified field continues to extend outward to the south, north, and west from the core campus.

Brockman Hall forms itself first within the warp and weft of this campus tapestry. The importance here is the unity and connection of the university through the extensibility and agency of the originating plan. The whole is a shifting field of campus passage about which Brockman emerges.

Three complementary principles give rise to the massing strategy for the building. First, we sought to integrate and extend the underlying substance of the campus tapestry and emulate the "thinness" of the best historic buildings. Second, we committed ourselves to forming the massing and the facades about the site's microclimate. Lastly, we set the goal of internal program organization that would maximize flexibility and collaboration across time.

The building program includes three basic components: laboratories, offices and conference rooms, and a lecture hall. To maximize flexibility, the basic massing was split into two blocks: a laboratory wing and an office wing. The vastly differing intensity of building systems needed to serve these two uses informed this decision. The extensive mechanical systems serving the laboratories could be concentrated in a penthouse immediately above. The offices with their lower ceiling heights and simpler mechanical services would be in a separate but connected structure. The corollary benefit of this organizational strategy is the passage of faculty and student researchers back and forth from laboratory to offices and conferences across the day and evening, fostering casual encounter across disciplines. The large lecture hall is located at ground level to one side of the through passage, with shared facilities on the opposite side. Together these heavily visited and more public ground-level spaces provide welcome activity that spills out to the adjoining passages and courtyards.

Finally, the microclimate of the immediate site gives form to every aspect of Brockman Hall. The Houston climate is hot and humid. Locating the taller and wider laboratory wing to the south provides welcome overshadowing of the courtyard to the north. This allows considerable glass at the offices in the courtyard, offering light and view while shielding them from unwelcome heat gain and glare. The two floors of the office wing are raised a full story above ground atop elegant, board-formed, tapered concrete pilotis. The resulting space is a covered porch at the center of the Science Quadrangle, an open and welcoming shelter from rain and sun that extends comfort and use of the exterior landscape. The narrow north-south and east-west passages through the building massing are slypes that accelerate moderate afternoon wind velocity and ventilate the shaded public space beneath the elevated bar of the building. A welcoming water feature provides evaporative cooling during the afternoon hours, enhancing the appeal of this space.

The design accepts this complex agenda—the physical form of the campus, the microclimate at the site, and the specific building program—giving equal agency to all three goals. The same principles extend to the eight distinct building facades, joined together by two glass bridges, that result from the split massing. Just as the massing itself deeply fuses Brockman to the campus and its climate, so too are the individual facades tuned to circumstance. The southernmost facade facing the central campus is informed by and references the vertical proportional systems of the historic Cram structures as well as the lineation and scale of the masonry striations at their base. It is largely opaque as it shields both the laboratories and the site from intense southern sun. The ventilated rain screen wall keeps the heat load off the laboratory walls. Just enough light is let into the laboratories through narrow vertical windows to provide daylight and orientation to time and place. The narrow east and west flanks are shielded from the low-raking sun angles by vertical fins. The north facades are glass. Both spandrel panels and windows are articulated with Penrose frit patterns to hint at the activity inside and to carry forward the tradition of iconography on Rice buildings.

The word "campus" embodies the idea of a collection of buildings in space. To test a work of campus architecture, one should first walk through the campus, then into, around, and through the new work. The test should be repeated from different directions, circling, using all the senses, to experience it fully within its place. Brockman Hall is seamlessly woven into the fabric of Rice University. The campus would be less without its galvanizing presence. Rather than extending historic forms, it extends principles. Utterly of its time, it speaks to its purpose to further the understanding of physics. And it does so within the intellectual and physical framework of Rice University.

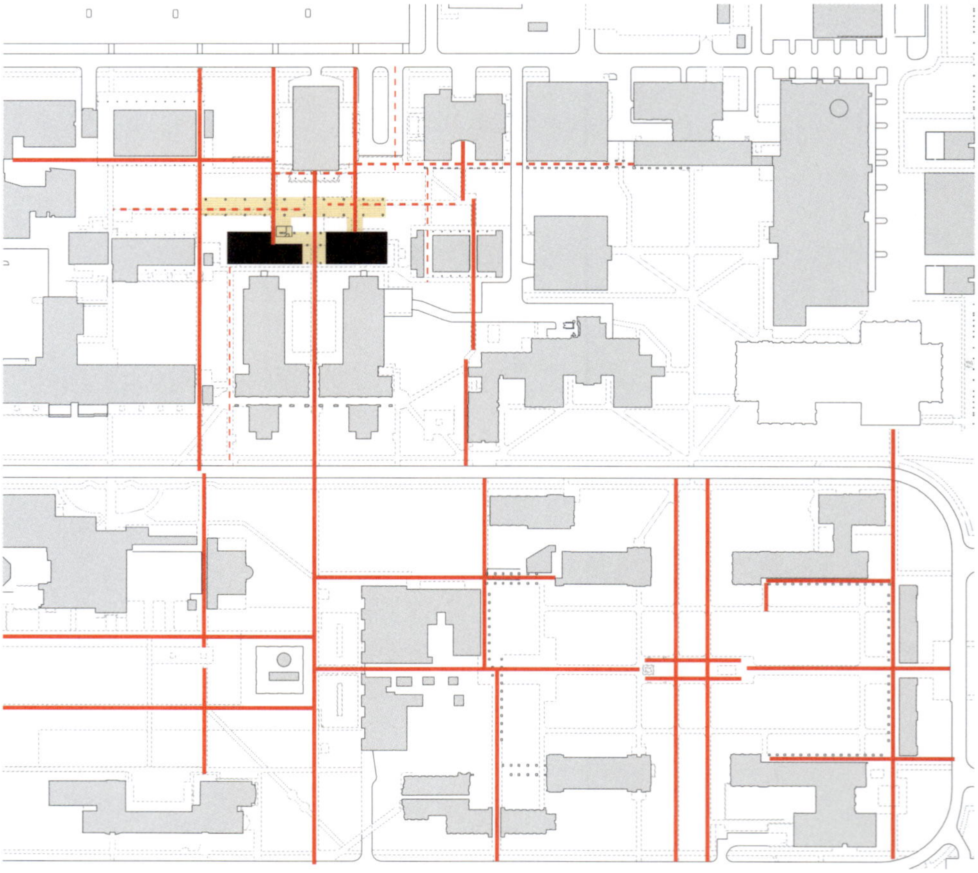

WARP AND WEFT

The brilliance of the originating Ralph Adams Cram master plan for the Rice campus is in its extensibility. It is not based upon set pieces, but rather upon networks of regulating lines that loosely define axis, edge, scale and proportion. Brockman is a large science laboratory, but more than one hundred years after adoption of the Cram plan, it fits easily within and extends the campus framework. The opaque limestone and brick bases of the original campus structures are reinterpreted with translucent glass block between brick bands. They allow light into the spaces beyond, and they glow at night, illuminating campus walks.

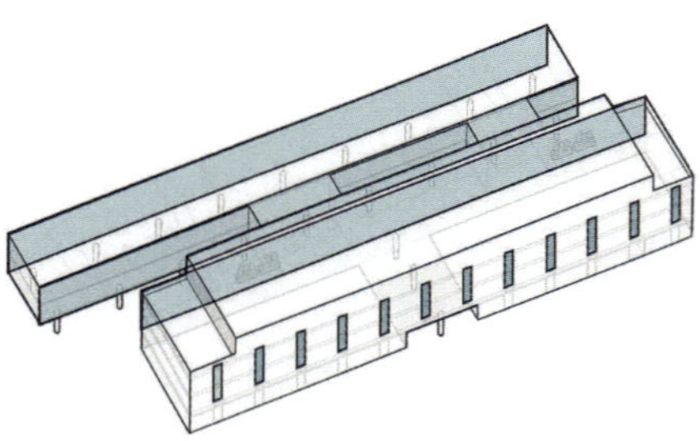

Daylighting

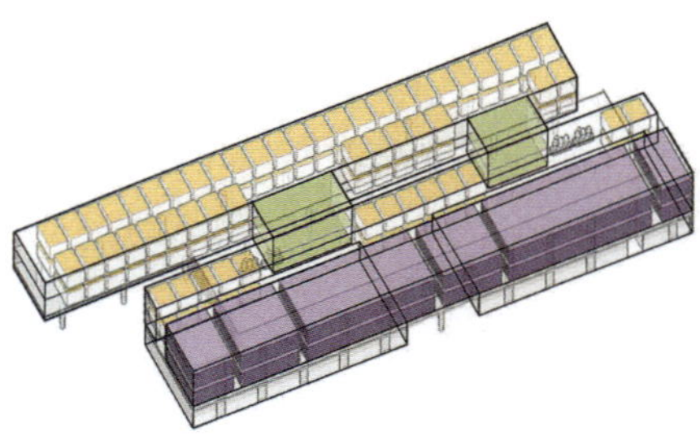

Program

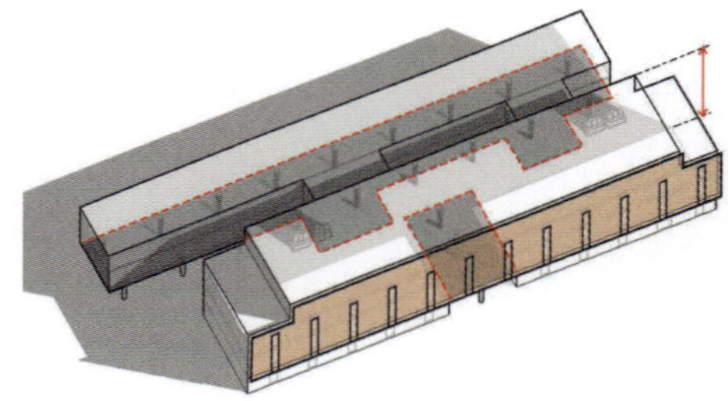

Shading

HUMID HOUSTON

Fitness to place extends beyond master planning and materials to the microclimate the building creates. Offices are enhanced by daylight and view that limit lighting energy and improve the work environment. Physics laboratories are the opposite. They require constant temperature and shelter from light. The tall laboratory bar with limited window surface and terra cotta baguette shading is positioned to the south, overshadowing the lower north-facing bar of offices.

The narrow open courts between the two wings provide shaded daylight for offices, and they channel wind across the shaded courts and walks below. The central north-south passage is a wind slype that accelerates winds through outdoor space, providing welcome comfort.

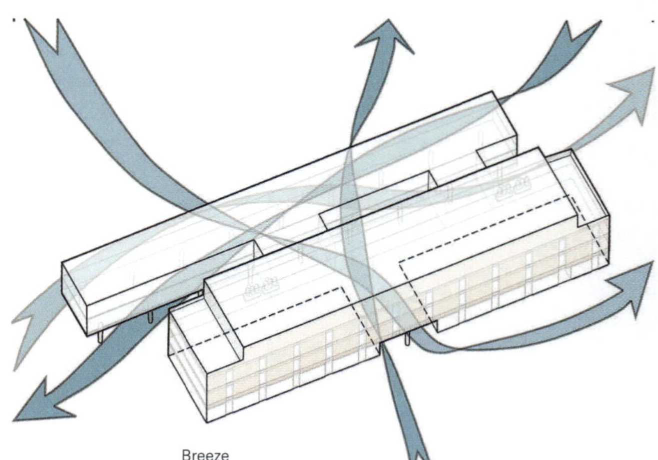

Breeze

TUNED FACADE

While the underlying material of the upper walls is largely taut glazing, consistent with the adjoining 1960s space science buildings, the specific forms and articulation vary based upon location and solar orientation.

The north-facing walls are covered with a leaf-like Penrose frit pattern. The walls within the light wells are shadow box glazed at the floor/ceiling cavity, except at the two bridge connections between the bars. The eastern and western ends of the office wings integrate vertical glass fins for shading. Above the base, the south campus-facing facade uses terra cotta rainscreen baguettes to both shade the wall and to extend the historic Rice red tile roofs to a contemporary material and construction system.

WHOLENESS

We believe this building, more than any other modern building at Rice University, understands it place on the campus. It participates in and extends the campus holistically without premiating any single moment over the totality of the experience of movement into, around, and through Brockman Hall.

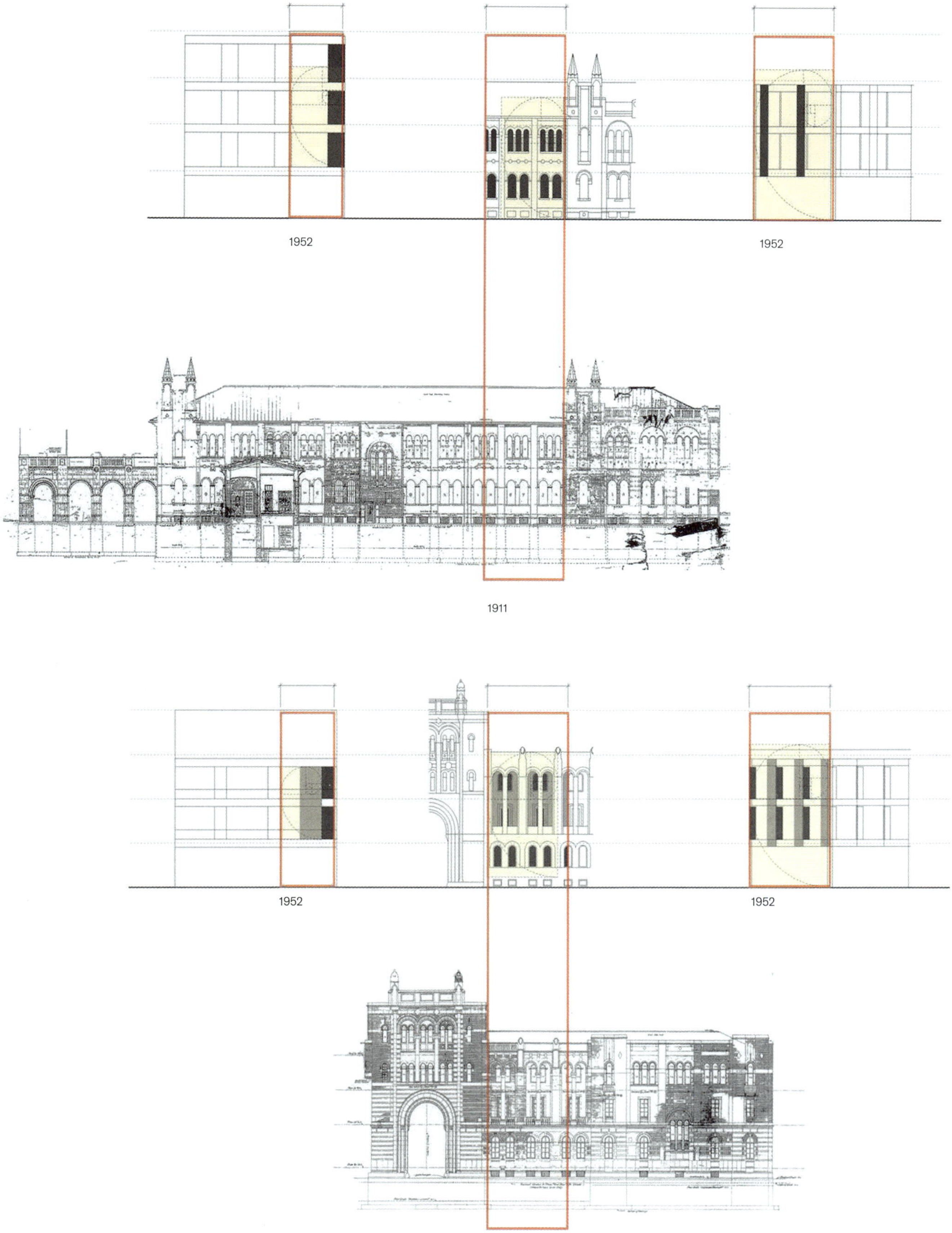

Lovett Hall, 1911

FULL-SCALE

We do not draw and pray. Full-scale mock-ups are a critical part of our design process. The terra cotta baguettes atop the glass block and brick base wall were first tested in our office for visual effect and to study edge terminations.

At the shaded court beneath the elevated offices, every detail was critical to success. There was concern that the space would feel too low, like a parking deck. We worked to make sure we had the proper height, then shaped the ceiling as an elliptical dome to give it visual lift. The concrete piloti that the offices above float upon are tapered to give a sense of the weight above. They are board-formed to create a landscape element drawn from the trees surrounding the court. The formwork was beautifully drawn by Fred Langford, an architect who specialized in concrete and building technologies for Louis Kahn at the Salk Institute, the Kimbell Art Museum, and the Government Center at Dhaka.

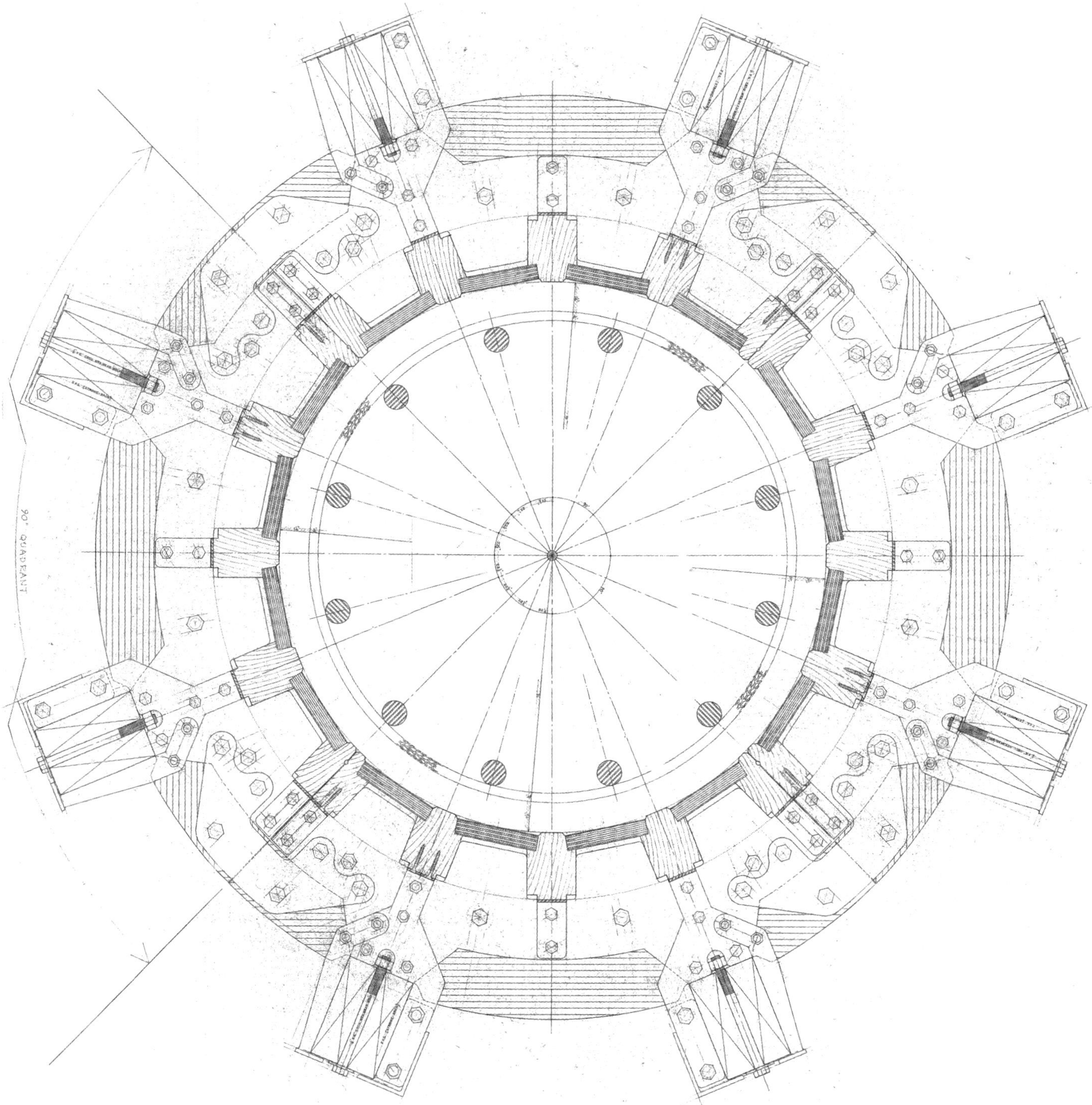
90° QUADRANT

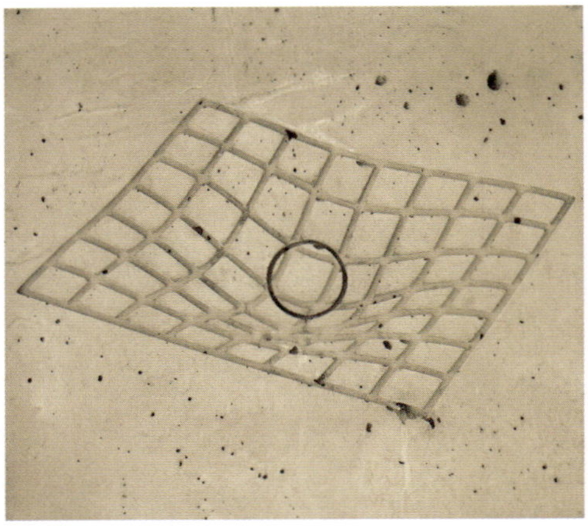

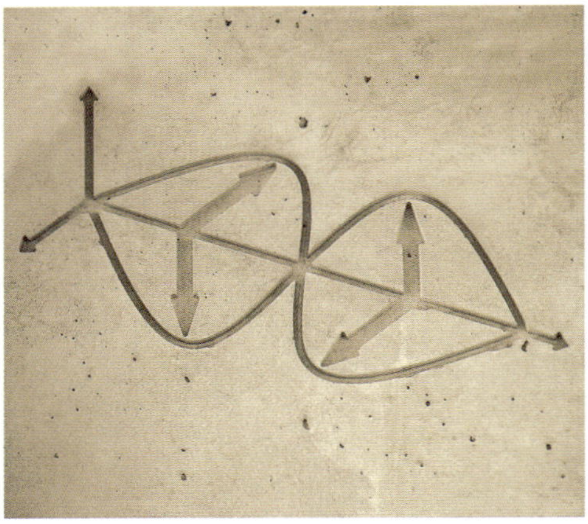

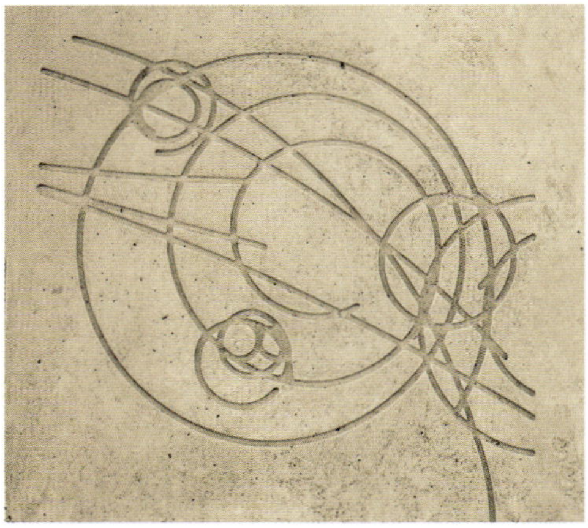

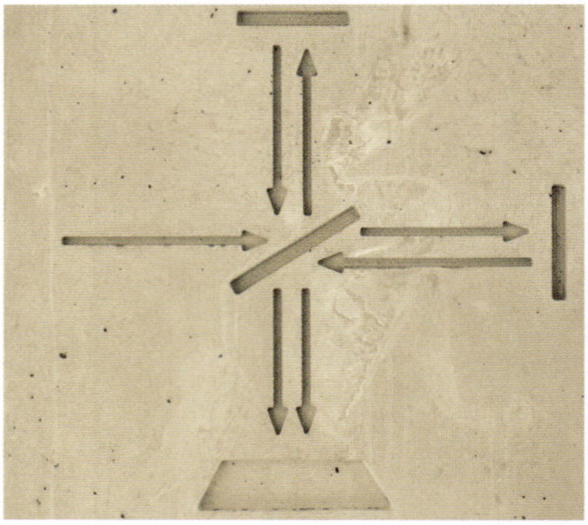

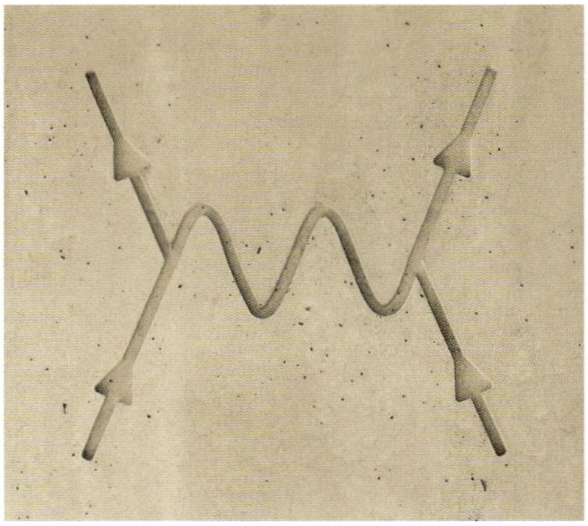

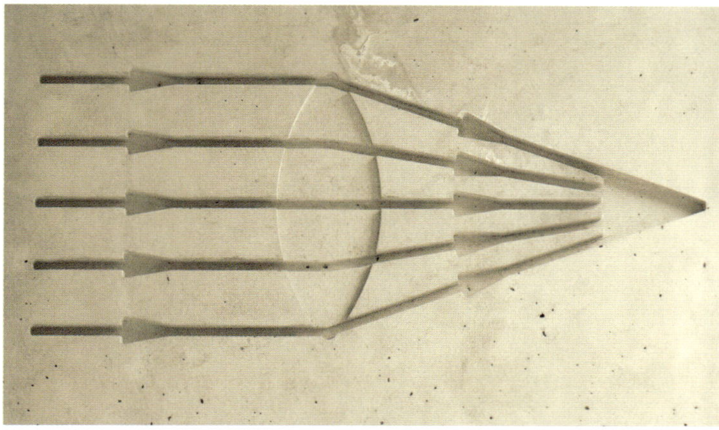

ORNAMENTAL

Nearly every Rice building has ornamental details integrated in its walls. These ornaments are occasionally built up of small tiles or carved into stone. They are generally iconographic and specific to the place and purpose of the building. We chose to integrate our details using a fully modern technique: casting in concrete. We made rubber molds and placed them inside the formwork before casting the concrete. When the concrete had cured, the forms were stripped. We asked the Physics faculty to give us the iconographic program for the castings. The abstracted representations range from Einstein's discovery that gravitational fields can bend light to the story of Schrödinger's cat.

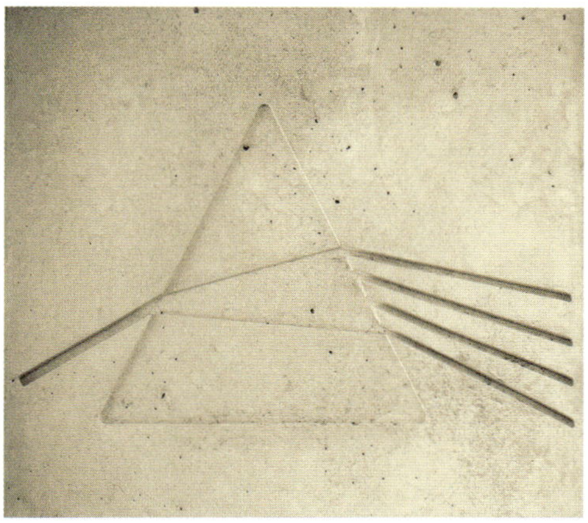

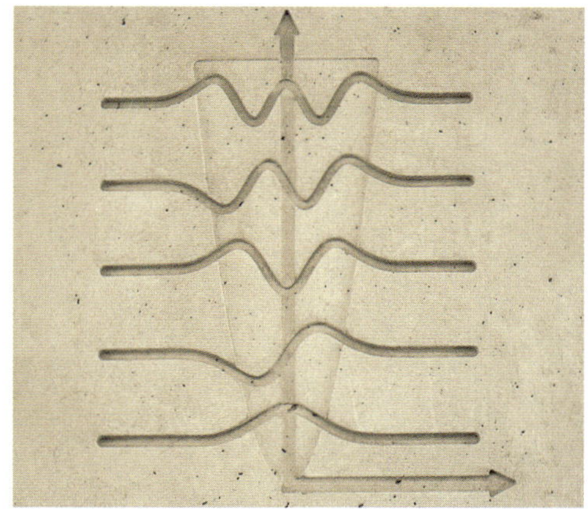

Morse and Ezra Stiles Colleges

Yale University

New Haven, Connecticut

There is much to admire and inspire in the body of work that was achieved by Eero Saarinen during his too-short life. Among his mid-twentieth century peers, he was especially fearless in his integration of new technologies that emerged in the wake of World War II to influence the often-resistant realm of architecture. Neoprene gaskets similar to those used for car windshields in the automotive industry are one such innovation he pioneered for architectural use in facade assemblies. His confidence was grounded in committed programs of research and prototyping that inspire us today. He built well, no matter how leading edge the application. Saarinen was equally fearless in his desire to never have a signature style, to look not at himself but at each unique client, place, and purpose as the instigator of architectural form. He was contextual through the 1950s—long before the word made its way into architectural discourse.

The historic context for Morse and Stiles Colleges, completed in 1962, was the much-loved group of ten residential colleges built at Yale from 1932 through the early 1940s. They were largely designed by James Gamble Rogers in a mix of collegiate Gothic and neo-Georgian styles, all modeled on Oxford and Cambridge precedents.

For Morse and Stiles, Saarinen studied the casual medieval architecture and urbanism of Italian hill towns, especially the famed towers of San Gimignano. The physical form of the two colleges divides at the center. A passage between gradually reveals and focuses us on the distant tower of the Payne Whitney gymnasium. The architectural volumes of Morse and Stiles together form three crescents and shape three courtyards. The largest of these is the great curving exedra that becomes the forecourt to the tremendous volume of the gymnasium. Two smaller, irregular crescents in turn define the internal courtyards of each college, where the focus is on the dining hall. A residential tower in each college completes the hill town reference, and together they further frame the gymnasium tower beyond.

During much of their first fifty years, Morse and Stiles were consistently thought to be the least desirable of the twelve colleges at Yale. We undertook a benchmark study to compare their facilities to the original ten colleges that had just been renovated. First, some history: At the end of WWII, students returned to Yale. The occupancy of the ten existing colleges grew and continued to swell into the 1950s. With this density came discontent and a decision to add the two new colleges. Surveys were used to inform the program for Morse and Stiles Colleges. What followed is a cautionary tale for all who use surveys to inform decisions. When asked, students of course overwhelmingly requested single rooms, but they were not asked whether they desired the preponderance of these to be "stand alone" or "in suite." Sometimes phrasing is everything. In the ten original colleges at Yale, the housing culture was mainly suites, groups of single rooms sharing a small living room. But owing to the surveys, Morse and Stiles were instead largely built with stand-alone singles and doubles.

A second aspect of the benchmark study that informed our work was a comparison of student life spaces across the whole residential college system. It showed Morse and Stiles to be significantly disadvantaged in both the available array and quantity of these spaces: fitness, shop and fabrication, music practice, small group performance, art making and exhibition, lounges and gathering. Further, dining facilities were undersized in both food presentation and preparation areas compared to the newly renovated colleges.

When we are working within a system or collection of similar buildings, we often undertake comparative benchmark studies. Here, the findings provoked programmatic change by depicting the residential system as a whole and highlighting differences between colleges. The study became an objective tool to rebalance the residential college system across the university.

For the housing at Morse and Stiles, this meant reconfiguration to add substantial suite-based living spaces and reduce stand-alone singles. Owing to the poured-in-place concrete construction and the irregular shape of nearly every room, the difficulties in this conversion were legion. But this change in the housing dynamic was the single most important social transformation at the colleges.

The student life facility shortfalls were resolved with a 25,000-square-foot addition shared between the two colleges. This addition is formed below grade about a sunken garden in a crescent-shaped courtyard at the juncture between the colleges and the exedra facing the gym. A new bridge carries pedestrians above the sunken garden, highlighting the drama of the moment at which they pass into the open crescent flanking the Payne Whitney tower. The sunken garden is a third courtyard, an outdoor room shared by Morse and Stiles. It gives light and access to a suite of student activity spaces that encircle it.

A concrete portico with a ceiling that slopes up to the daylight above surrounds the sunken court. The circulation portico is irregular in shape while all the adjacent program spaces are of regular geometric forms. This is an inversion from the original Saarinen structures in which all rooms were irregular and the circulation corridors rectilinear.

The original moat walls of the Saarinen building have been re-used in segments as part of the new walls that integrate skylights, bringing surprising and welcome light into the program spaces below. Sunken halls for socializing were conceived by Saarinen as rathskellers, but they have been transformed into light-filled commons by crystalline skylights that project through the terraces above.

We see our work here as an open dialogue with an admired predecessor. We have sought to edit, revise, and add to Morse and Stiles—not only to accommodate present needs, but more importantly, to gift them a future as places of desire, places to live, study, and play on a decisively different but equal footing with their peers in the ten original colleges.

LONELINESS

While students like privacy in their bedrooms, they do not like living alone. Perhaps the most important accomplishment in our transformation of these residential colleges is the conversion of many stand-alone single and double rooms into suites, each composed of a small living space with multiple attached bedrooms. The suite of two to several students is the foundational unit at the core of successively larger nested social groupings that distinguish a residential college from a residence hall.

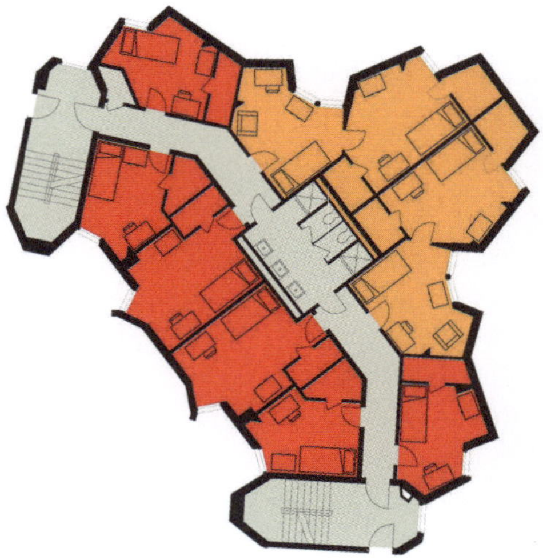

Original Saarinen Unit Plan

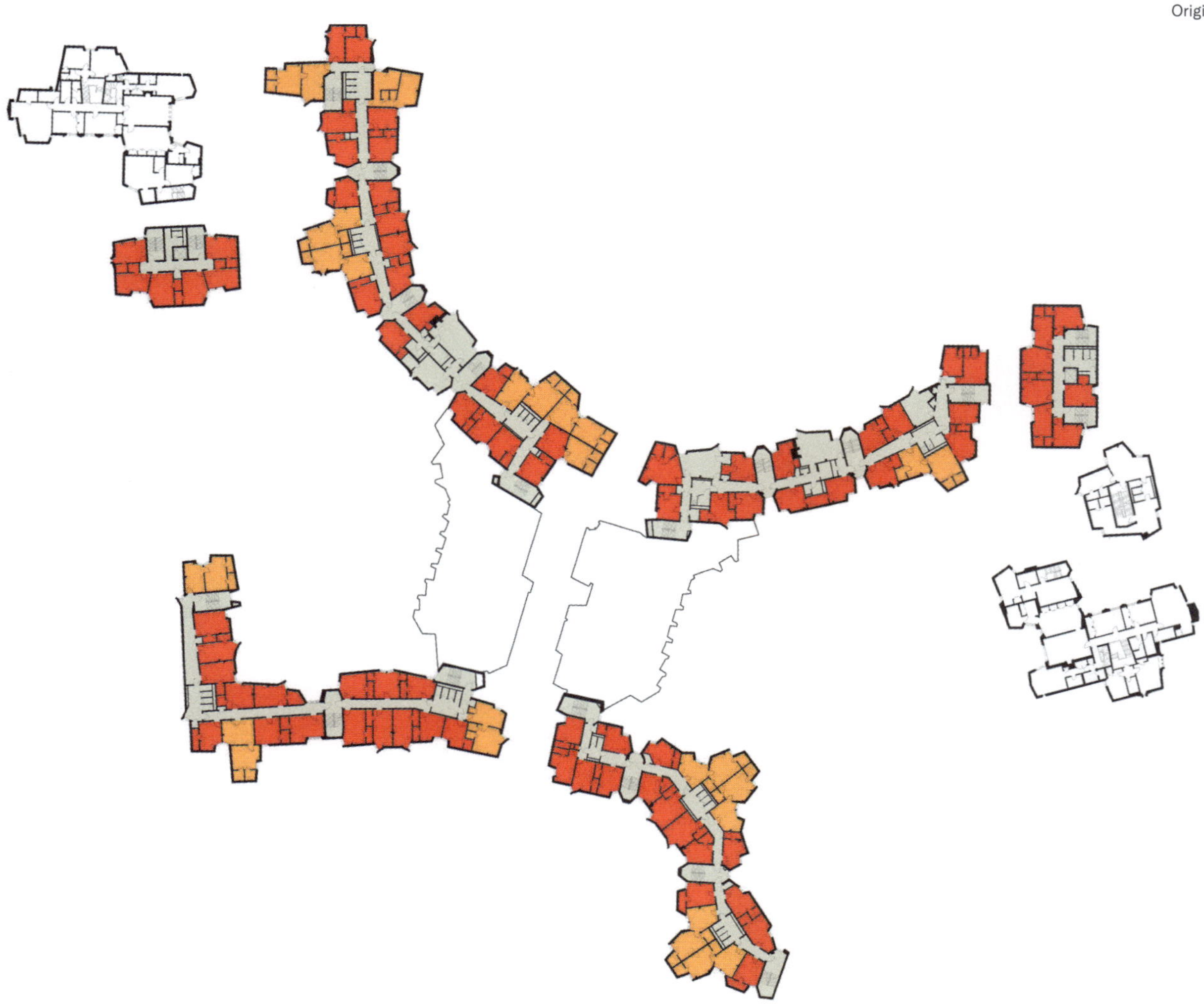

Original Saarinen Building Plan

Modified Building Plan

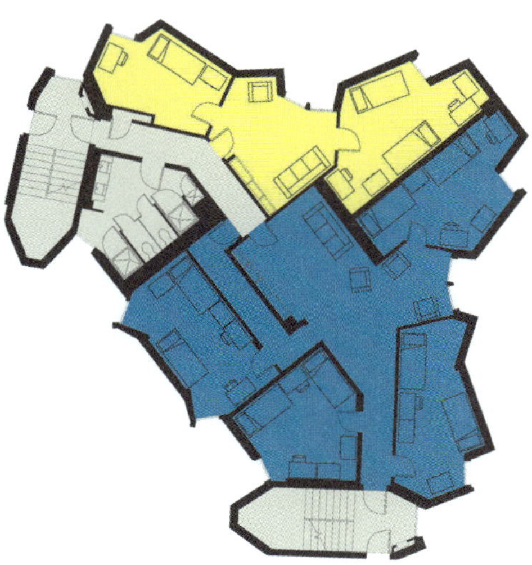

Modified Unit Plan

- Stand alone single
- Double room
- Three bed suite
- Four bed suite
- Five bed suite
- Six bed suite
- Seven bed suite
- Eight bed suite
- Circulation and baths

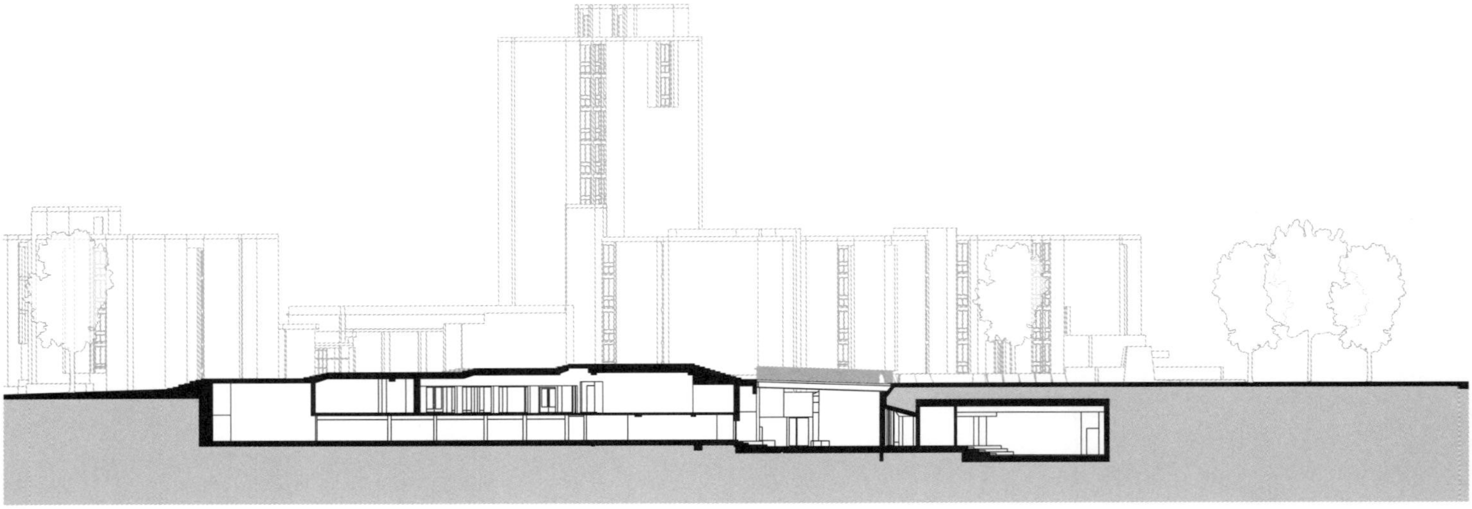

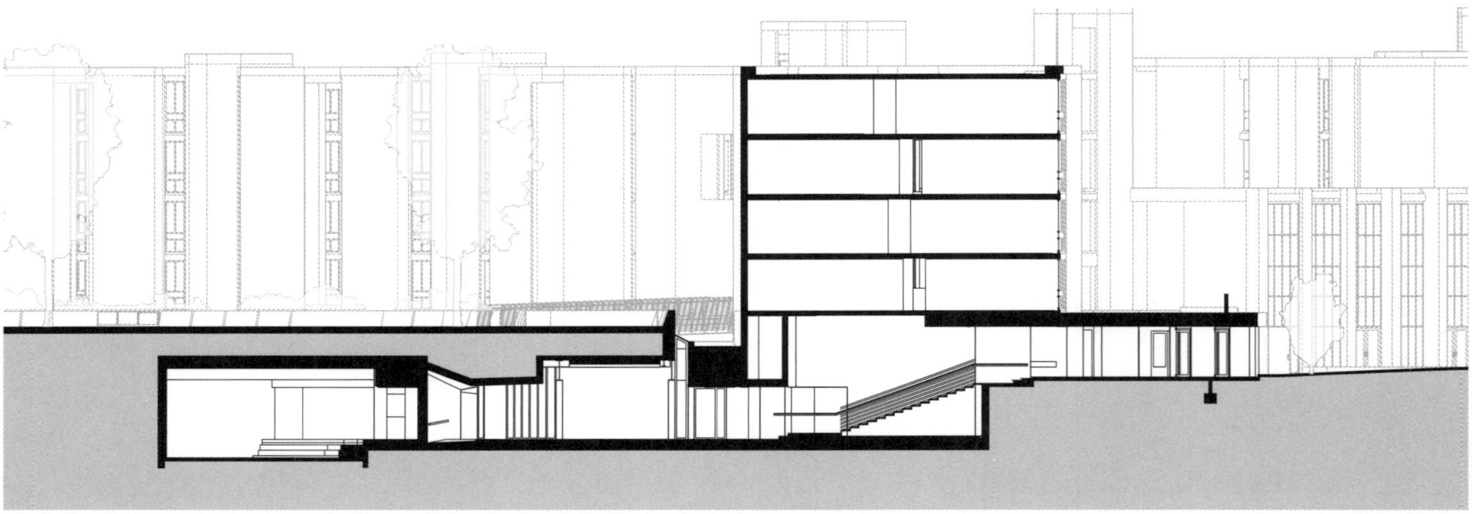

PRESERVATION

The sweeping curvature of the great courtyard at the base of the Payne Whitney Gymnasium tower is a focal feature of Morse and Stiles Colleges—and of the Yale campus. Saarinen's intent was to use the vast gymnasium (this black and white photograph is taken from the tower) as a wall to enclose this new elliptical space. A passage between the perimeter walls separating the two colleges opens at the courtyard to dramatically frame the gymnasium tower. The preservation of this treasured space and view required significant excavation and underpinning to the perimeter walls to construct the new activity center below.

VOLVO

ROOTS

The changes begin beyond the buildings at the landscaped courtyards. Boundaries between inside and outside, between buildings and grounds, are here blurred. The dining halls now open out with a wooden deck above terraced waterfalls that recycle site water. The desire to allow a large tree to grow again above the addition becomes an opportunity to form the new architecture below about nature above. The resulting tree-well is shaped about the root structure.

EXTRUDED

The Morse and Stiles Common Rooms were thought of as "rathskellers" by Saarinen. They are located below terraces with no light and view. The alterations to these rooms introduce light monitors on the terraces above, drawing daylight through the coffered radial structure into the transformed, new "living room" of each college.

SCULPTED

Art is integrated into the very fabric of Morse and Stiles. Costantino Nivola's cast concrete sculptures are integrated into the landscape and walls of both colleges. The new landscapes reintegrate these works at the center of the Stiles water feature and atop the new subterranean addition. Claes Oldenburg's 1969 *Lipstick (Ascending) on Caterpillar Tracks* was relocated from Beinecke Plaza to the Morse courtyard in 1974 and restored during this project.

MOSTLY MOATS

Most Yale residential colleges are surrounded by moats. These are both a reference to the predominant Gothic revival architecture and a practical way to secure ground-level residential rooms within the urban setting and admit daylight into the basements. Saarinen followed this precedent of moats at Morse and Stiles with low, sloping cast concrete and stone walls outboard of the perimeter building walls.

The new addition required disassembly of these moat walls. They were sawcut into several foot-long segments and stored off-site during construction. New board-formed concrete walls were cast as light monitors in the addition roof, admitting daylight into the new student activity spaces below. The original walls were then reinstalled as precast panels between the skylights, reestablishing the moat perimeter.

Charles David Keeling Apartments
University of California, San Diego

San Diego, California

The site for the Keeling Apartments is an edge, overlooking the dramatic coastal cliffs of La Jolla. The topography slopes gently from north to south, with western views out over the Pacific Ocean and eastern views to the campus and mountains beyond. The arroyos of the natural landscape give form to the meeting of architecture and land. While rain is scarce in San Diego, its arrival is often torrential. The entire ground plane at the Keeling Apartments forms itself about these opposite poles of scarcity and deluge. Along both sides of the building, following the pedestrian pathways, landscaped swales connect the rainfall to an ephemeral pool of gravel and boulders beneath the elevated end of the building that marks the southern entry to the campus. Designed to channel water to its ocean outlet, the swales become moats to control campus flooding when the system is overtaxed. The boulder landscape and planted swales—one of which transitions the grade with weirs to create overflow pools—are beautiful empty or full.

The whole of this assemblage is an architectural arroyo, guiding and absorbing people and water as they course across the site. It creates a constantly changing choreography of filtered movement, sound, sunlight, and shade that engages the senses and promotes an appreciation for the way in which daily life is interwoven with the natural landscape and the benign California climate. Perpendicular paths lined with infiltration plantings lace together the whole of the courtyard, creating a patterned and variable assembly of topography, nature, and human occupation, which can be observed in its totality throughout the day from the exterior walkways that screen the facades of these multistory buildings. This is a working courtyard that also provides a contained zone of serenity and beauty for its inhabitants, connecting them intimately to the natural elements.

The landscape does not end here on the ground, but is lifted up to the roof of the middle of the three buildings. There it becomes a green roof that connects, moves, and absorbs water and people across the roofscape. Part secluded courtyard and part aerial street that joins the two taller adjacent buildings, it rewards its users with expansive Pacific views, dramatic sunsets, cool ocean breezes, and fresh air sequestered far above the traffic lanes that edge the campus below. While the grade-level courtyard focuses inward and gives place to the communal life of the college, the rooftop courtyard projects outward, to the uninterrupted expanse of ocean beyond. The dual foci of these outdoor spaces, one inward to the academic community and the other outward to the world beyond, is a metaphor for the work of Charles Keeling, the Scripps Institute researcher for whom the complex is named, who first alerted the world to the possibility of human impact on global atmospheric carbon.

Architecture is at its most elemental—especially in this most elemental of natural landscapes—when composed of few materials. Rather than drawing attention to itself, such architecture creates a foil for the world it inhabits. Its surface becomes a palette to receive the movement of the sun across the hours of the day. This is superbly demonstrated by the nearby Salk Institute, created by Louis Kahn, largely with concrete and wood. The Keeling Apartments discipline themselves with a simple set of materials: concrete, fiber cement, and fiberglass.

Concrete is ancient and elemental: cement, sand, stone, and water. Fiberglass is the opposite; modern and composite: fiber and resin. Fiber cement falls somewhere in between, elemental materials formed by modern processes. Concrete is present at Keeling in two forms:

cast-in-place and precast. The frame, floors, and roof are cast-in-place concrete, in the white color typical of Southern California, acting as both structure and finish surface, inside and out. Precast concrete rainscreen panels with integral shading fins at window edges dominate the exterior enclosure, supplemented with areas of cement fiber rainscreen. Fiberglass gratings create the safety enclosures for open perimeter walkways and act as solar shades. They are an off-the-shelf industrial product—selected, not designed. In their own contemporary way, these too are elemental for their ability to satisfy myriad practical requirements. They are economical, lightweight, quick to install, and inherently structural; the color is integral and therefore fade-resistant; they are not subject to solar heat gain; they are transparent to the breezes; the depth of their grid blocks sunlight from oblique angles and provides visual privacy, yet they feel almost transparent when viewed at right angles from the interior; and most importantly, they do not deteriorate in San Diego's moist and corrosive marine environment.

The motivation to build the Keeling Apartments was an act of social reparation. The apartments draw undergraduates from a remote location on the other side of the campus into the physical orbit of Revelle college. All are now joined together in a living-learning community with dining and communal facilities at the center. The three new buildings, respectively five, eight, and ten stories high, form a C-shaped courtyard edged with the same volcanic stone walls that were used at the plaza fronting the first campus buildings constructed in 1964.

The relative position of the three structures is a response to microscale environment, with the tallest structure located to the north to minimize overshadowing of the courtyard, the opposing south bar three stories shorter to allow more sun to penetrate the courtyard, and the longest and shortest wing positioned to the west and elevated at the south end to maximize long views to the ocean and to allow afternoon sun to penetrate. Placing the majority of the units in wings with an east-west axis—the opposite of the way buildings are commonly sited in La Jolla—actually allows for more and better views of the ocean by taking advantage of oblique as well as direct views.

Since each residential unit extends through the full width of the building, every unit has views to the ocean on one side and, on the other, to the campus and mountains beyond. As a result, each also enjoys both morning and late-day sun and superior cross-ventilation, negating the need for air conditioning. The exterior walkways are positioned along the south- and west-facing edges of the buildings for solar control. Since occupants can access their rooms only from the exterior walkways, the facades are constantly animated by their movement.

Together, the fiberglass-screened concrete masses shape and control the passage of wind and sun across the site and passively protect their occupants by filtering the sun's glare, tempering its heat, directing the ocean breezes to ventilate the living spaces, orienting the views, and enlivening this place with an ever-changing dance of sun and shade throughout the season and the day.

The Keeling Apartments open our senses to place, drawing architecture into a compelling union with the elements. The collection of buildings listens to and responds to these elements. It is beautiful because its forms and materials are not arbitrary. Nothing can easily be added nor deleted. It is an act of holistic design that gives agency to those elements that sustain life.

FILTER AND FORM

Keeling Apartments give form to every aspect of its place. The courtyard is an edge to the campus along the Pacific Coast and concludes a main pedestrian passage. It collects storm water at this low point in the campus topography and filters sun and wind into the buildings and through the site.

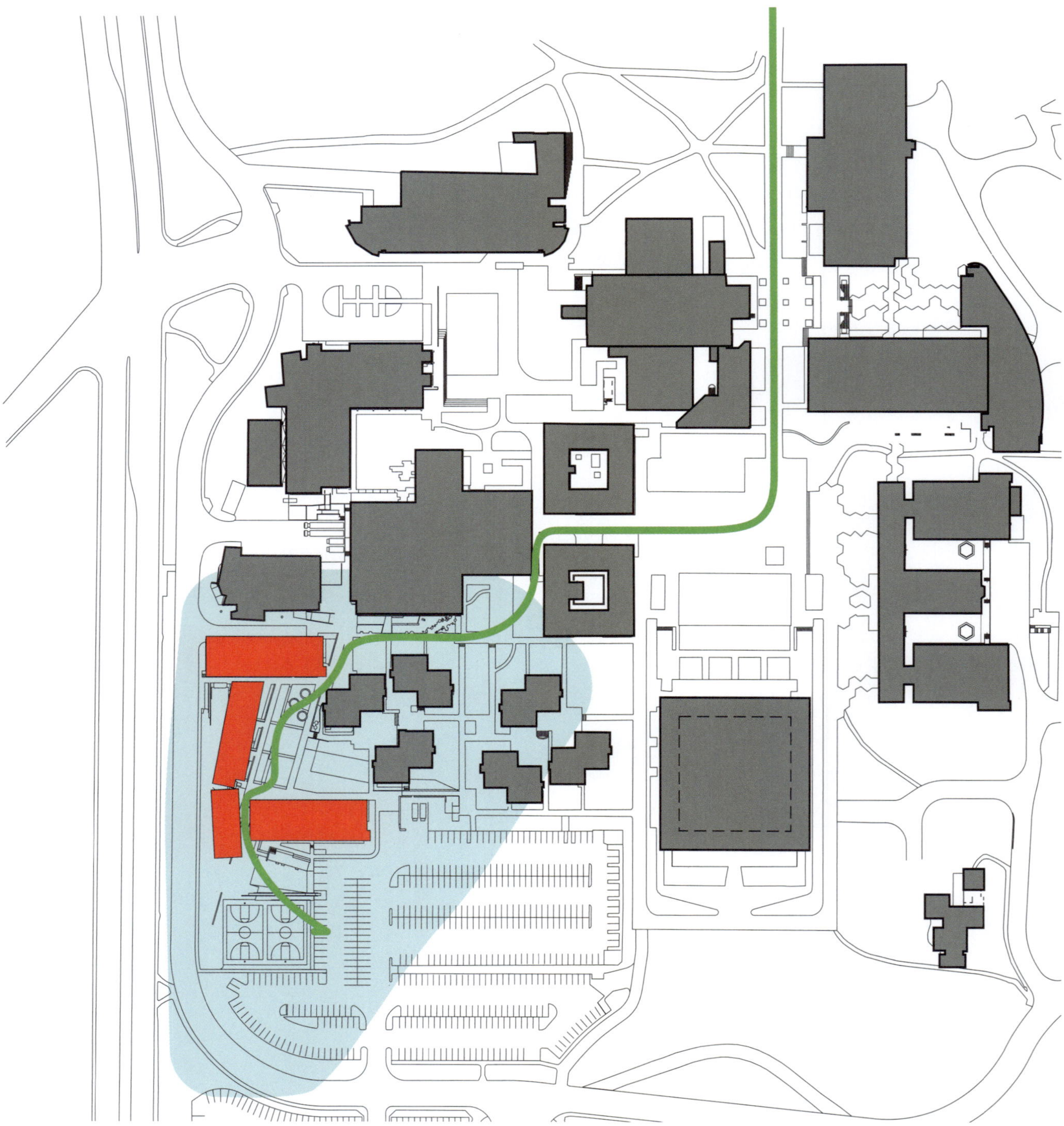

ARROYO

The backbone of the site is an arroyo.
While rain is infrequent, when it does arrive it is torrential. Rain that falls on the buildings and site makes its way into a system of filtration beds, stone channels, and wiers. The passage of people parallels this movement of water. Often storm infrastructure is buried below; here it forms the surface as a working landscape.

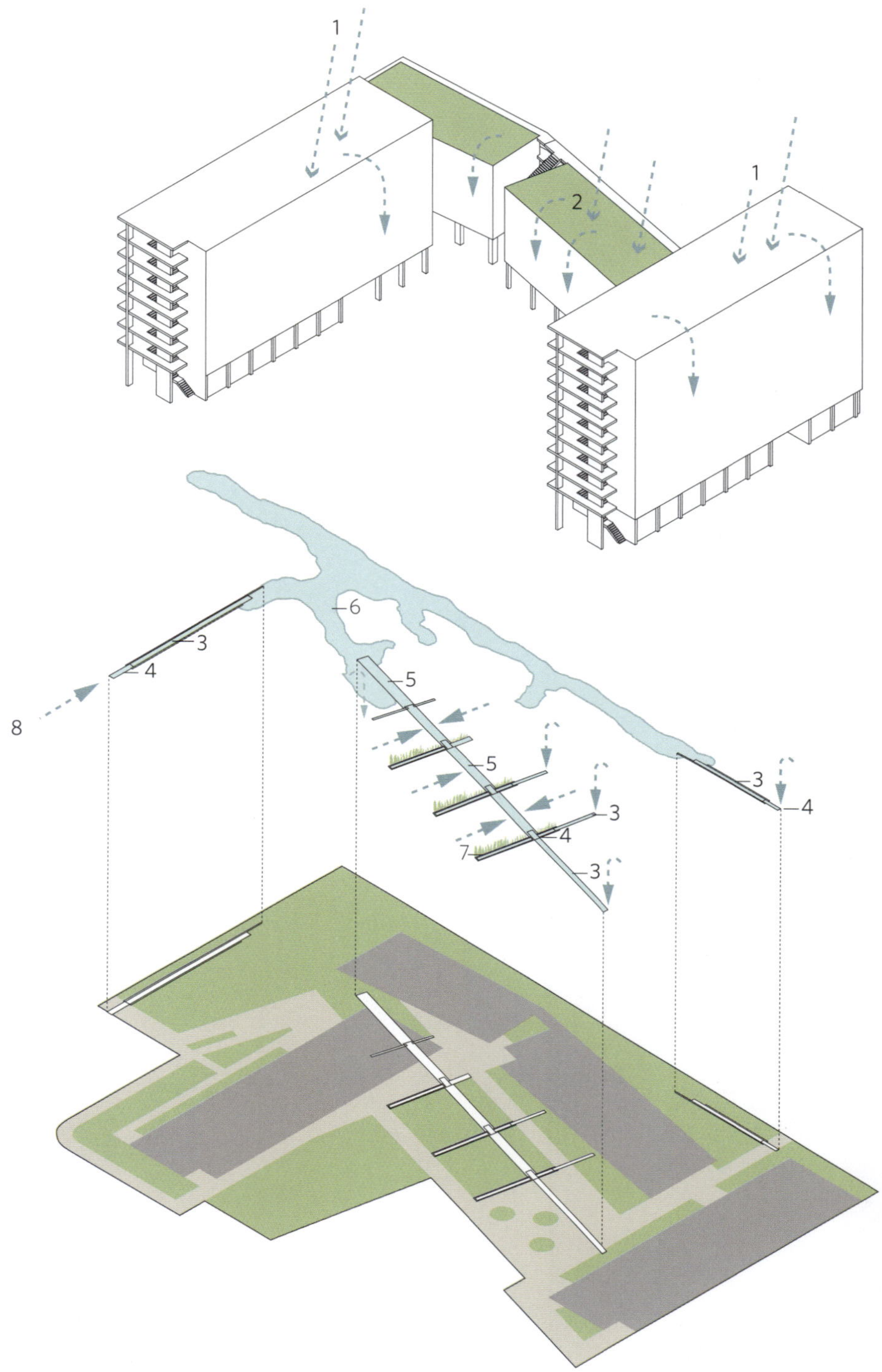

1. STORMWATER
2. VEGETATED ROOF
3. WATER CONVEYANCE CHANNEL
4. WEIR
5. ROCK SWALE
6. ARROYO
7. PLANTER WALL
8. STORMWATER FROM PARKING LOT

LIVING ROOF

The rooftop of the lower building that connects the two higher ones is also a working courtyard that manages water, insulates the building, and provides mid-level passage and connection across the whole of the Keeling complex. The plantings reflect the diversity of local vegetation that thrives in these alternating dry and wet conditions.

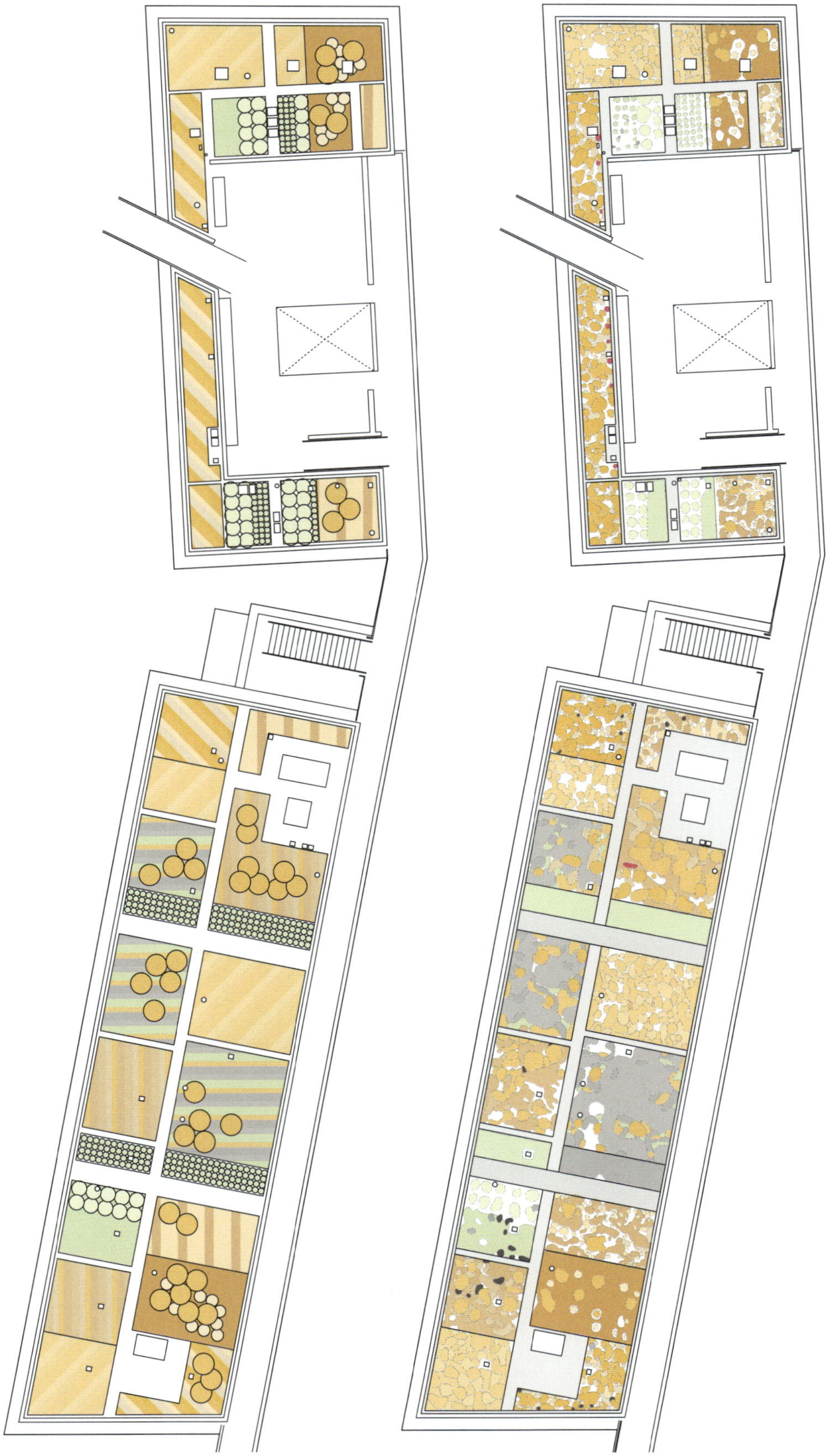

HOLES

Water flows from infiltration beds in the courtyard into channels beneath sidewalks. From there, it flows into an arroyo-like landscape of boulders, sand, gravel, and plants. The boundaries of architecture and landscape flow together beneath and between buildings.

Loose-laid volcanic rock site walls exist across the campus. We needed a more precise, structured version for this site. After eight mock-up attempts, we arrived at a hybrid solution that is both precise (cut at its edges) and irregular (textured across its face).

The whole of the landscape is a narrative passage among the natural and manmade.

SHADE AND SHADOW

Architecture is most compelling when elements have several purposes. Here the vertical shading fins are also structure for the balcony guardrails. Corrosion-resistant, off-the-shelf fiberglass gratings are typically used for factory floors. Here they are impervious to the salty air as well as opaque when viewed obliquely and transparent when viewed frontally. They paint delightful, shifting shadow patterns across the floors and walls. Solar gain on the west-facing low bar is lessened by a slight bend in its massing.

Winter

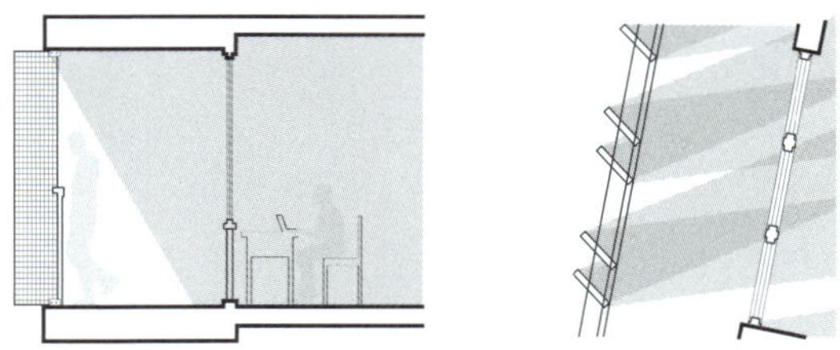

Spring and Fall

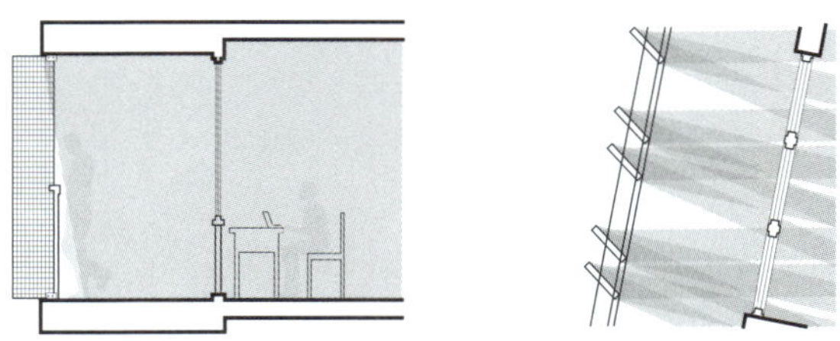

Summer

Quaker Meeting House and Arts Center
Sidewell Friends School
Washington D.C.

For nearly fifty years, the Sidwell gym was home to bouncing balls, squeaking sneakers, players' chatter, coaches' commands, bright artificial light—and, improbably, to weekly meeting for worship at this Quaker school. Quakers use the medium of contemplative worship to find the "inner light" within each of us. Silence and light are the program for a meeting house. But silence is anathema to a gym. So is the light of day. It was a stretch to think that when the gym was relocated beneath an adjoining field, the meeting for worship could find a true home of silence and light within the shell of the old building. The debate went on for months: Should the old gym come down? How could six hundred middle and upper school students come together to find light through silence in a space built for neither?

Quakers are caretakers and stewards of the Earth. Decisions to demolish and discard do not attain easy consensus. The old bones and materials of the 1950s gym still held economic and cultural value. The Quaker ethos here coincided with material reclamation and reuse. The old gym lived to see a new day as a place for worship as well as a center for arts and music. Not only did much of the structure and roof remain, but added materials including flooring and walls were reclaimed from Maryland barns and given new life here in the meeting for worship.

Attaining an atmosphere of silence and light has long been a challenge. The Quaker poet John Wittier is reputed to have said that even "nature is too garrulous" for proper silence in worship. This sentiment likely dates back to a time in seventeenth-century England when Quakers often met outside beneath trees for fear of retribution. What would the Quaker founders have thought of the repurposed Sidwell gym as a place for worship, surrounded by music and the arts below and beyond, within an active campus in a bustling neighborhood of an even busier city and region? On the other hand, where should a meeting for worship be at a Quaker school campus other than at its heart?

These conundrums create the tension and debate that are the soul of architecture. How can a meeting for worship be both at the center of activity and otherworldly? How might the medium of architecture both connect and separate? The answer here arrives layer by layer. Layers of use pass from the out of doors through a landscape veil to a defining building structure, lined by a threshold of building systems, with the totality made tactile and emotive through reclaimed barn wood and acoustical plaster. Each successive, purposeful layer traces a separation, an orbit about a core of silence and light. Nothing can be added nor deleted. We aspire here to what Leon Battista Alberti calls *Beauty*—that reasoned harmony of all the parts within a body, so that nothing may be added, taken away, or altered, but for the worse.

Quaker meeting houses within cities are often approached through walled gardens. The Quaker meeting at Fourth and Arch Streets in Philadelphia, near our first offices, is an exemplar. A tall brick wall separates the garden from the city. The garden within begins the transport of the mind and soul to a place of silence. At Sidwell, the existing central plaza functions as this garden. Reformed and renewed with this project, the plaza begins the approach to the meeting space. A sheltering portico, with a garden of sassafras trees layered beyond, continues the passage to silence between the plaza and the building. The meeting for worship would still be too garrulous if the central plaza were to lead directly to it. Instead, an embracing lobby hall mediates the passage, connecting the pocket garden to the worship space. It is yet another transition that allows for passage and a successive layer of quiet.

For a meeting space to elicit silence, a sturdy partition from the outside world is required. In this case, it is a wall both ancient and modern; ancient in its thickness at four feet. Modern in the layers of its make-up: structure; mechanical ventilation; heating and cooling; life safety systems; door operating systems; acoustical perfomance; display cases to the lobby; and finish materials. It is a wall that creates a true threshold from the world without to another within.

The meeting itself is a nearly square room. In keeping with Quaker belief, it has little hierarchy, no front or back. It is all sides. There is nothing at the center, just a void at the floor and ceiling. Worshippers line the four sides of the room in concentric rows of benches. Entries are centered in the lobby halls to the west and south of the room. A single floor riser lifts part of the bench seating up to the east and north for better views and greater intimacy. All can be equal in this room—young and old; pupil, teacher, and head of school.

Within the meeting space, slivers of diffuse light profile the top and sides of the north wall. The light from above is only felt, not seen directly. The source is obscure, mysterious, at times magical. Never have two simple insulated skylights, cut into the roof of an old gym, accomplished so much. Placed at alternating depths, four acoustical plaster ceiling planes overlap, creating a rotational movement about the light-filled central void and concealing both the natural and artificial light sources. Spiraling about the center, the ceiling actively gathers worshippers into the light as it filters down to the open floor, bathing the central void in silence.

The lower level of the old gymnasium underwent a similarly dramatic transformation, in which former locker rooms and showers gave way to a new Arts Center. North-facing glass block windows were replaced with transparent glazing, drawing daylight into the art rooms. The concrete structure of the gym floor was exposed with new, artfully organized building systems, providing a highly flexible and loft-like space for art making.

The framework of the old gym provided yet another opportunity to knit the campus together. When enclosed, a previously inaccessible exterior alley between the old gym and the adjoining Arts Center offered the prospect of passage from the central plaza to the lower campus beyond. This addition, with its hallway, new stair, and elevator, is an important piece of campus urbanism. It centers the campus anew about the meeting for worship and makes the entire campus accessible. The new wood-clad, L-shaped structure wraps two sides of the old gym, offering a music rehearsal hall and practice rooms. It cantilevers out above and shelters exterior walks and a stair and elevator to the new below-grade fieldhouse.

SILENCE AND LIGHT

In a Quaker meeting for worship, the community reflects in silence as individuals seek their own inner light. The physical focus is a void at the center of the room. The landscape settings and architecture wrap the meeting in successive layers of space. Here at the Arch Street Meeting in Philadelphia, each layer removes distractions from the city beyond the walls.

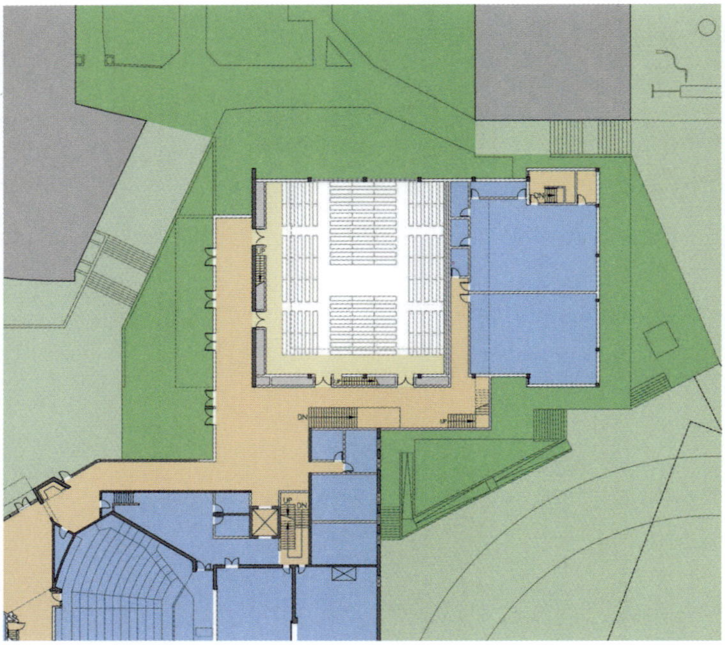

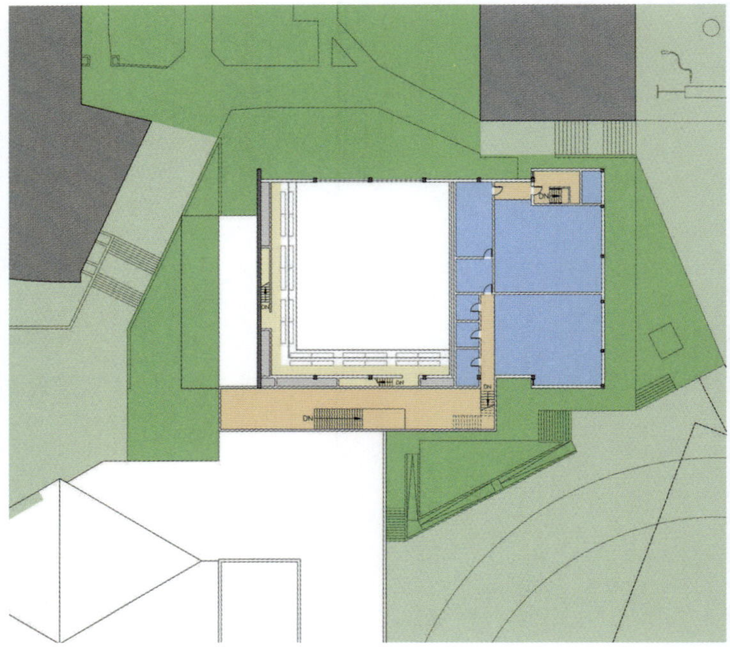

SPIRITUAL SPACEMAKING

A Quaker meeting at a school is different. Rather than a standalone space for worship, this meeting must be both at the center of and separate from daily activities.

The diagram that became the meeting for worship is here surrounded by campus buildings (grey), paved walkways and courts (light green) fragmentary landscapes (dark green), arts and music programs (blue), hallways (beige), and the thickened perimeter wall of the meeting (yellow).

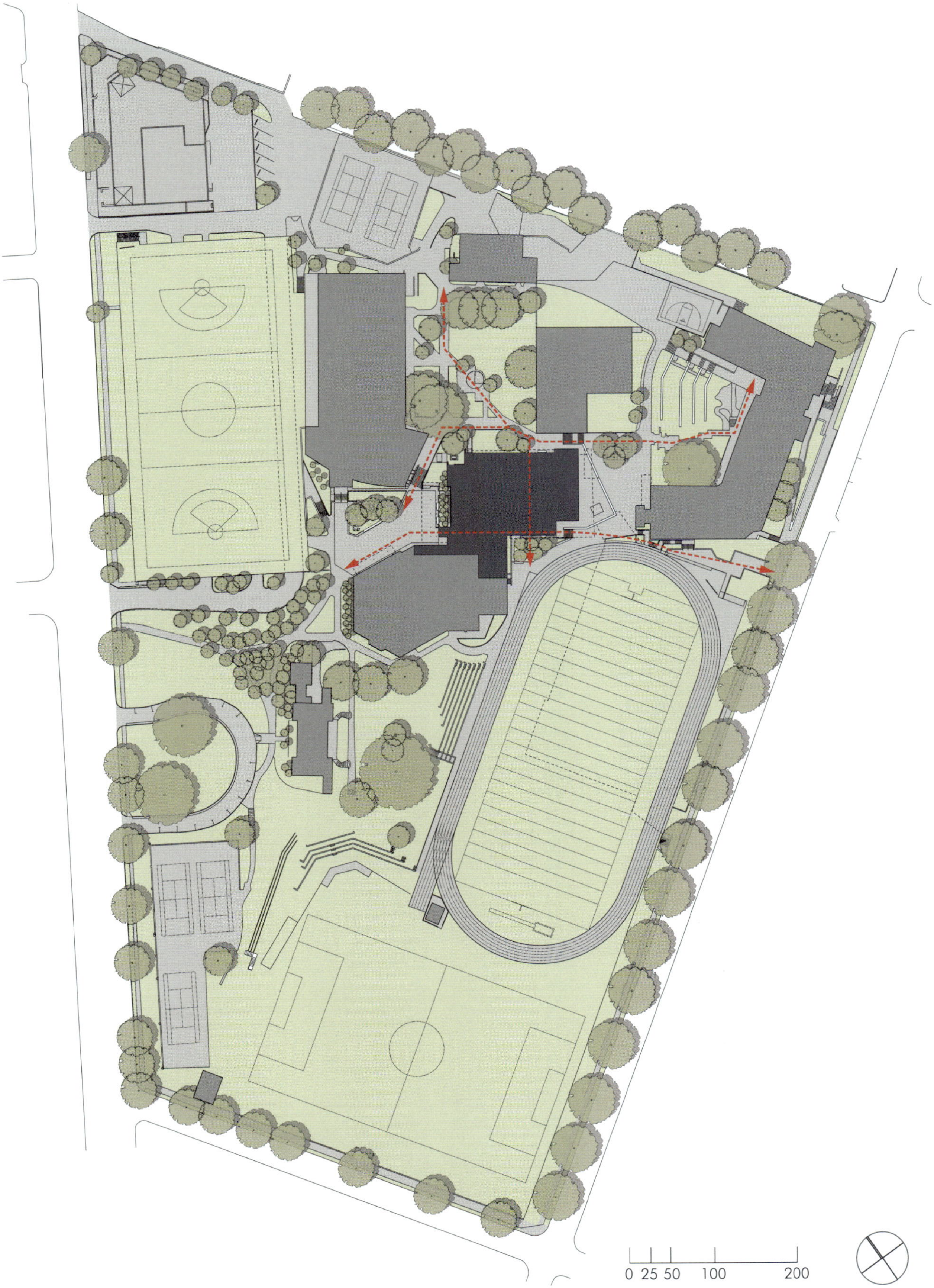
0 25 50 100 200

MAC
WRESTLING
CHAMPIONS
2002
MAC
BASKETBALL
CHAMPIONS
2007
MAC
SOCCER
CO-CHAMPIONS
2007
MAC
WRESTLING
CHAMPIONS
2008
MAC
SOCCER
CHAMPIONS
2008
MAC
CROSS
COUNTRY
CHAMPIONS
2008
ISL
LACROSSE
CHAMPIONS
2008

FITNESS

How do we transform a banal 1950s gymnasium into an evocative meeting for worship? Successive architectural layers including porticoes, pocket gardens, hallways, thickened walls, slivers of light, and wood plank liners all insulate students in the meeting from the sounds and senses of daily campus activity.

FOUND PASSAGE

The meeting for worship is simultaneously separated from the campus and connected to it. Interior and exterior stairs link the central campus square to the Middle School and athletic facilities below and the neighborhood beyond. An unused alley between prior generations of buildings became an opportunity to reintegrate separate buildings into a new campus whole. The red stair wall says, "Come this way."

SIDWELL FRIENDS

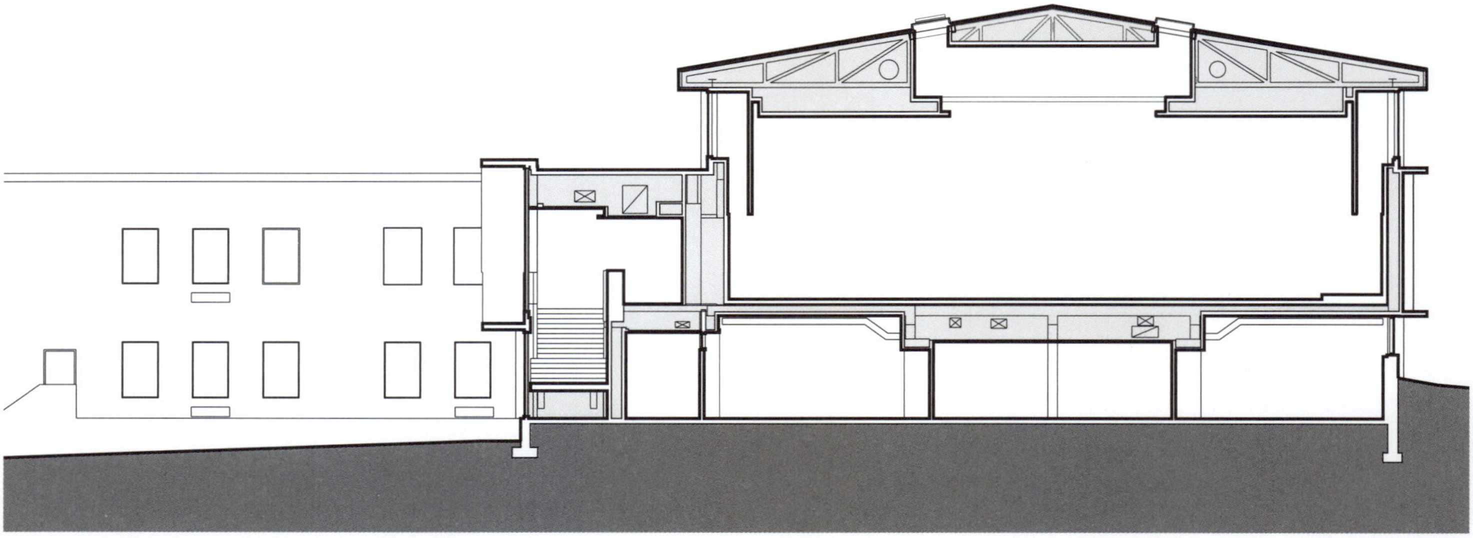

QUIETING

Two flat skylights were added to the old gym roof. They cannot be seen from below. Mysterious light filters down through the rotating planes of the ceiling, illuminating the meeting for worship.

Bands of metal line the thickness of the perimeter walls and provide space to conceal contemporary building systems. Planes of wall and ceiling float in front of clerestory windows, rendering the source of light invisible.

Here's Hoping that it Rhymes for a Reason

Center City Building
University of North Carolina at Charlotte

Charlotte, North Carolina

This tale of two campuses is very much a parable of American urbanism since World War II: in the city, out of the city, and back again. The University of North Carolina at Charlotte traces its origins to 1946. The first offerings were evening classes at Charlotte's Central High School. With support by business leaders, the city, and the county, Charlotte College evolved and eventually became state supported. Like so many postwar urban families, corporations, and institutions, in 1961 Charlotte College migrated ten miles out of the city—to a thousand-acre suburban site, becoming the University of North Carolina at Charlotte in 1965. Just forty-five years later, this iconic addition to the city skyline marked the reverse migration back to the city center, an urban campus in downtown Charlotte.

Previously, the university had leased a few spaces for classes in the city, but more students were living and working downtown, and demand had shifted. University presence was needed to forge an identity in the central business district itself. The selected site is in the burgeoning First Ward. The program that evolved is unique, in part driven by the large amount of space that was needed, coupled with the high cost and limited availability of land. Even in urban settings, universities often atomize by department. Each discipline almost always has its own place and geographic identity within the broader campus. The radical idea here was that all schools of the university would share space. There would be no departmentally dedicated teaching and office space. While this sort of "hoteling" strategy is increasingly common in office environments, where employees reserve their workspaces on an as-needed basis, it remains rare in academic institutions. In addition to the capacity this system offers to maximize the scheduled use of space and lower cost and environmental impact, it also physically integrates disciplines in shared classroom and office environments.

Each of the university's divisions and schools provided input on desired teaching spaces, offices for professors, and space for multi-disciplinary interaction. Significantly varying program requests were categorized and streamlined into fundamental types to be shared by all schools and departments. Agreement on these types allowed the project to move forward. Teaching spaces were defined as seminar rooms, tiered classrooms, and flexible studios; offices as open, shared workspaces with adjacent meeting rooms available for private conversations; and social spaces as informal lounges adjacent to vertical circulation, linking floors and oriented toward views of the city skyline. In order to sustain long-term flexibility, the building core is located at the northern edge of the site in contrast with conventional central-core configurations. This strategy allows open floor plates that are adaptable to change in academic program, enrollment, and teaching style long into the future. Positioning the core to the north also places opacity adjacent to a private developer's site with unknown program and design, whereas the occupied space receives abundant natural light and views east, west, and south.

In a city of many commercial office towers, it was important that the university distinguish itself and establish its institutional presence. The twelve-story tower is organized in four neighborhoods, or blocks, each three stories in height. Above the base, the program for these three-story campus sectors is similar. Each has two floors of classrooms coupled with one floor of academic offices, except at the top where a mechanical penthouse occupies the uppermost floor. Conceptually, these blocks are each a familiar campus-scale academic building within the larger twelve-story structure that is the urban campus. An atrium lounge connects the three levels within each block, encouraging the use of stairs, promoting informal encounter, and relieving pressure on elevators. The blocks lend university scale and form within the vertical campus while supporting cross-disciplinary interaction.

The three-story blocks gain external presence through rotation of two blocks off the building and city grid. In addition to making the campus sectors legible as academic neighborhoods, the resulting cantilevered overhangs provide welcome shading of facades below to the south and east. Within the gridded curtainwall, a mix of opaque and transparent glass with fritting is used to develop a high-performing building envelope customized to specific orientation. The fritting and opaque curtainwall panels are densest at the southwest corner where summer heat gain is most intense, gradating to more transparency at the southeast and northwest corners. Approximately 40 percent of the facade area is transparent, optimizing daylight and views while minimizing heat loss in winter and heat gain in summer. It is this expansive and holistic assembly of strategies that results in the high performance of this LEED Gold building.

The internal neighborhoods within the blocks of the Center City Building support and extend the teaching mission of the university by returning to its urban roots. These neighborhoods focus first inward, enveloping students and faculty in communities of classrooms, seminar rooms, offices, and meeting spaces. At the same time, the new building projects outward, engaging and extending the evolving urbanism of the First Ward.

The building program at the three-story base is developed to engage the public with the university. The streetscape level houses a bookstore, gallery, and café off a landscaped plaza, providing continuous pedestrian activity. These facilities are equally at home in commercial and university settings. A large auditorium and lecture hall occupy levels two and three above the street. They are a sort of piano nobile, an urbane elevated principal floor scaled to the adjacent plaza and the park beyond and connected by an atrium that begins at street level. At the building scale, the distinctive massing of the Center City Building anchors the south edge of the new four-acre urban park atop a below-grade parking structure.

The assembled image is one of a holistic nested urbanism that traverses all scales of the city. It begins in the region; then focuses its lens on the city; followed by a park within the city; and the university on the park. It anchors the university with an active commercial streetscape and large-scale auditorium that invite both the public and students within, and concludes with academic neighborhoods of classrooms and offices that educate and support the student—building a fully urbane university campus.

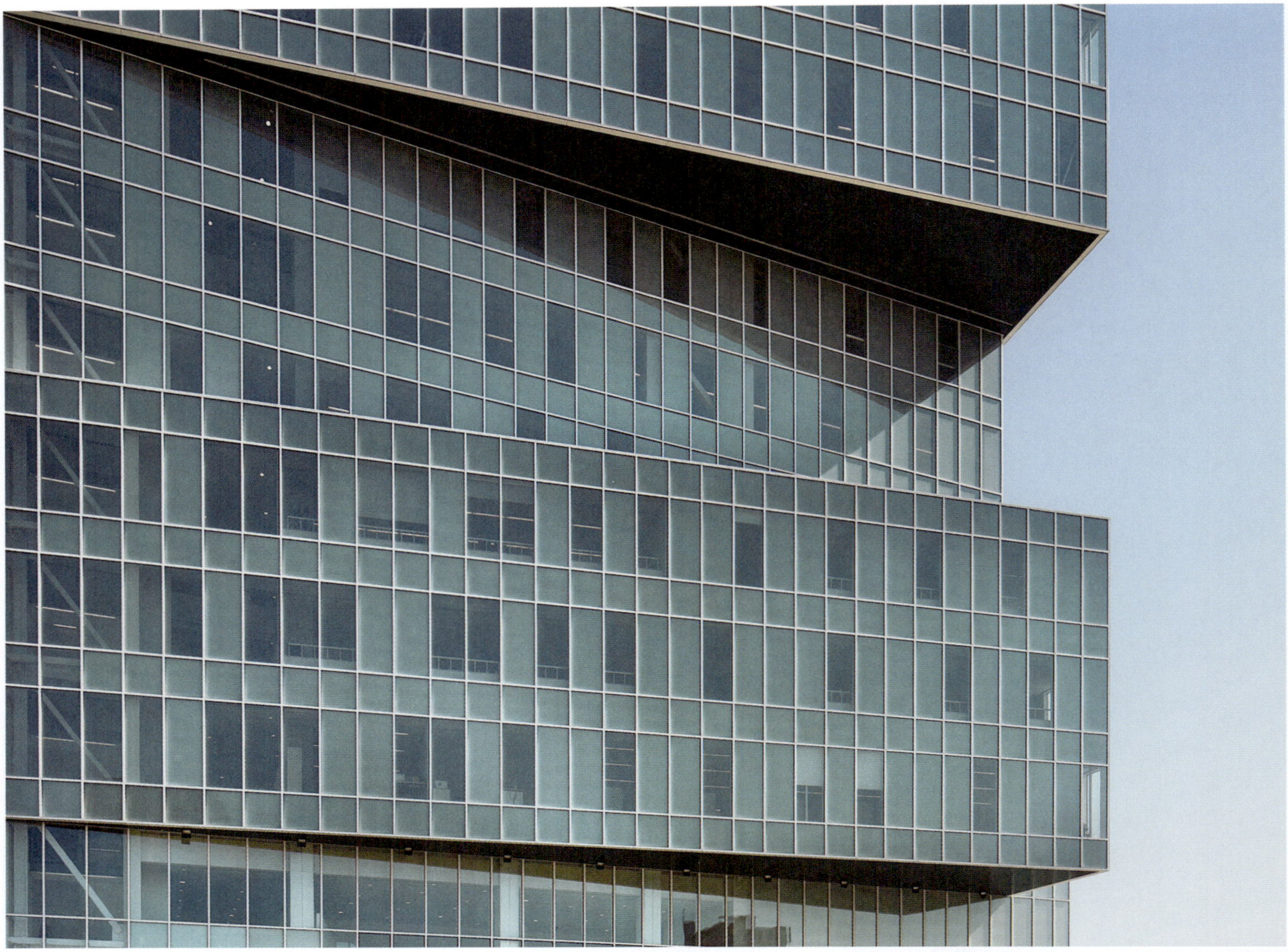

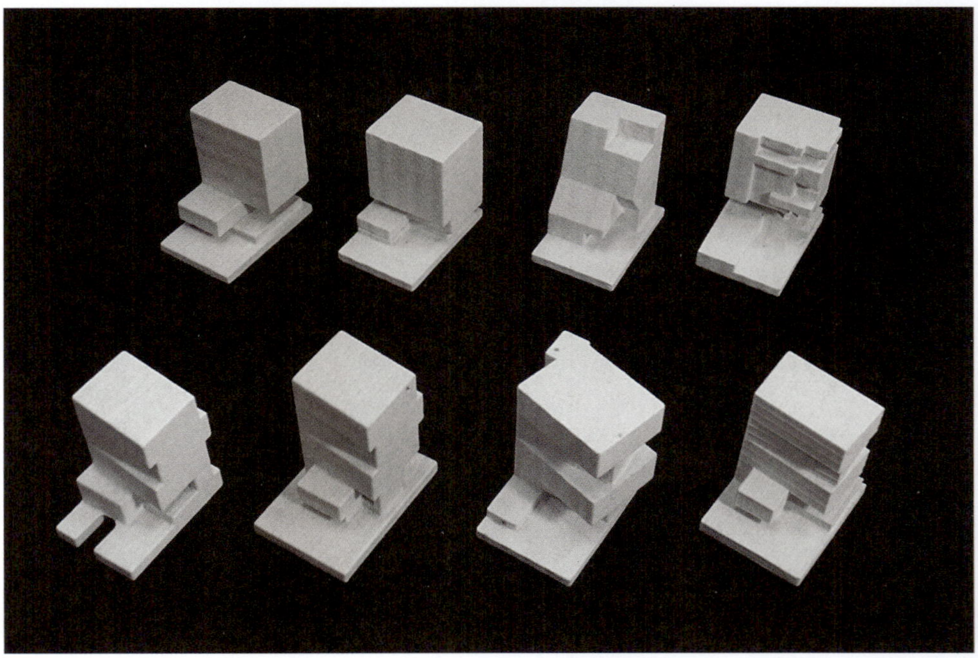

MASS ROTATION

The rotation of the massing has two purposes. First, it expresses the fragmentation of the program into four components: the two-story base has public facilities, including not only the galleries but a large lecture hall, classroom, and seminar room; meanwhile, each of the three triple-story components above contains a program unit complete with classrooms, conference rooms, offices, and work space. Second, the specific location and orientation of the rotations are developed to overshadow the elevations and minimize solar gain.

GRADATED GLAZING

While the Center City Building appears to be uniform in its glazing, the overall window-to-solid ratio is forty percent. Spandrel panels are employed at floors and ceilings and between windows. It is this ratio that produces a high insulating value across the entire building envelope. Glass fritting was also evaluated through gradation studies to vary and optimize its density across each elevation. The result balances clarity of vision while minimizing heat gain.

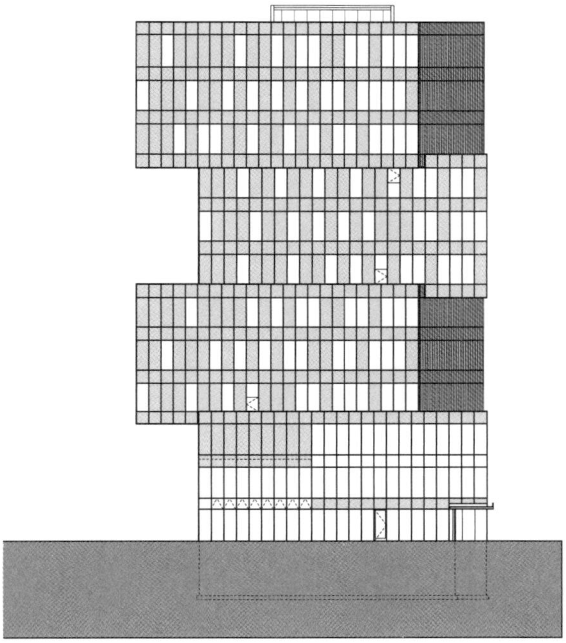

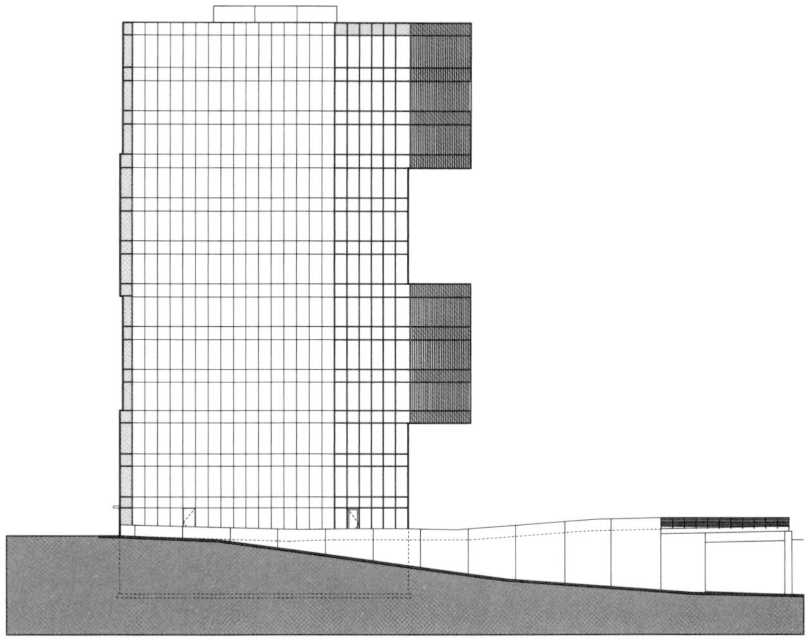

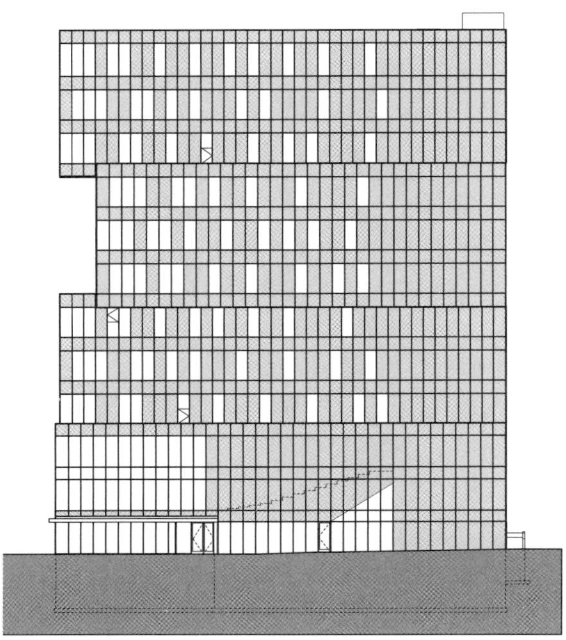

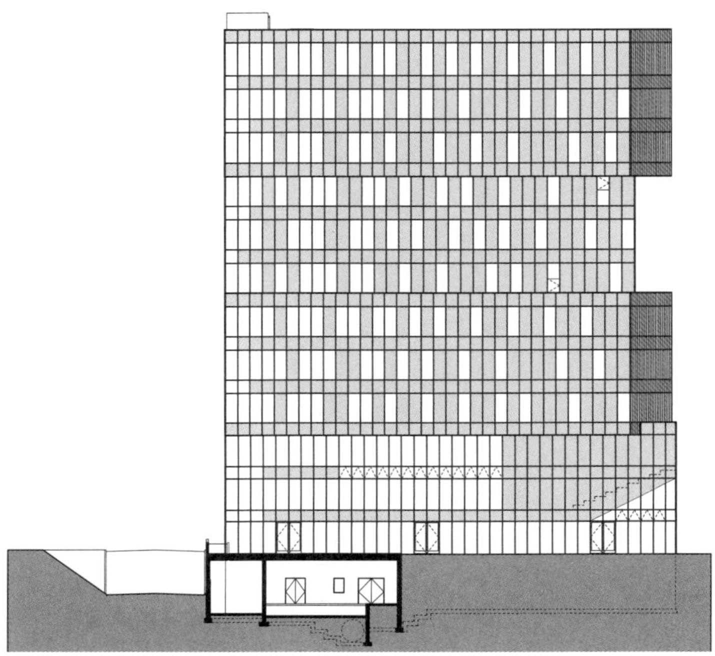

HINGE

Groups of buildings organized about and defining outdoor spaces make up a campus. How might the intimacy and diversity of this concept translate into a single high-rise urban structure? Open stairs here unify two levels at the ground into a single place that serves as a campus center. Similarly, open stairwells in each of the three-story academic units above connect the floors as individual buildings nested within the whole. The open stairs and the spaces they reside within are in effect the landscape grounds and neighborhoods of this new urban campus.

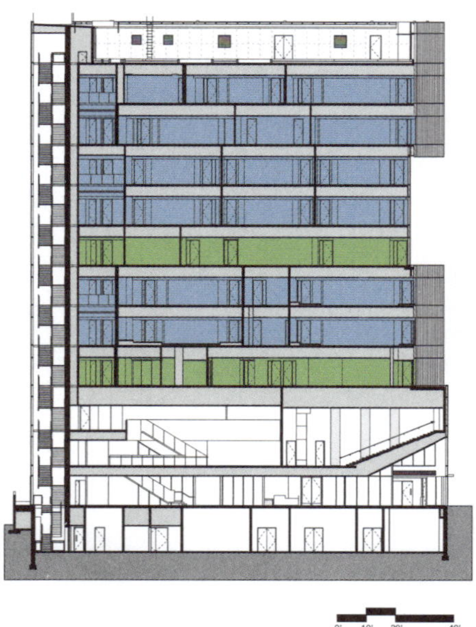

EXTENSION

The lens of this new campus focuses both in and out. The interiors throughout are open to views within. At the perimeter, daylight penetrates deeply, with expansive views to the city beyond. The life of this new urban campus is everywhere, beginning in the park that it shares with the city, extending through the community spaces at ground level that open the campus to the street, and then on up through the internal campus neighborhoods above.

Edgar N. Putman Event Pavilion

Edgar N. Putman Pavilion

James A. Michener Art Museum

Doylestown, Pennsylvania

Architecture often begins its story decades or even centuries before a glimmer of desire presents itself. The seeds of this new room were sown long before the Michener Museum of Art came to exist. The Putman Event Pavilion in a very real sense began to form itself in 1884. This is the year that the well-known Philadelphia architect Addison Hutton completed the Bucks County Prison in Doylestown, Pennsylvania. In its time it was a model of prison reform in the United States. The prison was a vast rectilinear room, open to the sky, enclosed by massive, twenty-five-foot-high stone walls. Unlike most prisons today, it was very much part of Doylestown, the seat of Bucks County. It presented a dignified address on the adjacent street, just a block from the historic center, with an urbane entry through the central arch of a pedimented stone pavilion.

This entry pavilion and half of the original prison walls remain. The other half of the imposing perimeter wall, along with the prison cells and interiors, was demolished in 1986 to make way for the Michener Museum and a new public library. The 1884 Addison Hutton pavilion is now, a century later, the museum entry. The visitor today passes from the street through the stone archway into an outdoor entry court, facing another fragment of the nineteenth-century prison. The museum entry becomes a more recent third wall in this entry court. The volume of this outdoor entry court is intriguingly about the same as the volume of the new Putman Event Pavilion placed on the north side of the building.

Conscious or not, these sorts of dimensional and spatial continuities form themselves when generations extend architectural conversations across time. The Michener Museum uses the two historic prison walls to frame its front door. But the attitude toward the remaining stone walls was far less decisive. These walls are of exceptional mass, height, and texture. Enclosing the museum's sculpture garden on the north side of the building, they create an outdoor room that is remarkable because it is about sky and foreground, not horizon. Rather than the horizontal planes that so dominate our daily viewsheds, the focus here is down on the ground and up at the sky. The museum entry assimilated the corner walls of the old prison perimeter, but with little engagement of their mass and texture. In the largely opaque galleries beyond, there was no dialogue between interior and exterior. The space between the galleries, the rooms within the rooms of the old prison, and the massive walls beyond were just that—space, not form. The massive stone walls could only be experienced from the outdoor courtyards, not from within the galleries.

Prior to our interview for the new event pavilion, the prevailing planning idea was that the pavilion should simply extend the entry lobby farther into the garden. This would have only compounded the lost opportunities of the original museum, burying even more of the old prison wall. Further, it would have done nothing to draw event visitors into the museum and its collections.

Our proposal was to develop a glass pavilion as a transparent object in the middle of the sculpture garden. This new pavilion stands free of the stone wall, with passage on all sides. It creates two terraces within the sculpture garden, making the landscape of the sculpture court more specific and useful. While the terrace to the west extends the lobby with stone paving and café seating, the east terrace is more pastoral, with a lawn and water feature that serves as a play area for children.

The pavilion entry in our design is from deep within the galleries. Guests traverse the breadth of the collection, experiencing the internal worlds of paintings and sculptures before they emerge into the vast outdoor room defined by the stone walls of the old prison. The Putman Event Pavilion is in effect an elegant glass vitrine, a transparent room within the much larger stone room of the old prison perimeter. The contrast between the juxtaposed rooms is what makes the whole so compelling. One is old, solid, and textured, with each stone and joint laid by hand. The other is new, transparent, and machined. They are symbiotic in the fullest sense of the word. While from utterly opposing times and material worlds, the presence of each transforms the perception of the other. The wall is more wall. The glass is more glass. The people in the glass vitrine at the center of the sculpture garden themselves become part of the assemblage, on display at the center of the art. At evening weddings, the theater of the space is on full display. The shades are lowered and the lights are off within the pavilion. Guests roam the sculpture courts within the walls before dinner. Then the lights come on, and the shades rise. The pavilion becomes a welcoming lantern, a box of light that beckons inward.

The craft of the stone wall is in the thousands upon thousands of decisions made by masons as they selected and fit individual stones into the expansive walls, forming and pointing each resulting joint. A century and a quarter later, the craft of the glass walls is the opposite. Our task was to render the joints between the glass panels as few and minimal as possible, yet still build a wall that performs in structural and environmental terms. The aesthetic, technical, and craft challenges presented by the glass vitrine lie in its minimalism. But the presence of the massive and beautifully textured stone walls beyond demanded nothing less. We set out to eliminate both vertical and horizontal structure between the glass panels. At more than twenty-three feet in height, the dimensions of the individual panels were at the far end of what is possible.

We went overseas to a German manufacturer for help. The resulting individual panels are made up of five plies of glass: three laminated plies plus an air space plus two laminated plies. The air space creates a thermal break between interior and exterior. The laminations depend upon an innovative, clear structural adhesive to attain the strength they require at this monumental scale. The massive 3,500-pound panels sit on edge beams at the floor and are attached beneath the roof, with only structural adhesive between them. The result is clear vitrine walls with only thin, shallow floor-to-ceiling lines between.

There is a certain magic in the clarity of intentional contrast as a way for architecture to converse across time. While we are here single-minded in our pursuit of this clarity, the architecture is far from simple. All is painstakingly crafted. The roof structure rests upon the museum wall with a pair of elegantly thin steel columns poised independent of the glass perimeter, and doors to the adjoining sculpture gardens are mounted to the ground within slender frames. Simple elegance is the most difficult of all accomplishments.

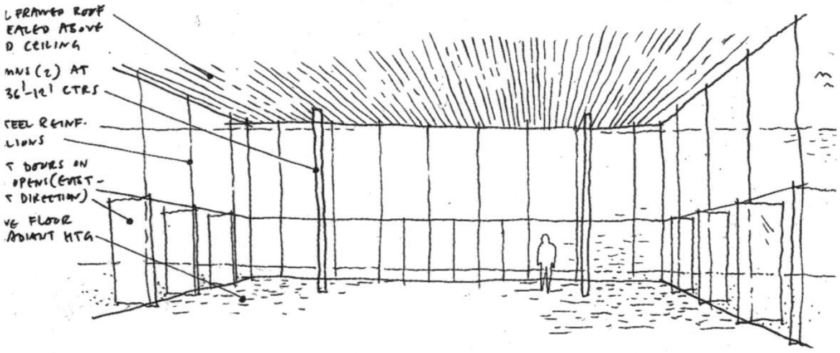

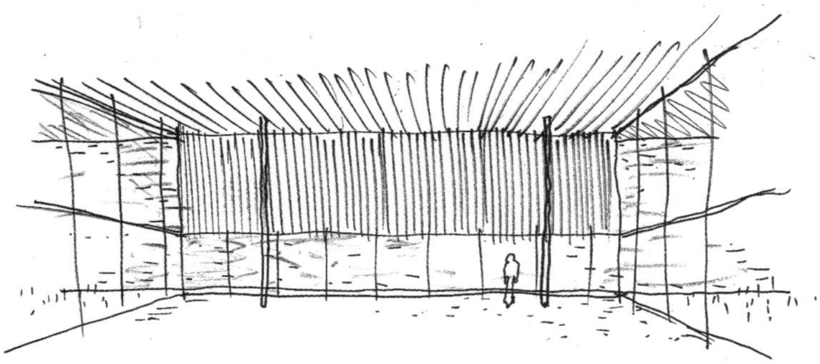

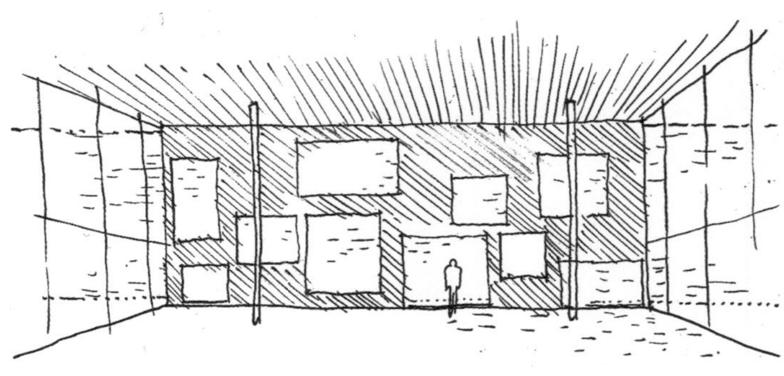

VITRINE

Our approach to this project was unusually preemptive. Normally our architecture emerges over time, through circumstances we uncover as we research and come to know the client and the place. Here, we went into the interview with an idea for a glass pavilion, really a vitrine, in the middle of the museum sculpture court. While this was not what the client and the board had been thinking, they immediately saw the power in the idea and hired us. The completed building stays true to the idea depicted in the interview sketches, with the exception of the removal of the horizontal mullion.

HELD CAPTIVE

The dominant feature in the museum sculpture garden is the nineteenth-century prison wall. One would think that dividing an expansive garden into two separate rooms would diminish the whole. But the new glass pavilion at the center proves this wrong. The resulting spaces to either side enhance the experience of the sculpture in more intimate settings, and the eye-level views through the pavilion along with the reflection of the sky on the upper levels of glass render the gardens dynamic and ever-changing.

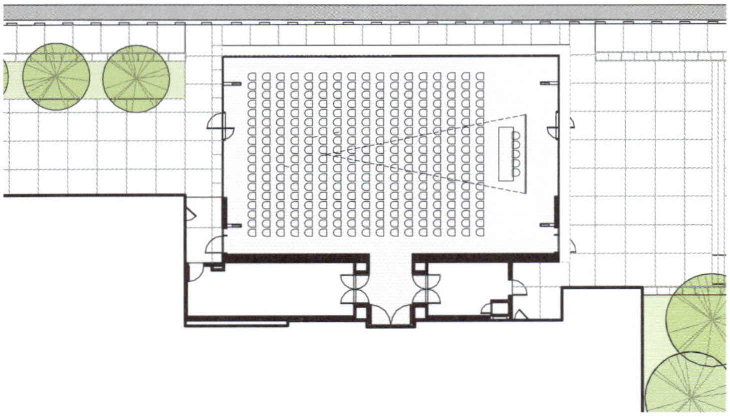

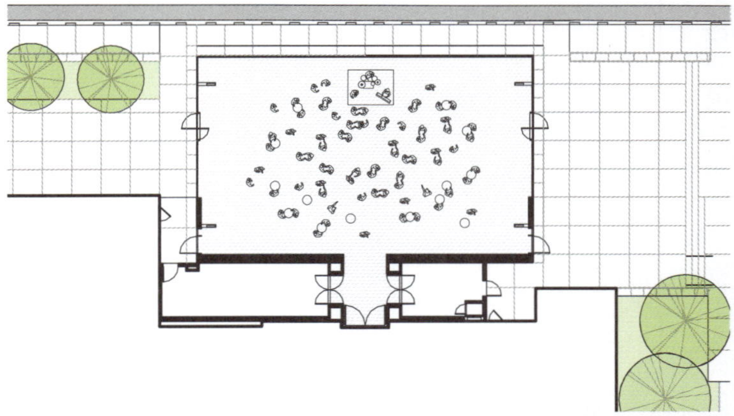

EVENTFUL

The pavilion is a flexible event space. It accommodates weddings, musical performances, lectures, and receptions. Its location draws guests through the museum galleries on their way to and from events.

The vitrine is itself a performer. For evening events in warmer weather, the translucent shades are closed while guests mingle in the gardens. The effect is that of a softly glowing lantern set upon the ground within the old stone walls. When the event is ready to begin, the shades retract, signaling all to enter.

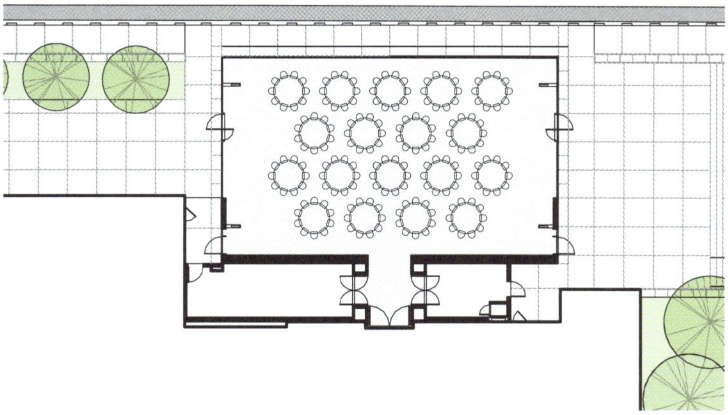

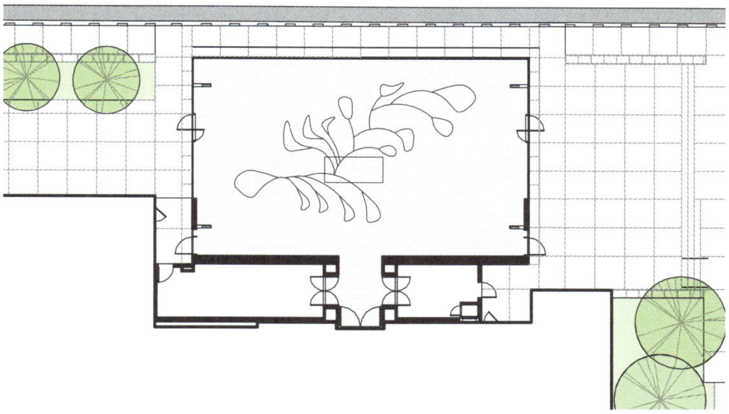

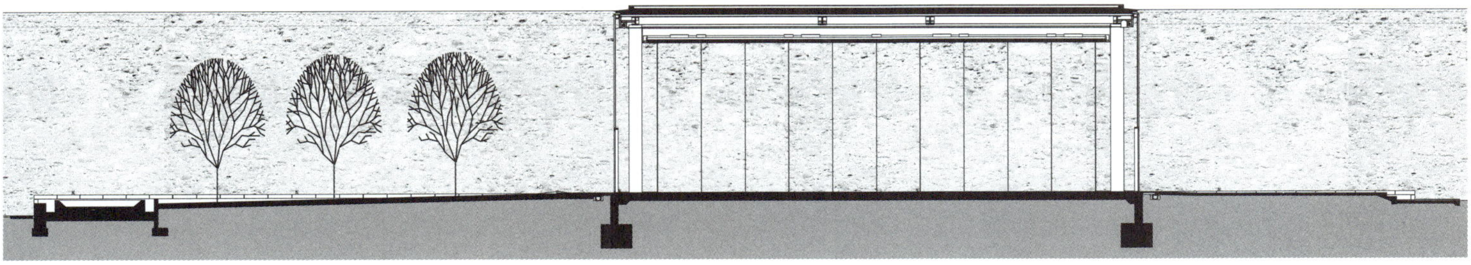

STRUCTURAL GLASS

Our certainty about material at the outset allowed for deep research and development of the glass technology and structural system necessary to realize the ideal of the glass vitrine in the garden. Through collaboration with the German manufacturer, we were able to eliminate all mullions between glass panels. The resulting individual panels are twenty-three feet tall and five feet wide, attached to structure only at the bottom and top, with structural silicon adhering each panel to the next at the vertical joints.

PLACEMENT

Individual panels are composed of five layers of glass: three at the outside, then a gap to create an insulating airspace, then two more layers at the inside. Advances in the laminating interlayer make this scale of panel possible.

The resulting units weigh over two thousand pounds. Extreme care was necessary in manufacturing, shipping, and erection. Extra panels were delivered in case of damage. In the end, only one panel had to be replaced owing to delamination at the edge.

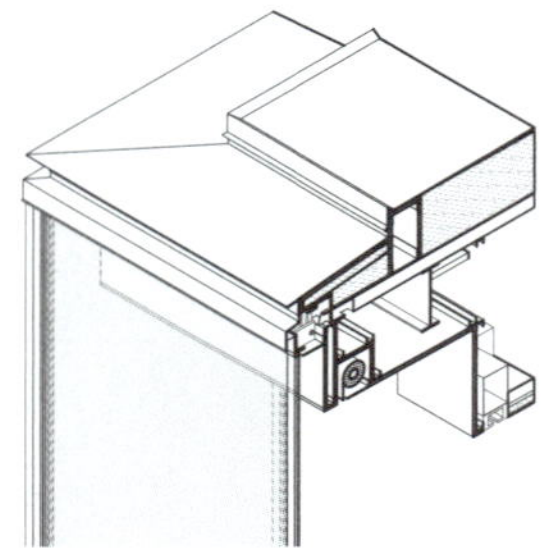

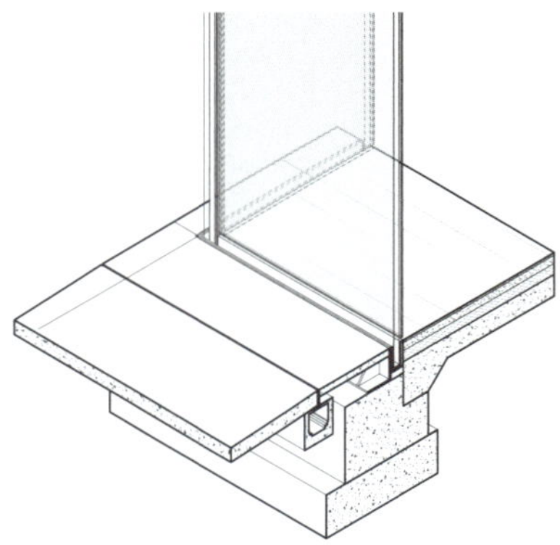

Dilworth Park
Center City District
Philadelphia, Pennsylvania

Philadelphia's City Hall stands at Center Square in a city of noted squares: Washington, Franklin, Rittenhouse, and Logan. All were plotted by founder William Penn in his famous 1683 plan for the origin of Philadelphia, though at the time the place "Centre Square" would occupy was still uninhabited countryside. The city had not yet grown that far west. Today, the location could not be more important to the soul of the city.

Center Square was home to the nation's first centralized water works at the turn of the nineteenth century as the city expanded westward from its origins along the Delaware River. Later, with the relocation of the water works to the Schuylkill River, Center Square became the site of a new City Hall—the grand building we know today—in 1901. Instantly recognizable for its 548-foot high clock tower topped by an Alexander Milne Calder sculpture of William Penn, it remains the nation's largest municipal hall. A mid-twentieth century rerouting of the streets surrounding Center Square created a two-and-a-half-acre apron to the west, expanding the square with the multilevel Dilworth Plaza completed in 1977.

Dilworth Plaza was from the outset more of a place to move through than to be in. It struggled to fulfill its civic promise. Elevated above the adjoining streets by stairs and walls, the plaza was forbidding and inaccessible, with a center that could not be occupied.

The civic objectives of our transformation were simple. First, level the entire park to the grade of the adjoining city. Second, define the park as an urban oasis with a green belt of trees and plantings at its perimeter. Third, develop the center for daily use across the seasons and for large events like celebrations and protests. Lastly, provide compelling access to mass transit worthy of this privileged location at the heart of the city.

The art of collaboration evolved to new extremes as we developed the park. Center City District retained Urban Engineers to lead our collective efforts, organizing our work as well as that of OLIN, the landscape architect, and CVM, the structural engineer. Our collective work had to interface with SEPTA, the regional transportation authority, across many dimensions, from access to and design of the new transit station below to scheduling of transit service interruptions.

The best way to comprehend the role of Dilworth Park in the transit infrastructure of the region is to think of it as a vast urban train station without the lofty shed above the tracks. Imagine 30th Street Station without the station itself. The entire mass transit structure of the city and region comes together beneath Dilworth Park, including the two major subway lines, the subway-surface trolley system, and access to regional rail lines. Developing circulation connections from the park to the transit hub below and threading structure through the dense web of that transit network was exacting work. Transit needed to remain operational with only occasional suspension of service.

But the transit work below ground was not our only challenge. Philadelphia City Hall is a monument that dominates the memory and sense of the city. How could a plaza and transit entrances at the base of a structure of this magnitude participate in and support its monumentality? That is the central conundrum we faced with this project.

Our answer lay in part in Étienne-Louis Boullée's great, unrealized Cenotaph to Sir Isaac Newton. Taking the top of the spire above the west face of City Hall as our geometric center, we circumscribed an arc that intersects the surface of Dilworth Park below, resulting in our profile for the mass transit entries at the base of the circle. The sweeping arc of the transit pavilions is derived from and locked into City Hall. It is the cradle that supports the monument and links the new transit entrances to the grand landmark.

What material and structure might we use for transit pavilions flanking the front door to City Hall, where the sheer magnitude and weight of the masonry walls tend to overwhelm? How could we make an entry to the city from the underworld of mass transit that glorifies the light of day and celebrates the life of the city? How could these pavilions both appear and disappear, be and not be?

Glass can have both qualities, but its conventional metal framing and support structures scale it—rendering it building, not sculpture. To be worthy of presence before this, the largest all-masonry building in North America, we needed to work with a single material. Just glass—no metal. Recent developments in structural glass laminates and structural sealants allowed us to accomplish this objective. Our earlier work on large-scale frameless glass panels at the Putman Pavilion for the Michener Museum informed the project. Seven plies of structural glass laminates make up the seventeen-foot wide, 180-foot-long arc of the roof. Five plies compose the cantilevered side walls. A structural silicone joint fuses the two together.

Can casual and monumental civic placemaking coexist? Can Dilworth Park, with its obligation to respect and enhance the historic monument that is City Hall, also become a front yard? It seemed to us more necessary than ever to try. As our sense of access and connection to government has eroded, we envisioned this small park at the base of City Hall as a daily draw, a place to go, not just a route to pass through.

A white steel pavilion is central to the programming of the new park. It anchors the north edge and shelters not only a major stair and elevator to mass transit below, but also a café and visitor information station. The pavilion is an elemental concave steel structure—almost temple like—supported atop six steel columns. The glass and metal panel-enclosed café nests itself within the space defined by four of these columns, offering casual meals, coffee, and opportunities for lingering. Interior café seating extends to an adjacent outdoor terrace with additional café tables and casual seating, all set within the larger plaza by a U-shaped stone bench.

The programmable fountains atop the flat scrim of the north plaza invite passage and play in warm months. An ephemeral artwork by Janet Echelman curves its way through the fountain jets, tracing the subway lines beneath the park. Mists of water rise through stainless steel gratings and are illuminated by colored lights as subway cars pass below. In winter, a skating rink takes the place of the fountain. The lawn panel to the south is home to picnics and ball tosses. The whole of the plaza is now the place to go to meet, to play, to rest, to reflect, to use mass transit, to celebrate, and to protest. Somehow City Hall, this great urban monument, feels a bit closer to our daily lives. Without moving, its place in the city has changed.

CENTER SQUARE

Ever the visionary, William Penn positioned five squares within the river-to-river gridiron plan of his "green country town," with Center Square at the heart of the future city. At the end of the eighteenth century, nothing was more important to the growth and prosperity of the city than a safe and reliable source of drinking water. Center Square became the site for this critical infrastructure. When demand outstripped capacity, the pumping station at Center Square was replaced by a water works at the site of what is today the Philadelphia Museum of Art. Always rising to address the most important needs of the growing city, Center Square later became home to City Hall.

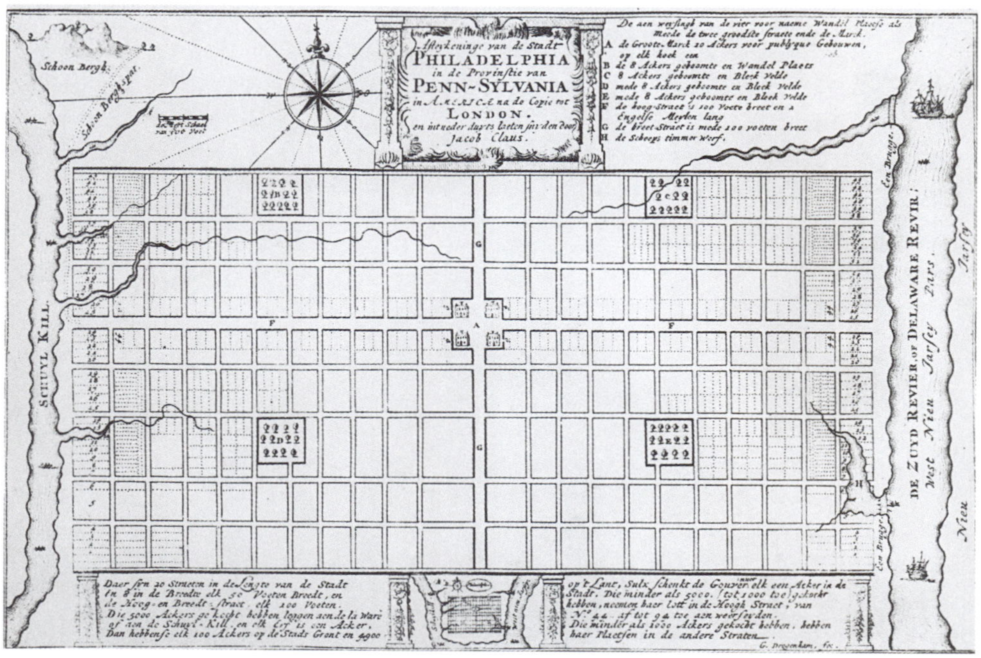

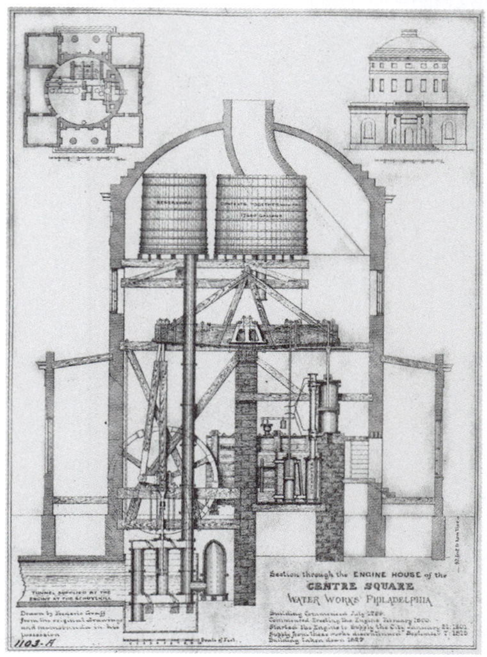

36928-B
9-7-38

UNSUNK

A street relocation enabled the 1977 development of Dilworth Plaza on an expanded apron to the west of City Hall. The entire northern half of the 1977 plaza was sunken below grade for access to mass transit below. The southern half was elevated above grade with long runs of imposing stairs. Neither was accessible to the city in physical or perceptual terms. It struggled to attract users from the outset.

The new plaza reestablishes the street level and rings it with greenery. A lawn, water feature, and café are an oasis at the center. Dilworth Park is now a welcoming front yard and porch to City Hall, a destination for the city that draws four million visitors a year.

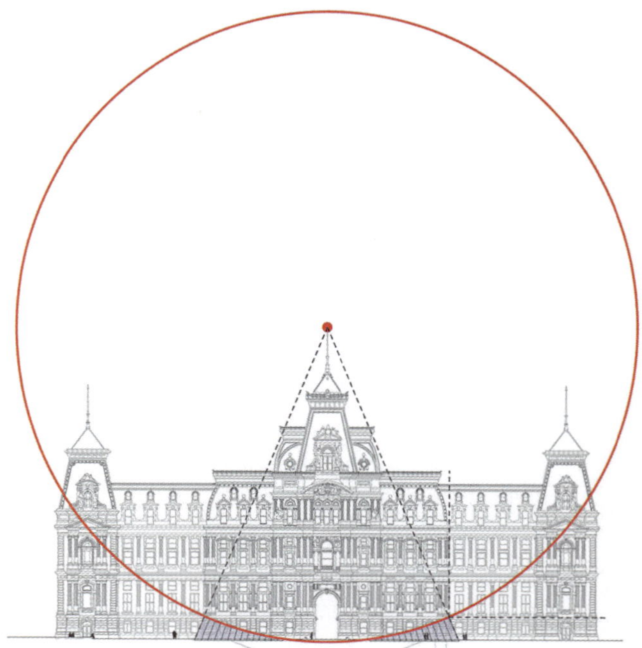

CRADLE

Transit access from the plaza to the subway and trolley concourses below is through a 180-foot glass arc. This arc is geometrically fused to City Hall and the concourse below. Centered on the spire atop the west pavilion, the arc is a cradle that visually and symbolically supports City Hall, framing it along the east-west Market Street axis of the city. Both transparent and present, it simultaneously defers to and celebrates City Hall.

GLASS AND STONE

Both vast in scale and solid, City Hall is the largest all-masonry building in the world. Like City Hall itself, the arc is composed of a single material: glass. It has no supporting metal frame, which would diminish and scale it. The resulting structure is a tour-de-force of glass engineering.

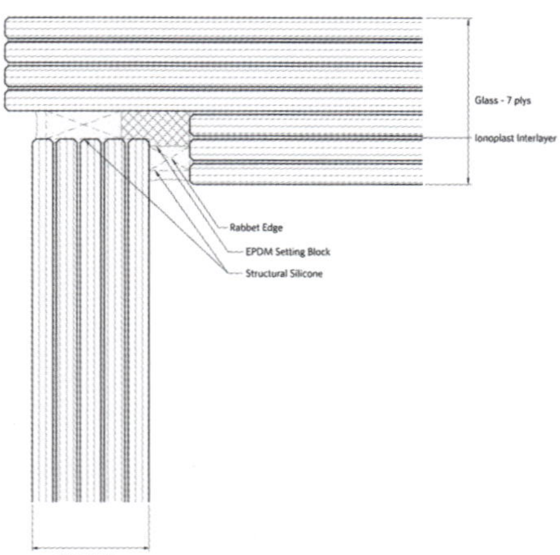

GENTLE TRANSIT(ION)

The entire structure that supports the plaza, glass arc, elevators, stairs, and café had to be threaded through functioning subway, trolley, and regional rail lines. Only occasional and short service interruptions were allowed.

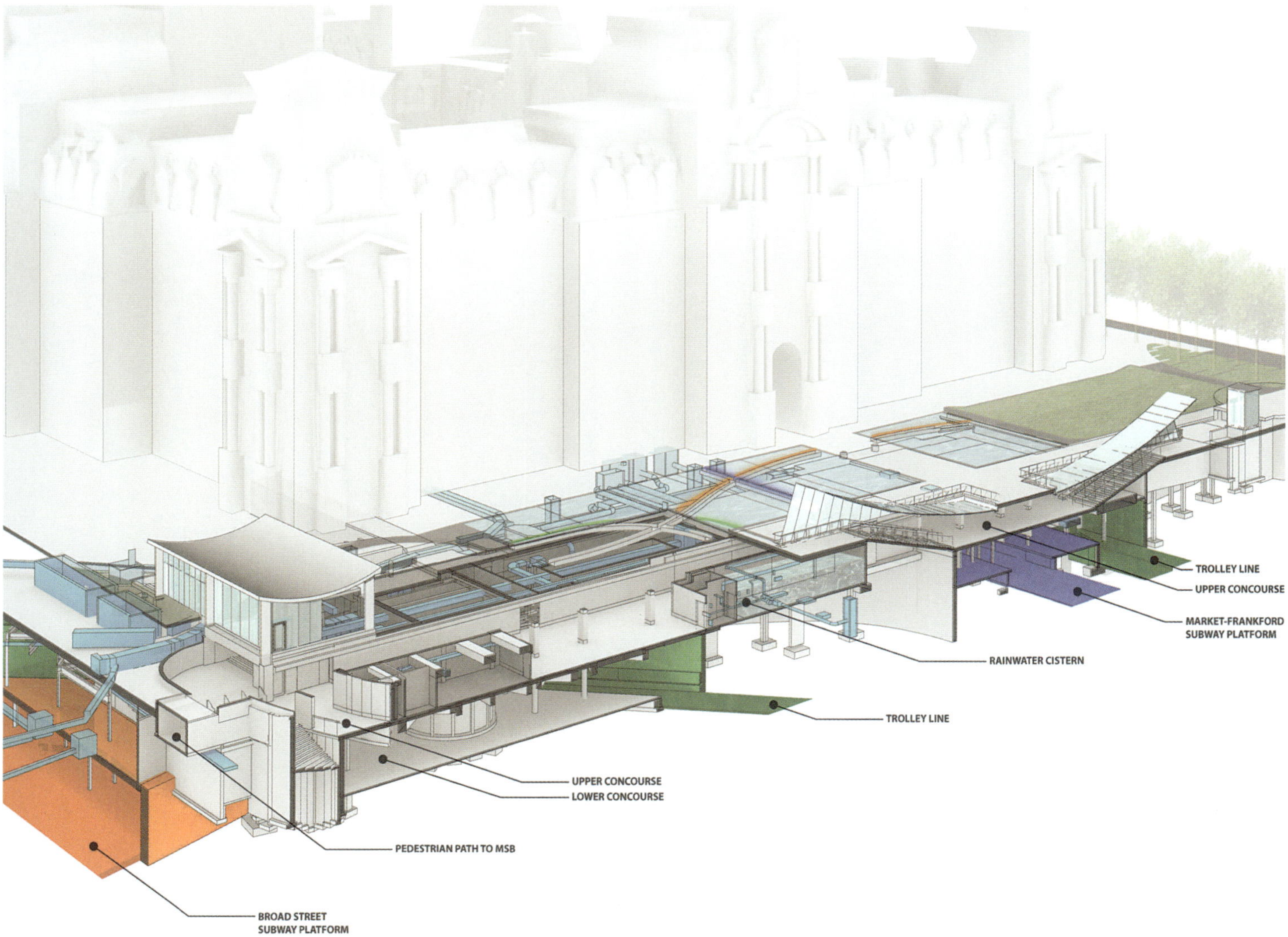

ASSEMBLE

Before City Hall was even an idea, Center Square had from the outset been a place for the city to gather. Dilworth Park returns this civic role to Center Square.

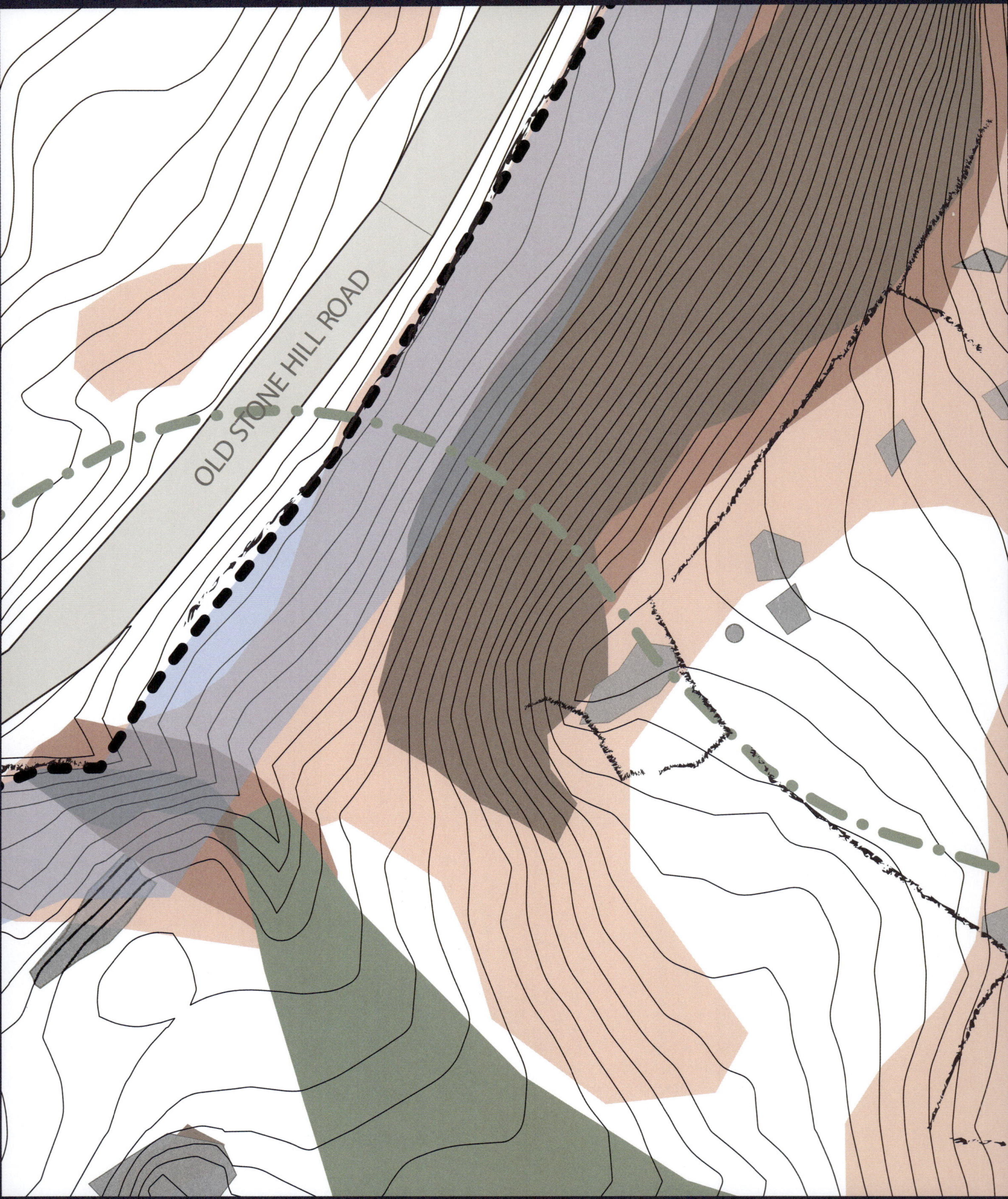
OLD STONE HILL ROAD

Pound Ridge House
Private Residence

Pound Ridge, New York

The tranquility they felt at their first visit drew the owners to this steeply sloping forested site. Their brief to us was simple but not simplistic: "To live in a house in the woods, of the woods"—to feel the presence of the outside inside. Enthusiasts of contemporary architecture, they were highly engaged in the design and construction process. This commitment facilitated a series of unanticipated solutions—programmatically, tectonically and materially—that gave rise to unexpected outcomes.

The owners are also collectors. Much of their art is architectural: a set of prints from Giovanni Battista Piranesi's *Imaginary Prisons*, an M.C. Escher print, Frank Stella paintings. They see the house as both a vessel for and part of their collection. The art resides between floor-to-ceiling windows that curatorially frame views to the natural surroundings. Prints and paintings exist side by side with vistas to the forest and moments of intimate proximity to the immediately adjacent rock cliffs.

As long-time residents of Pound Ridge, they knew the landscape well. The geology of this particular site appealed to them. It begins at a low elevation with a seasonal stream in a wetland. From these beginnings, it climbs more than a hundred and fifty feet up and across a boulder-strewn slope to the crest of Pound Ridge. Much of the original land purchase is deeded to a land conservancy.

The site as we know it today was largely formed more than ten thousand years ago as the last glaciers receded north along the East Coast across what is today Westchester County, just north of New York City. These glaciers scoured the underlying granite ridges, leaving behind cliff-like rock outcroppings and sediment with vast rock forms strewn about. In earlier times, the site was agricultural, with fieldstone walls partitioning the steep slopes. Fragments of these stone walls remain, engaging the cliffs and boulders in a delightful conversation—back and forth between the forces of nature and those of man. The house is an opportunity to extend this dialogue.

The placement of the dwelling within the landscape came to us almost immediately as we explored the site on foot. Near the top of the ridge there were two remarkable rock "rooms," one a full story above the other, with a small ravine between that carries runoff from the cliffs above to the stream below. The back wall of these two rock rooms is the uppermost cliff of this remarkable geomorphology; the front wall is lower and more heavily scoured. Filled with glacial till, the spaces that remained between cliff and ledges were perfectly suited for this dwelling. It seemed the site had been waiting ten millennia to complete itself with this home.

Sometimes program shapes site. Sometimes site shapes program. Here program and site exist in a true marriage. The lower rock room naturally circumscribes a stone-wrapped service wing, with the bedrooms above. The upper rock room encloses the living spaces. An entry hall in the lower rock room houses a stair that rises to a glass-enclosed bridge over the ravine, connecting the lower and upper rock rooms. The geological envelope and the architectural program here coincide in a single enclosure of architecture given form by geology.

We think of this dwelling as both an evocation of the classic New England saltbox and an environmental critique of Philip Johnson's nearby Glass House. We embraced the natural environmental traditions of the site and region, and passive house principles for construction and operational efficiency. Single-pane, all-glass walls at the Glass House become high-performance structural insulated panels and triple-glazed windows. Upon enclosure, the house was pressure tested, and infrared thermography was used to map thermal gaps in the envelope. These gaps were sealed during the quality control process. A geothermal well field below the house's footprint provides cooling and heating through radiant slabs within the highly insulated architectural envelope.

Working within the rock rooms, we sought a light touch. Spread footings nestle within the adjoining cliffs and boulders, placed so that we could fully avoid blasting and rock hammering. Stone sentinels brace the house ends against lateral movement, and likewise a pair of stone abutments support the glass-enclosed bridge. A masonry fireplace anchors the far end of the living room as it opens out along the ridge. The lower service level is simply exposed concrete and stone. Should the house ever become a ruin, these sentinels and stone walls would remain, just as those of prior generations did. Beyond concrete and stone, structure, insulation, and enclosure are integrated via structural insulated panels for walls and roofs, swiftly and carefully erected by a small crane. Floor-to-ceiling windows strategically infill the remaining voids.

We sought materials for the home that were of the place, not necessarily in it. The materials that exist at the site are stone (ridge and glacial boulders) and wood (the forest). We considered both early on, and to varying degrees both have made their way into the home. The base, fireplace, and the bridge abutment are stone, and soffits, ceilings, floors, doors, and windows are wood. But it was the broader sense of the natural place we were seeking—not just the geology, but the sky, the earth, the passing of days and seasons, the weather. In short, the ephemeral as well as the permanent. Our interest in engaging these transitory shifts led to the idea of using reflection to enhance the full experience of this place across time, weather, and season, yielding a compelling counterpoint to the relative permanence of the geology.

In contrast to the Glass House, there is not a single material heralded here, but rather four that compose the upper-level envelope: polished stainless steel that offers a mirror-like reflection; brushed stainless steel that abstracts and refracts the general tonalities of weather (grey or bright) and season (green or golden or white); coated copper that does not reflect but rather receives the contrast of shadow and light from trees or clouds upon its surface; and lastly, transparent glass at the windows that allows one to actually see inside or reflects the outside depending upon the time of day and relative quantities of light. These four materials are our palette. They are the paint we use to capture the wonders of time and change—qualities that are rarely so immediately and continuously present in architecture.

BEGINNINGS

The geological setting for this house extends across vast terrain that can be best understood through telescoping scalar maps that encompass the region, then focus inward on the immediate Pound Ridge area, and finally the specific 15-acre property. The underlying metamorphic gneiss bedrock begins well to the south in New York City. The ridge that today encloses the house was scoured from this bedrock 10,000 years ago by receding glaciers. Glacial till and loose boulders, some organized as fieldstone walls during earlier agricultural inhabitation, are scattered across the steeply sloping site below the ridge.

Pound Ridge, New York

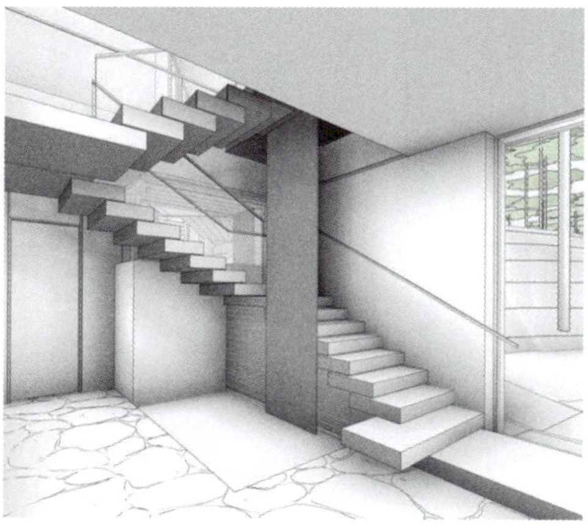

STONE SENTINEL

A small ravine spills down from the ridge above between two rock rooms, one ten feet above the other. These two rooms became the primal architectural enclosures for the dwelling. A sloping bridge over the ravine connects the "given" rooms. Stone walls lift the bedrooms above a garage in the lower rock room. Stone sentinels, one a fireplace, the other an abutment for the bridge, anchor the ends of the upper room. A concrete stair ascends from the entry to the main level.

When the house is long returned to the earth from which it came, these rock walls, sentinels, and stair will remain.

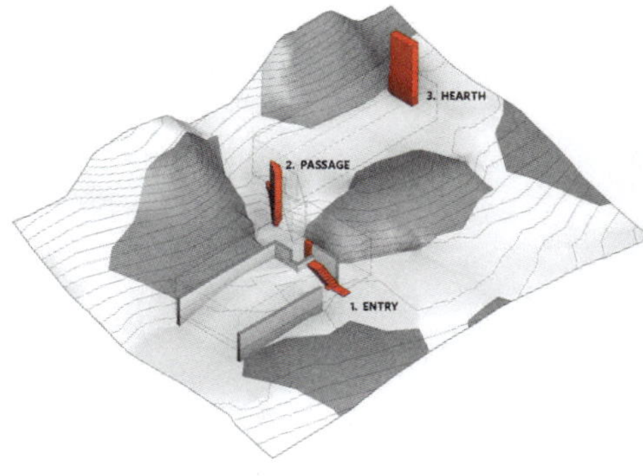

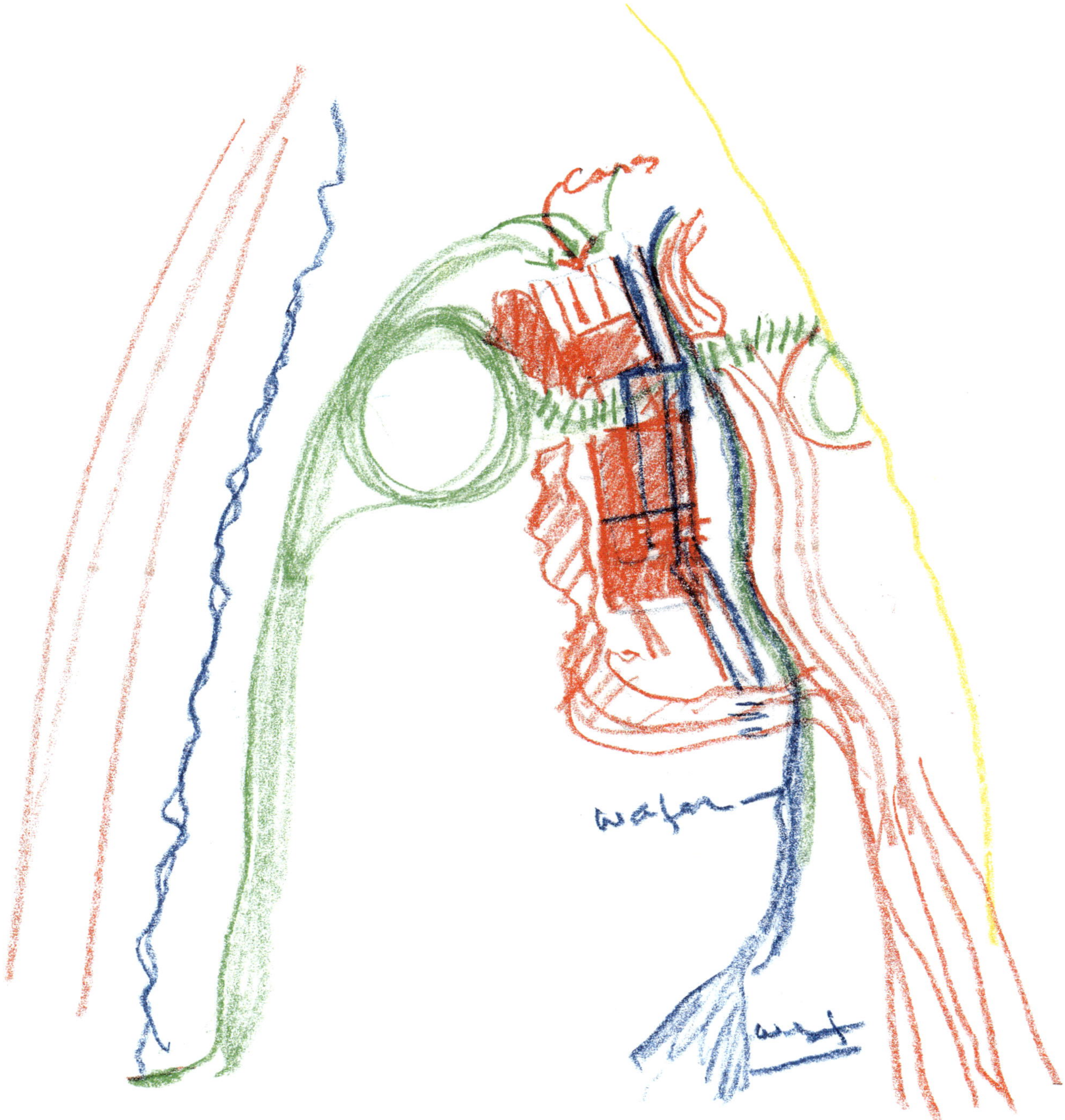
Cars
water

ROCK ROOMS

We sought to be simultaneously in and of the site, touching the geology as lightly as possible. The foundations of both the upper and lower wings are within a few feet of the rock ledges behind and in front. A parting in the rock ledges to the north allows for a driveway and access to the garage below. The encircling rock escarpment to the south extends the living room and porch outward along the ridge.

Remains of earlier field stone walls and new stone walks lace through the dwelling and across the site, joining one rock outcropping to another. New trees and shrubs further define outdoor rooms.

CAPTURING MOOD

Nothing is ever permanent, not even the rock rooms that bound this dwelling. While even ten thousand years may be a mere blip in geological time, it is slow time compared to the seasons and weather. The ephemeral time that the walls of Pound Ridge House celebrates is the opposite of geological time. It is fast time, changing with the hour, the weather, the seasons. While geology is stoic, the walls of this house are moody.

EVALUATING PATTERNS

Art, durability, product availability, panel cost, elimination of bird strikes, and construction detailing coincide in these facade studies. There are four materials that make up these walls: brushed stainless steel, polished stainless steel, coated copper, and glass. We modified one material choice based upon weathering of the site-installed mock-up. Metal panel types varied in cost. We used algorithms to generate random patterns that would optimize facade system costs and would not present large uniform expanses of reflective material that might confuse birds. We then tuned the patterns by eye.

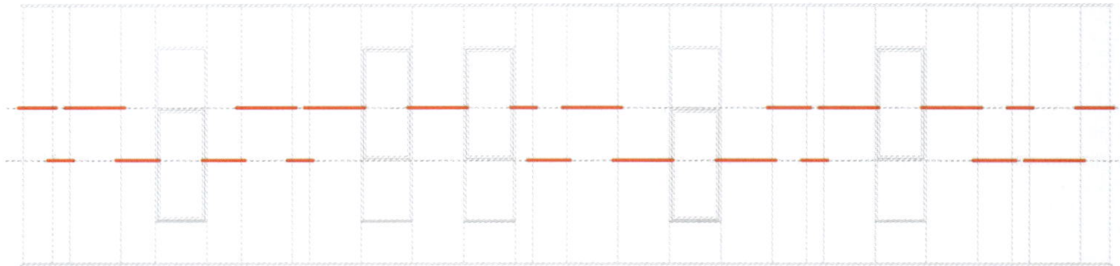

REGULATING LINES

PANEL SIZES

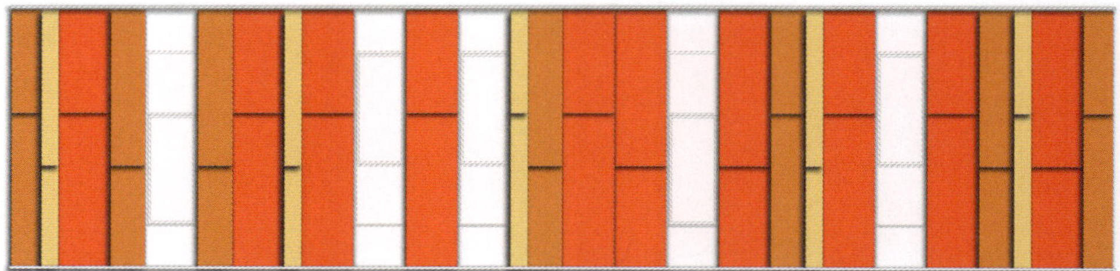

DEPTH

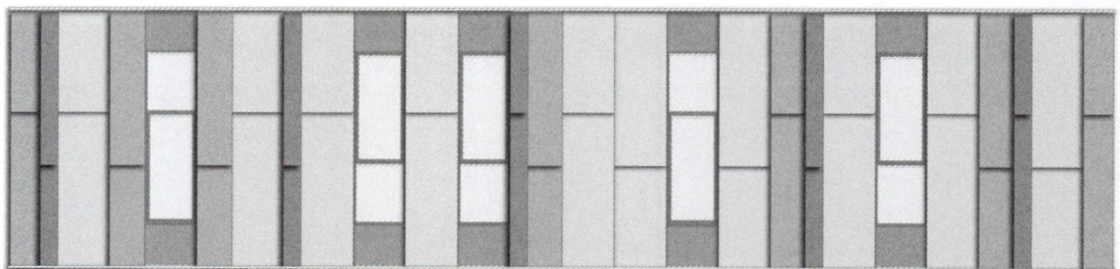

MATERIALS

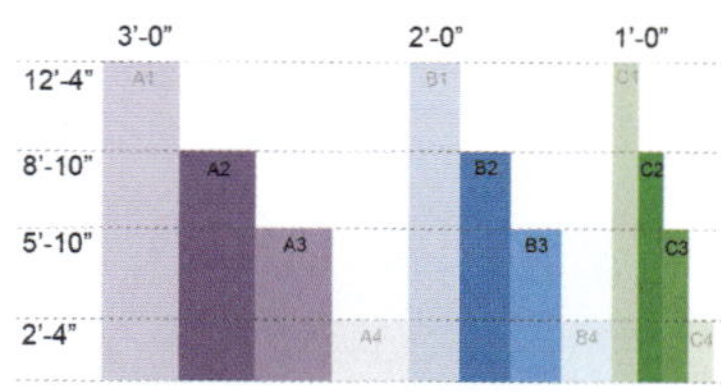

2 HEIGHTS x **3 W**IDTHS

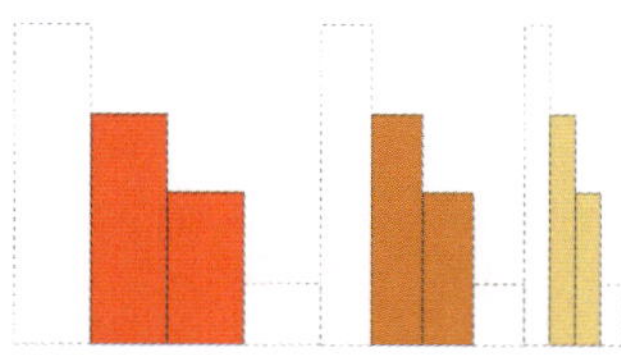

3 DEPTHS

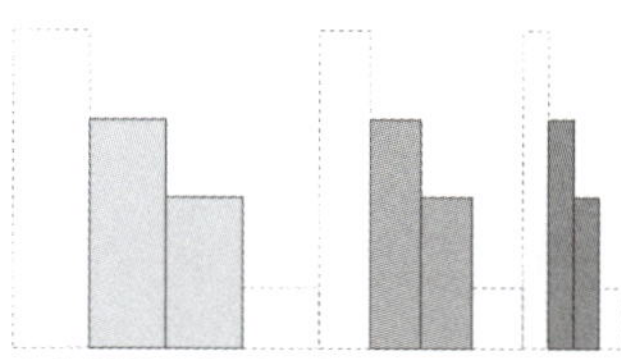

3 MATERIALS

	#	sf	%
A1	0	0.0	0.0%
A2	10	265.0	37.3%
A3	10	175.0	24.6%
A4	0	0.0	0.0%
B1	0	0.0	0.0%
B2	7	118.5	16.7%
B3	7	78.3	11.0%
B4	0	0.0	0.0%
C1	0	0.0	0.0%
C2	5	44.2	6.2%
C3	5	29.2	4.1%
C4	0	0.0	0.0%
	44	*710.0*	*100.0%*
0.5"	20	440.0	62.0%
1.0"	14	196.8	27.7%
1.5"	10	73.3	10.3%
2.0"	0	0.0	0.0%
A	20	440.0	62.0%
B	14	196.8	27.7%
C	10	73.3	10.3%
D	0	0.0	0.0%

Consortium for Building Energy Innovation

Penn State University

Philadelphia, Pennsylvania

The two adjoining structures that comprise the Consortium for Building Energy Innovation stand in the Philadelphia Navy Yard, close to the Revolutionary War birthplace of the United States Navy along the banks of the Delaware River. The naval base settled into its present site at the foot of Broad Street in 1876, and flourished through World War II with as many as 40,000 workers. Just fifty years later, however, it was decommissioned in 1996. The Navy Yard has since undergone redevelopment as a 1,200-acre business, industrial, research, and development campus. Today, it is a startlingly wonderful mix of decommissioned aircraft carriers, battleships, and frigates floating among contemporary offices, industry, and a hotel—all housed in an eclectic assemblage of new and renovated structures. It is a fitting home for the Consortium for Building Energy Innovation, which dedicates itself to energy efficiency retrofits for commercial buildings.

Like the recent rebirth of the Philadelphia Navy Yard itself as a commercial campus, the Consortium is a tale of something old and something new. The something old portion, the Center for Building Energy Sciences & Engineering, occupies a repurposed World War II-era recreation center, Building 661. The something new portion, the Center for Building Energy Education & Innovation, stands across the street in a new glass- and brick-clad structure that defines the edge of a new park. Together, the two buildings initiate a satellite campus for Penn State University within the larger campus of the Philadelphia Navy Yard.

While each of the buildings offers specific constraints and opportunities, the initial challenge for us was establishing a dialogue between them. This conversation of necessity begins with the planning and form of the existing structure. The new building ideally both extends and responds to the old one while simultaneously forging new relationships to place and program. The whole of the Navy Yard site is formed about an underlying rectilinear street grid, not unlike William Penn's original 1683 plan for the city of Philadelphia. The site planning strategy for the Consortium respects the existing Navy Yard grid while also developing formal, campus-like relationships and connections between the two structures. The symmetrically positioned front door of the former recreation center extends its entry with a mid-block passage across the street to a walkway along the south edge of League Island Park, where it arrives at the entry to the new building. Wood-decked plazas at the front doors to both buildings visually connect the two. The new building further connects from its front door out to the elliptical walkway in the park and in the opposite direction to the street. The assemblage of the park and the two structures is fused through landscape and pedestrian walks into a nascent education campus within the vast Navy Yard campus.

Our first project was a complete retrofit of Building 661, unused since 1996. We worked to transform the World War II-era, neo-Georgian recreation center into the Center for Building Energy Sciences & Engineering, a headquarters for the Consortium and its member organizations. The renewal is itself a physical demonstration of the Consortium's mission to reduce energy usage by 20 percent in existing commercial buildings. It functions as a living laboratory for advanced energy retrofit technology, with "state of the shelf" tools and systems deployed throughout the building to demonstrate energy-saving solutions that can be readily replicated on a regional scale. Within this living laboratory, offices, collaborative workspaces, and conferencing facilities house researchers and grantees along with staff dedicated to public education and outreach.

The massing of the building directly reflects the three original program elements. Two side-by-side gabled sheds, one housing a pool and the other a gymnasium, join the more refined red and white neo-Georgian head-house paralleling the street. A lobby, lockers, offices, and other recreational spaces were located at the street front, with passage through to the pool and gym in the clear-span sheds beyond. Within an existing structure like this one, the most transformative design acts are often a form of editing. Coupled with decisions about restoration and renewal of historic fabric, the architects' use of selective deletion, alteration, and addition adjust the past to a newly envisioned future.

The first act of design in this transformation was to make the two separate athletic spaces into a single unified structure. Demolition of the wall that separated the gym and the pool completely changes the interior into an expansive, light-filled volume for events and exhibitions. To enable removal of this wall, new angled steel braces were added to stabilize the exposed glue laminated wood arches. Combined with new steel balconies along both perimeter walls, open steel stairs, and exposed steel trays for building system distribution between the roof and arches, the result is a lively conversation between the old wooden arched structure and the new steel insertions to accommodate programs and systems. Two refurbished linear skylights fill the upper balcony workspaces, the main level offices, and the central atrium with daylight.

Across the street, the newly built Center for Building Energy Education & Innovation supports the education and outreach agendas of the Consortium. It is managed by the Penn State School of Engineering and serves students, building managers, building energy auditors, and practitioners. The facilities include classrooms for hands-on training with building mechanical equipment, on-site and distance-learning classrooms, an auditorium, and an exhibition and training gallery. The energy education programs are enhanced by the design of the building itself. Glass-walled mechanical rooms, each with heat recovery, are dispersed between classrooms. Brick screens shade the exterior, and green roofs provide additional insulation.

The massing, position, and internal planning of the new education building reinforce both street- and campus-making in this area of the Navy Yard. It is long and low, with a single-loaded gallery hallway providing classroom access at both levels. This planning strategy stretches the full length of the block, establishing streetscape to the south and a clear edge for the new League Island Park to the north. The resulting definition and urbanity add to the dual sense of an emerging urban campus. Within this volume, classrooms alternate with office and mechanical spaces along the south flank of the bar, culminating to the west in the double-story volume of the lecture hall and lobby. The exterior south-facing elevation parallels the spatial plan inside with alternating solid brick walls at service spaces and predominantly glazed exterior walls at classrooms. The classroom walls are recessed glass bay windows, with open brick screens partially shielding them from south sun. The cladding strategies modulate the classrooms from dark to light: opaque brick to the immediate side of the teaching wall, brick-screened glass alongside the seating area at the middle of the classroom, and open glass at the rear entry wall of the classroom.

This streetscape elevation sits well within the context of the adjoining brick industrial warehouses and fabrication facilities. The north-facing park elevation lines the internal two-story gallery. Its base is brick, with alternating glass and translucent insulated panels above to maximize interior daylight and views to the park. The west facade facing the renovated structure across the street cantilevers the auditorium lobby out above a walled rain garden. Meanwhile, the street corner opens to a light well that admits controlled light and view into the auditorium lobby as well as water through the circular roof compluvium to the rain garden below. It is an engaging moment at the intersecting streets that allows intimate views into the sheltered rain garden and through views to the park and the renovated Consortium Building beyond. At this corner, the Navy Yard is coming of age again, but now as an urban campus forged about education and research rather than industry.

VESSELS

The Navy Yard is a gritty, diverse, and wonderful place for a new commercial office park. There is nothing like having a decommissioned aircraft carrier for a neighbor. Water figures throughout, with a harbor functioning almost like a vast piazza for ships, streets of water incised into the yard, and piers extending their fingers out into the Delaware River. Rail tracks, paved roads, and bridges trace and span the water.

Hundreds of vast buildings populate the space in between the infrastructure. Several story-high interior volumes are everywhere. A history of daylighting the workplace is on display. WWII-era toothed dormers and walls of factory glazing sit side by side with earlier roof ridge dormers and arched portals in brick walls.

STATE OF THE SHELF

The project began with two objectives. First, create a home for the Consortium for Building Energy Innovation in Building 661, an old recreation center (the 661st building erected at the Navy Yard); second, use this historic building as a tool to demonstrate "state-of-the-shelf" energy-saving retrofits in existing buildings. Instead of an addition to Building 661, a new classroom and office building was added across the street.

The two buildings together anchor and frame the south edge of League Island Park, the historic site where the Navy Yard began. The building entries connect across the street and to the park, creating a conversation between buildings and open space that initiates an educational campus within the Navy Yard. The new building is a backdrop for the park, and the park is a borrowed landscape for the building.

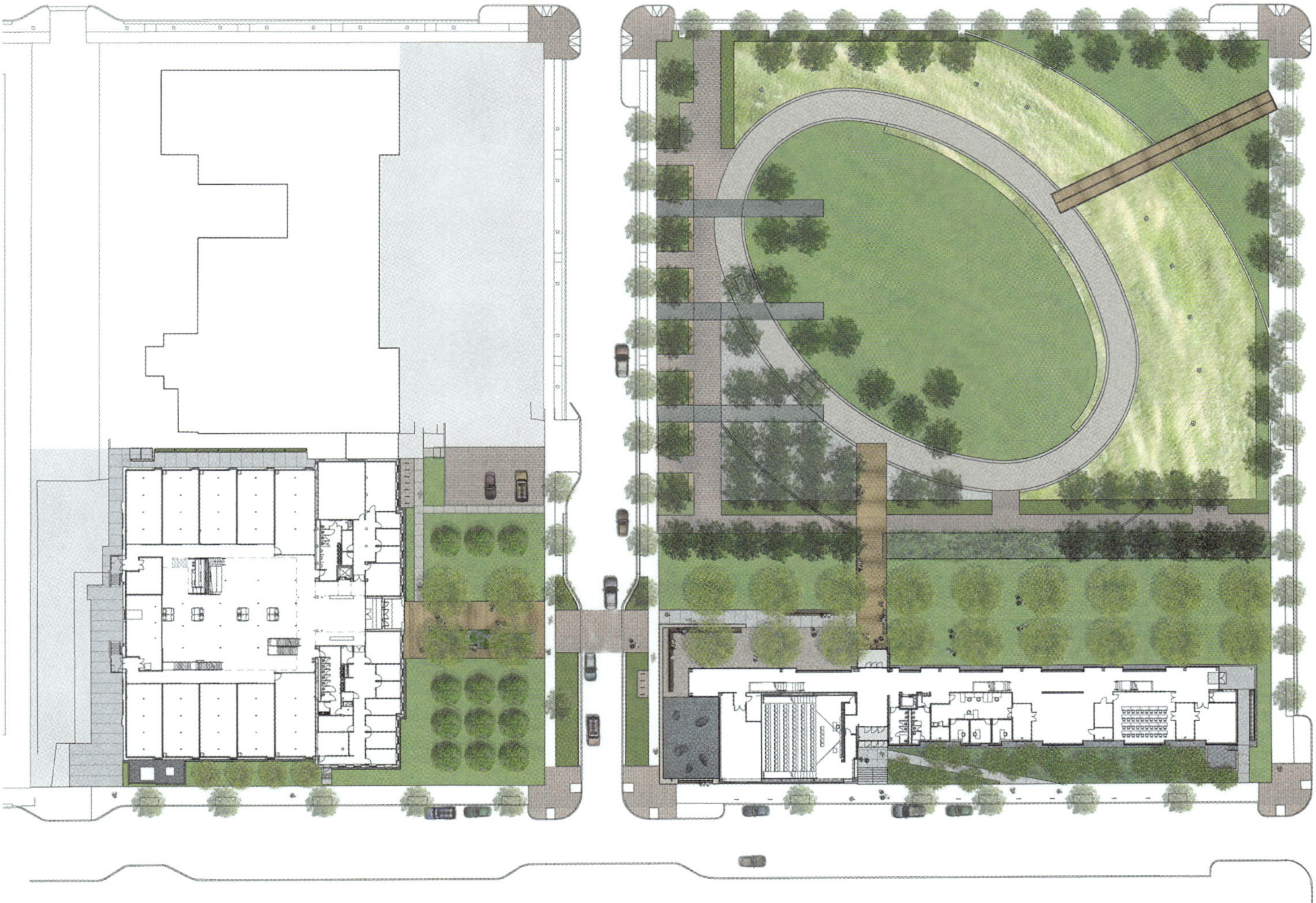

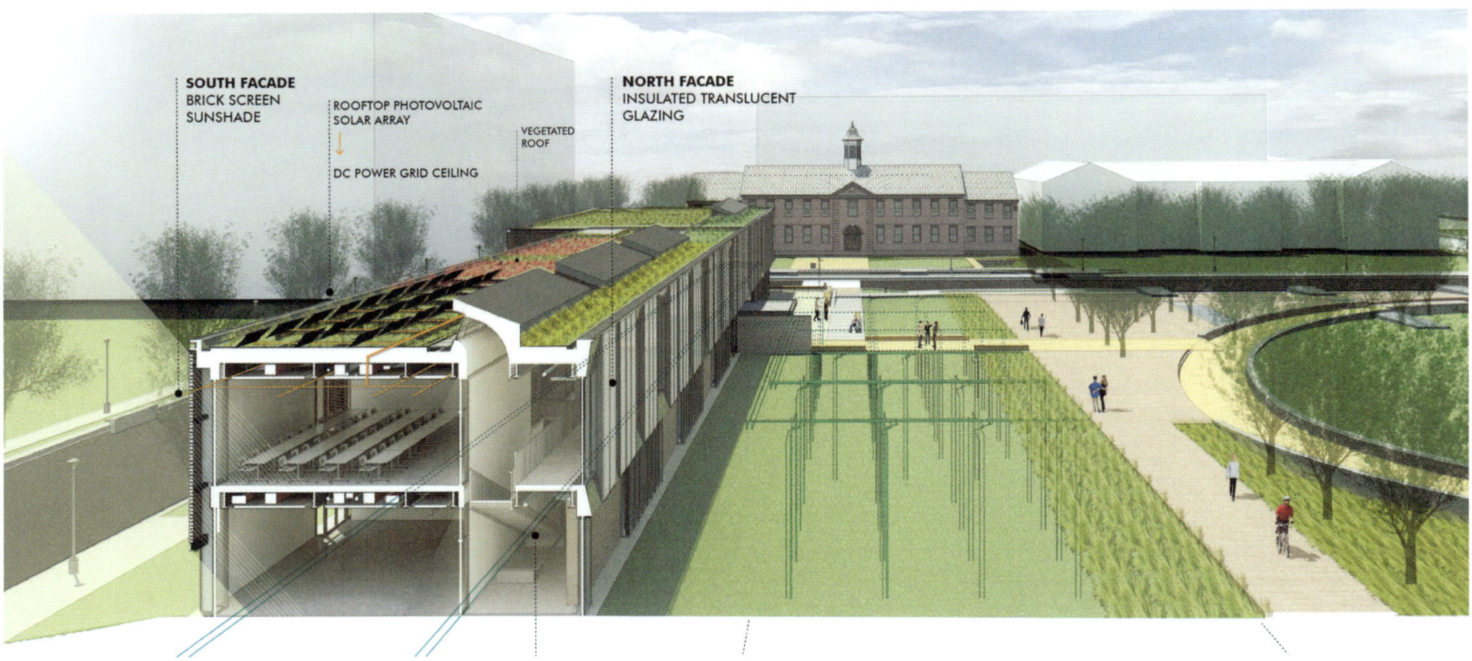
SOUTH FACADE
BRICK SCREEN
SUNSHADE
ROOFTOP PHOTOVOLTAIC
SOLAR ARRAY
DC POWER GRID CEILING
VEGETATED
ROOF
NORTH FACADE
INSULATED TRANSLUCENT
GLAZING

THINK TANK

An act of removal in an old building can be the most important act of design. By removing the masonry shear wall separating the pool and gymnasium, the old recreational building became a new center for the Consortium. A skylit event atrium is flanked by offices, work rooms, and conference spaces.

DOWNLOAD-BEARING WALL

The renewal of the 661 Building is a physical demonstration of the principles of energy innovation the Consortium was founded to advance. Innovation begins with passive strategies. Toward this end, our focus was on enhancement of the building envelope.

To measure performance of the existing wall, we introduced energy sensors, then heated the interior and let the building cool down, measuring energy transfer through the wall. We then used this information as a benchmark to assess improvement strategies. Paybacks were modeled for varying amounts of insulation as we sought optimum envelope energy performance.

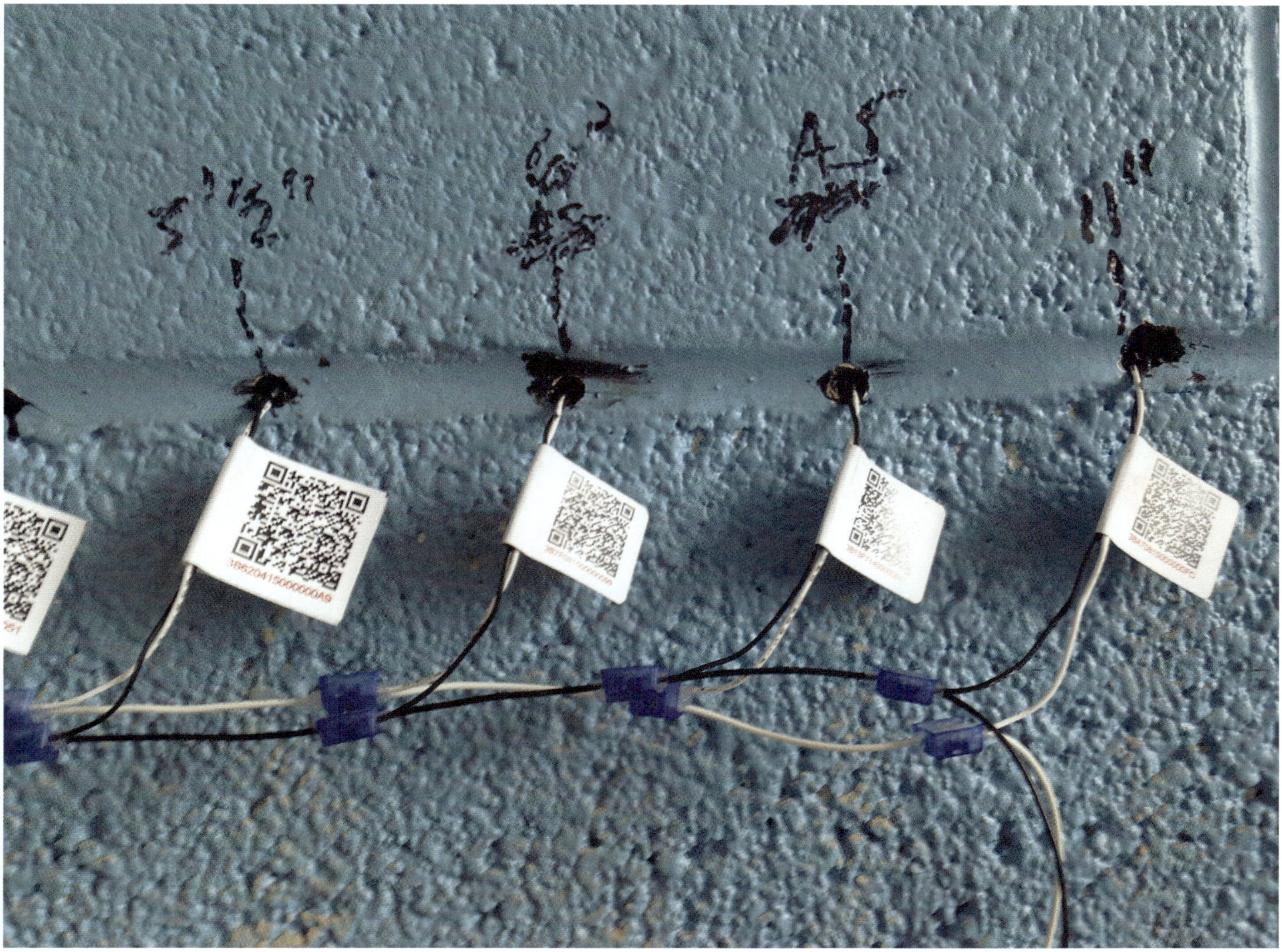

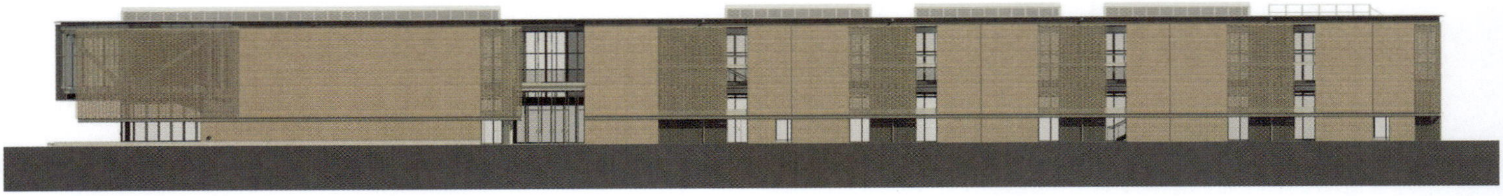

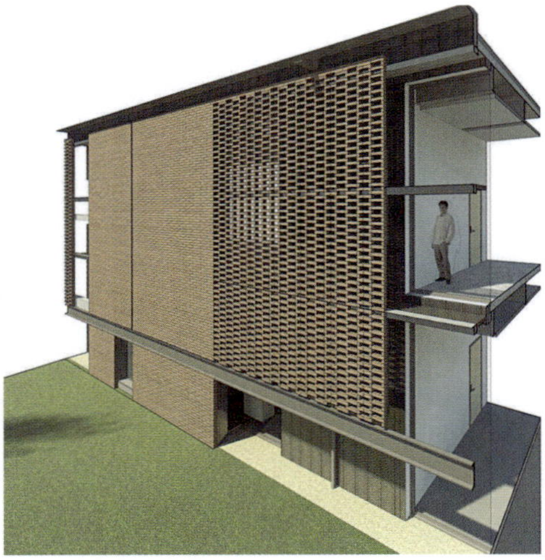

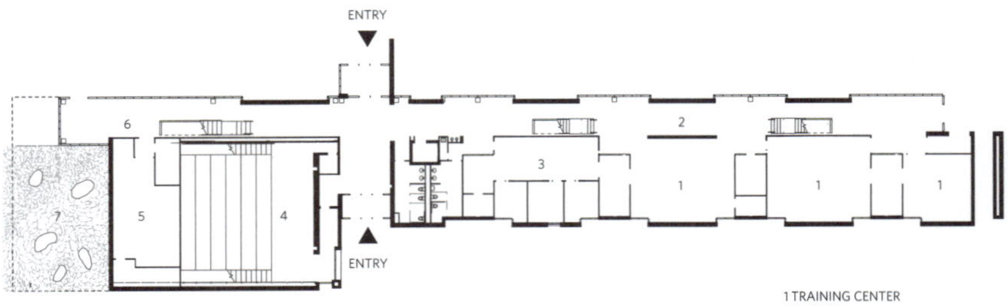

1 TRAINING CENTER
2 GALLERY
3 OFFICES
4 LECTURE HALL
5 MECHANICAL
6 EQUIPMENT GALLERY
7 ROCK GARDEN

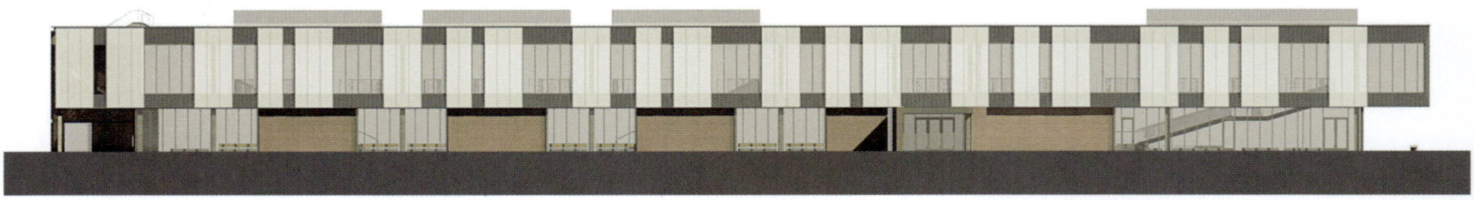

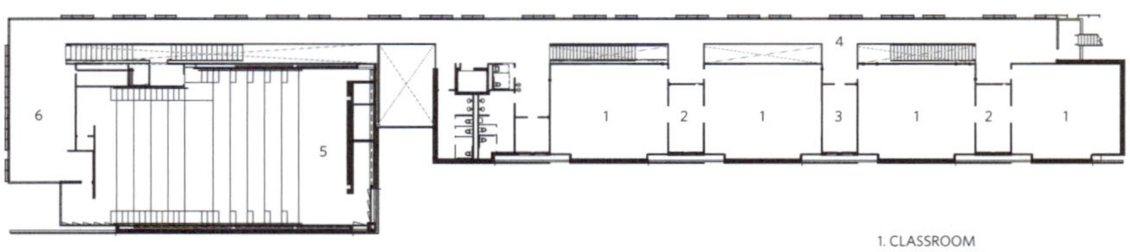

1. CLASSROOM
2. MECHANICAL
3. INSTRUCTOR PREP
4. UPPER GALLERY
5. LECTURE HALL
6. UPPER LOBBY

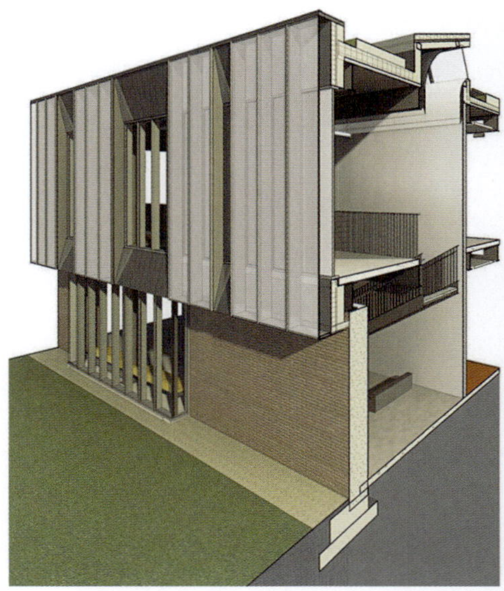

LONG AND LOW

The new building is long and low, stretching the full length of the block. Within the context of the Navy Yard, it feels almost like a ship. The north park-front wall is a combination of floor-to-ceiling glass and translucent insulating panels. Coupled with south-facing skylights, it introduces daylight and view to the double-story hallway beyond. The south street-facing wall couples solid brick panels with deeply inset glazing at the edges of the rooms. The brick screens admit filtered daylight while shading the interior from solar gain.

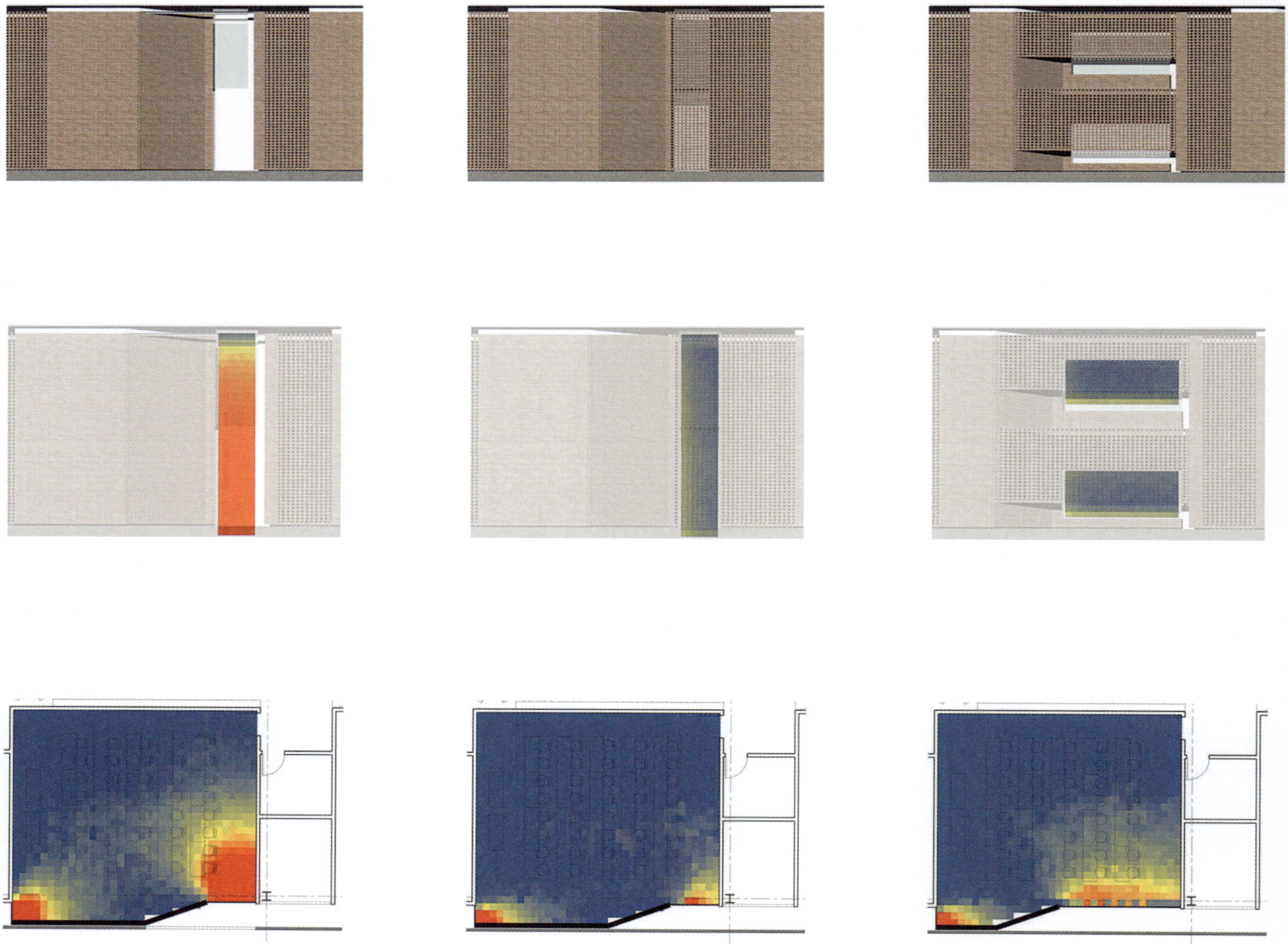

FIXED GLARE

We sought classroom interiors that were tuned to accommodate room darkening for audio-visual needs while also introducing daylight, view, and glare-free interiors. Windows that align with the rear walls of classrooms allow for the penetration and reflection of daylight and view. Windows at the front instructional wall are set back and screened by the perforated brick to introduce diffused daylight without glare on the instructional and projection wall.

Different approaches to window locations and sizes were modeled and iterated during design as we sought to optimize the overall window-to-wall ratio at 40 percent.

PRIGIONI
9

River House Renewal
Harvard University

Cambridge, Massachusetts

The idea of the residential college was brought to higher education in the United States by Edward Harkness in the early 1930s. His inspiration was the decentralized colleges of Oxford and Cambridge. Harkness was an activist whose substantial philanthropy focused on education. His money came with transformative agendas or not at all. The residential college was his central contribution to American university education, and his bequests established the residential college systems at both Harvard and Yale that exist to this day. Even with full funding, the idea was not an easy sell in the US, where the fusion of living and learning was novel. Students at the time lived largely unsupervised in either rooming houses or dormitories. It is a measure of Harkness' vision that versions of this model continue to transform the American residential campus at all scales, large and small, public and private.

At its core, the House (as they are called at Harvard) is a social structure. It extends the personal and intellectual growth of the student from the classroom to the residence by enveloping the student in ever larger layers of community: from the individual student to the room or suite with roommates; to the entryway or hall; to the greater House. Community space and adult support and supervision are associated with these larger layers of community. At Harvard, graduate student tutors live in small apartments dispersed among groups of approximately twenty-five students. At the level of the whole House, a senior member of the faculty lives in and supports the House, along with an academic dean and House administrator. A dining hall, lounges, library, seminar rooms, and student activity spaces provide the physical structure that draws the House community together over meals, learning, and activities.

The River Houses, built in the 1920s and 30s, comprise a National Register Historic District along the Charles River. Like all buildings, they began to change upon completion of construction. There is no such thing as stasis in architecture. The relentless forces that alter our buildings are many: weather and wear; advancing technology; codes and regulations; changing styles; and evolving programs. Over the course of almost a century, these factors accumulate, increment by increment. They add up to massive change: some seen, some unseen; some good, some destructive. The design of renewal is a comprehensive effort to reset the clock. The art of renewal is in the simultaneous transformation of the physical architecture, moving the clock both backward and forward. Certain aspects of the physical fabric, such as the exterior facades and roofs, dining halls and libraries, require preservation. They need to return to an originating state, but with contemporary systems inserted unseen beneath their surfaces. Others, such as student rooms and activity spaces, demand transformation. They need to evolve forward to support contemporary and future realities. The craft and creativity lie in developing an architecture of artful time management that recognizes and balances the differences and ratios between continuity and change. If there is not enough continuity, we lose memory and orientation to time and place. If there is not enough change, we lose utility and relevance.

The most dramatic alterations we introduced at the River Houses were driven by patterns of circulation and movement. These alterations evolved from the regulatory environment encapsulated in contemporary life safety and accessibility codes. For example, the River Houses were organized around vertical entryways. Student rooms opened onto stair landings, none of them accessible to those with reduced mobility. Nor did this organization provide a second means of egress needed in case of emergency. On the other hand, these vertical entryways had evolved into desirable layered communities of students: collections of rooms about each landing and the assemblage of landings into an entryway.

The planning art here is one of balanced fusion: Keep enough of the existing vertical system to extend memory, while inserting new lateral connections to make the Houses fully accessible, with two means of egress for safety. We created a hybrid circulation system by mostly retaining the intimate vertical communities while expanding them with others horizontally. These horizontal communities allow the tutors to be more centrally located among their advisees. This both/and solution preserves and extends, offering more, not less.

The complete transformation of the lower levels of the Houses supports and supplements all that transpires above. Originally the basements were used mostly for mechanical, storage, and limited athletic spaces and, as such, provided the sole underutilized resource that the River Houses afforded. Reprogramming of the lower level also allowed us to create an accessible, full-building circulation route. Destinations along this route draw students into, around, and through the new world of the lower levels. A gracious new stair gives the activities below presence at the entry lobbies. Passage is through activities: a pool and game room, a student-run café, an exercise room, a party room, art and maker spaces, and laundries. These new spaces are an urban streetscape, interior to each house, giving rise to unexpected encounters and conversations.

Together, this renewal gives rise to parallel visions of student life in a dialogue across time—one above grade in the historic structure, the other juxtaposed below in a new world. The original 1930s community spaces are formal: wood paneled Georgian dining halls, libraries, seminar rooms, and common rooms with ornamental plaster ceilings and beautiful chandeliers. These period rooms are justly treasured by generations of students, but they do not fully accommodate the evolution of student life across the more that eighty years since the founding of the River House system. The new lower levels make the historic world above work better, complementing the formal with the informal. The common rooms above, designed for seated and orderly conversation, find their analogs in a connected suite of new social spaces below: games, fitness, music practice, café, and big screen spaces. The inward focused wood-paneled seminar room above still has its uses, but so does the new smart classroom below.

In the original buildings, the lower levels had little presence or connection to the Houses above. The transformed River Houses use differing strategies, derived from circumstances unique to each, to give the lower levels presence and connection. At Stone Hall, a sunken garden extends the new multi-purpose lounge, café, and meeting room to the outside. At McKinlock Hall and at Dunster House, gracious single-run stairs from grade-level lobbies physically and visually connect the historic upper levels to the compelling world below. In some circumstances, the dialogue between historic and new form is a side-by-side affair rather than above-below. An exterior alley at McKinlock Hall was enclosed with a skylight roof to become both a new front door to McKinlock from the river side and an extension of the House dining and meeting spaces.

Throughout the River House district, the idea of renewal extends beyond a collection of extraordinary buildings to a way of life. Materials and systems are renewed and replaced to reset the relentless material clock of architecture to another eighty-plus years. So too is the life within this community adjusted to time and circumstance. As a social system, the Houses exist to educate and support the whole student, doing so through connections across histories and the present, as well as connections between people, ideas, ways of life, and beliefs. The aim of the building renewal is to reinvigorate the architecture as the vessel for a deeply connected and resonant way of living and learning.

Renewal of prior architecture is also a compelling way to program new architecture. The contemporary revival of the residential college model of living and learning owes much to what we have learned from renovating and adding to these historic structures. Programs and forms are richer when they emerge across the fullness of time.

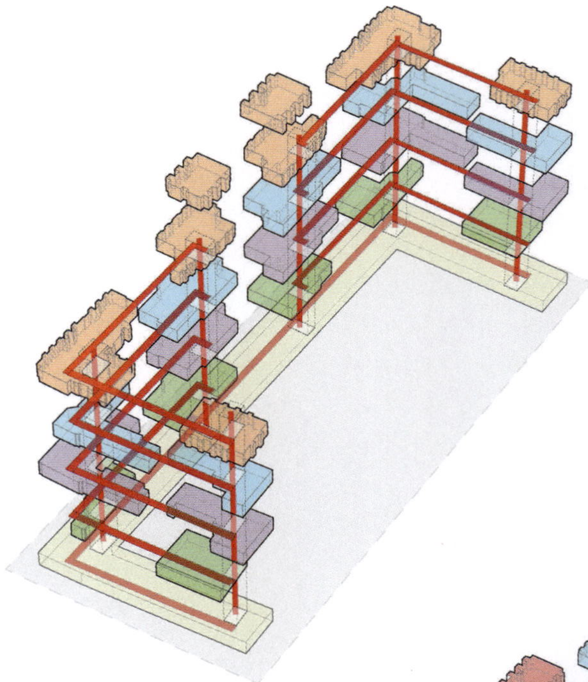

CONNECTIONS

The River Houses were developed at Harvard in the 1920s and 30s along the banks of the Charles River. Five of the original Houses were entirely new: Dunster, Winthrop, Lowell, Eliot, and Kirkland. Three others are combinations of earlier structures and additions from different eras: Leverett, Quincy, and Adams. The last, Mather House, was built in 1970. The original Houses were fragmented into distinct vertical communities that shared an entry and stair.

The fundamental planning transformation in the present house renewal is the insertion of lateral hallways at each floor, including lower, basement levels. These lateral connections, coupled with elevators, resolve both emergency egress and accessibility requirements. They also add a new layer of lateral community and oversight centered around tutor apartments.

WIDENER LIBRARY
MASSACHUSETTS AVENUE
ADAMS
MT AUBURN STREET
KIRKLAND
LOWELL
QUINCY HOUSE
DE WOLFE STREET
ELIOT
WINTHROP
PLYMPTON STREET
MILL STREET
LEVERETT
MEMORIAL DRIVE
LEVERETT TOWERS
CHARLES RIVER
WEEKS BRIDGE
DUNSTER
MATHER

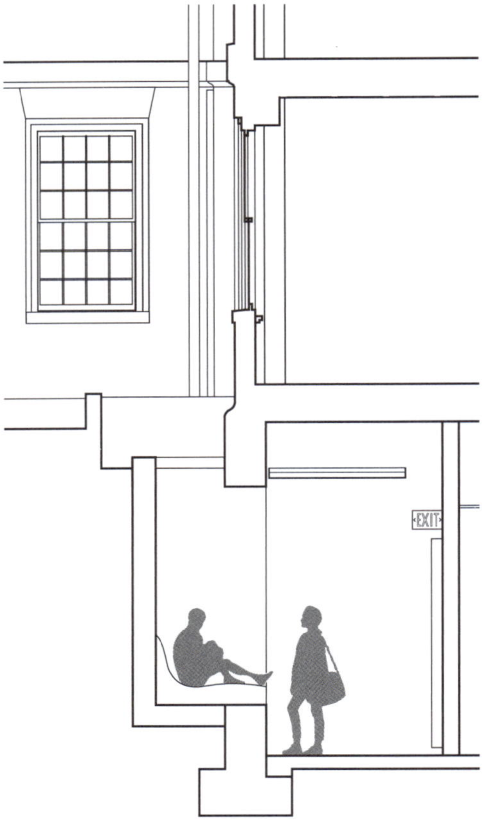

OUT FROM UNDER

The lower levels of the River Houses were conceived as storage and mechanical basements. Over the years, informal activities moved into the unused space. Replacement and reorganization of mechanical systems along perimeter walls, along with a new perimeter hallway, offered transformative opportunities for activity spaces. Wells and courts introduce daylight into these former basement spaces.

POWERED UP

The residential House ideal is at its best when the House is also the classroom. At Stone Hall, this is literally so. At the instigation of the Dean, we introduced a “smart” classroom in the lower level of the residence hall. Monitors are everywhere. Sliding white board panels allow every wall to be a writing surface, even the glass switch wall to the hall. Everything is wired and powered. The desks are self-contained, mounted to chairs on wheels.

LIGHT ALLEY

McKinlock Hall at Leverett House was already the product of additions across time when we started our work. An exterior alley had been left between two generations of building to allow light to penetrate. We added yet a third generation of dialogue to this conversation, enclosing the alley with a skylight and transforming it into an entry commons for the House. The original exterior walls remain. Adjoining grade-level rooms were lowered and converted to a seminar room and lounge/meeting space. Spillover dining and casual study now fill the old alley.

PRUDHOMME
9

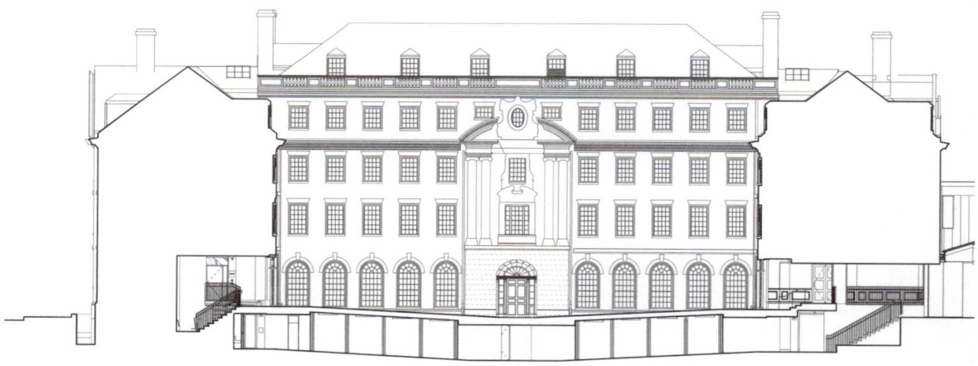

EQUAL ACCESS

Editing is especially important when working within historic architecture. A single intervention along the internal courtyard wall that connects all three wings of McKinlock is the incisive moment of design here. A basement hallway addition makes the whole of McKinlock accessible at the lower level and connects it through elevators to all public and residential floors above. It also doubles as an art gallery. Further, the walls of this passageway addition support the exterior ramps above that make the two corner courtyard entries accessible. It is simple, concise, and unlocks the whole.

SYSTEMIC CHANGE

In the renewal of historic buildings, architecture often chases infrastructure. The River Houses were not designed to distribute the vast array of building services required today. Strategies that accumulate and rationalize infrastructure are among the most important acts of design.

Perimeter walls become dense vertical chases at the lower level. Pipes and ductwork branch off into vertical chases that service perimeter heating, electrical, voice, and data systems at each floor. Accessible architectural enclosures follow, with form and system each modifying the other.

WEATHERING

The first obligation in the renewal of historic architecture is always the restoration of the exterior walls, windows, and roof. These systems begin their inevitable passage of decline the moment they are set in place. There are many forces of change at work here, including weather, changing codes, and standards of comfort. Roof flashings and slate are replaced after seventy-five years of freeze-thaw, rain, and snow. Leaking single-pane windows are replaced with insulated double-glazed systems that are fully weather-stripped. A temporary building is built around the building to complete the work of renewal.

Ortlieb's Bottling House

KieranTimberlake

Philadelphia, Pennsylvania

The city of Philadelphia is most often associated with events and places surrounding the founding of the United States of America. Less well known is its dominance as a center of industry and manufacturing throughout much of the nineteenth and early twentieth centuries. The setting for our architectural office is the Northern Liberties, one of the oldest sections of the city, situated along the Delaware River. With its ready access to river transportation, early regional roads, and rail lines, the Northern Liberties was once an epicenter of American manufacturing. Small row homes for workers were interspersed with manufacturing shops and plants of all scales throughout the neighborhood, making diverse products from saws to textiles, paints, steel springs, and leather goods. Poplar Street defines the northern edge of our office. It was once a rope walk, a narrow street lined with rope makers who used the street itself as a workshop, making rope to support the maritime industry.

By the middle of the nineteenth century, German immigrants began to introduce beer brewing into the Northern Liberties. There is a historical marker at the corner of our building identifying the site at which John Wagner from Bavaria brewed the first lager beer in America in 1840. These early breweries were successful. Henry F. Ortlieb and successive generations developed Ortlieb's into a major regional brand between 1869 and 1981, when it was bought by Schmidt's.

The bottling plant that is now our office was the last structure erected by Ortlieb's in 1947, just after World War II. It is a two-story building with a full basement. The topmost level housed the bottling equipment in a vast 35-foot high hall dominated by a light and ventilation monitor extending the full length of the building. Full-height factory glazing floods the space with light along the west and north flanks. The street level contained a large cooler room along with storage areas and a loading dock. The bottling plant is on the National Register of Historic Places as one of the few manufacturing buildings left in the Northern Liberties.

The entry and lobby to our workspace is through the fabrication shop. Our shop is our storefront, our window, and message to the city: History is alive, there are still makers in the Northern Liberties. This location was in part pragmatic, as the old beer-loading dock was the ideal place for our shop. But more importantly, it says much of what you need to know about us. We think in large part through making. The passage from our maker spaces at the entry level through our lobby and into the workplace above had to be direct and compelling, an open invitation to move back and forth freely through the worlds of thinking and making. Our red stair symbolically and practically fuses making and thinking once again into a single enterprise. It arrived as a singular piece from Zahner's fabrication shops in Kansas City, made of heavy folded metal plate that does it all: it is structure, walking surface, and guardrail in one. The diagonal open riser plates are threads that allow view through while stabilizing the single run stair. The roller plates at the bottom suggest a ship stair that can be lifted, reminding us metaphorically of the tenuous relationship between design and making in the modern world.

The upper level of Ortlieb's is a vast gabled shed filled with daylight. We see and feel this light as it moves across the days and seasons. Daylight, time, and weather are very present in our workdays. At times it can feel almost like an office cathedral, uplifting us with its soaring volume and light.

Light and air are life-giving elements. Almost all the light in our office is free. The expansive factory windows coupled with overhead light monitors afford a workspace positively infused with daylight. This old building designed for manufacturing is a potent reminder of how far we can get to comfort through design that uses what nature already supplies. Since most of our work is on screens, even on the dreariest of days we want little else. When needed, each work surface has an individually controlled task light. Much of our air is similarly free. Just as the original design invites daylight into the interior, so too does the building invite natural ventilation through extensive operable windows at the walls and overhead monitors. We continue to use the operable windows and exhaust fans in tandem with supplemental heating and cooling to minimize energy use. A raised floor creates an efficient plenum through which we can move low velocity air tempered for heating and cooling, as well as a flexible path for power, voice, and data. Individually controlled diffusers at the floor provide the capacity to adjust air quantity as necessary.

We believe that life is an experiment. We look at the world we inhabit and seek an ever better way forward. How could our office space itself become an experiment? No large office that we know of in Philadelphia functions without air conditioning. The Ortlieb's bottling plant was designed for natural ventilation and functioned for decades without air conditioning. Could it work as an office without air conditioning? We tried. We developed and installed sensors throughout the building to better understand and tune performance. We developed and recorded detailed digital surveys about how each employee was feeling throughout the day. In short, we "sailed" the building based upon the collected data. We conducted night flushes to precool the building's thermal mass, we opened and closed windows based upon humidity levels and the building's natural rhythm of heat gain and loss, and we added large shop fans and personal desk fans to improve our ability to tolerate higher temperatures.

Ultimately, when our rituals could not overcome the Philadelphia climate, we added a cooling tower and learned how to operate an office building in mixed mode, using natural ventilation whenever conditions allow. We now improve by increments as we continue to develop the logic statement that transitions the building automatically from passive natural ventilation to cooling. With each iteration, we improve comfort while reducing consumption, until we reach net zero.

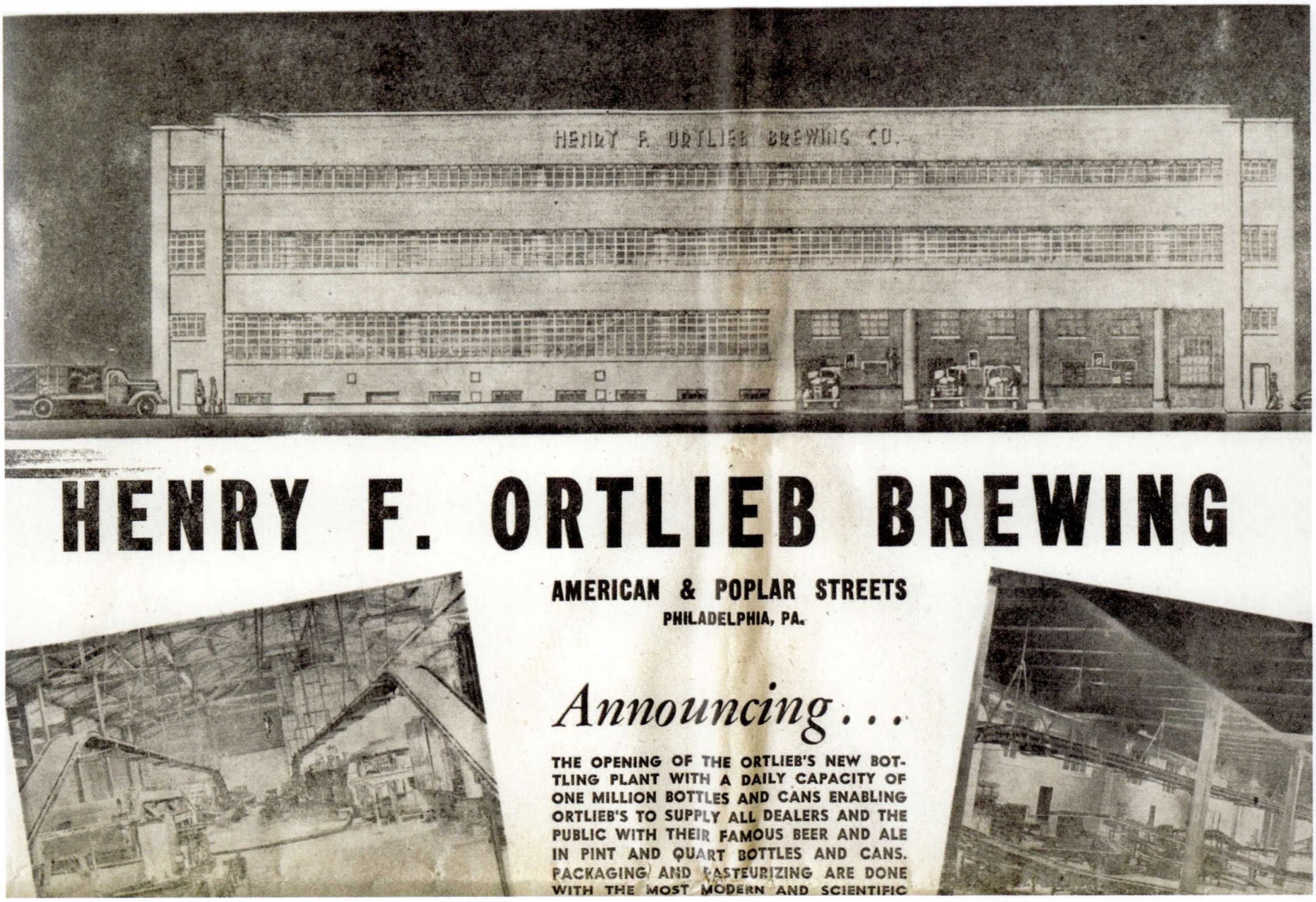

HENRY F. ORTLIEB BREWING CO.

HENRY F. ORTLIEB BREWING

AMERICAN & POPLAR STREETS
PHILADELPHIA, PA.

Announcing . . .

THE OPENING OF THE ORTLIEB'S NEW BOTTLING PLANT WITH A DAILY CAPACITY OF ONE MILLION BOTTLES AND CANS ENABLING ORTLIEB'S TO SUPPLY ALL DEALERS AND THE PUBLIC WITH THEIR FAMOUS BEER AND ALE IN PINT AND QUART BOTTLES AND CANS. PACKAGING AND PASTEURIZING ARE DONE WITH THE MOST MODERN AND SCIENTIFIC

A COLD ONE

The 1947 state-of-the art bottling plant for the Henry F. Ortlieb Brewery is now a state-of-the-art experimental home for our firm. The old loading dock is today the entry to a prototyping shop that enables exploration of leading edge architectural and engineering fabrications. The studio space itself is an experimental platform to explore natural ventilation, mixed mode ventilation, and other energy reduction and measurement strategies in an actual office setting. The Mister Softee truck was a way to ease the pain of an excessively hot day during our first summer.

Philadelphia, Pennsylvania

MAKING

The structure was designed to support heavy equipment on all levels as well as the movement of palletized products. Heat generated by the bottling equipment was exhausted through operable windows and a rooftop ventilation monitor that extends the full length of the building.

Seventy years later, all these features provide great bones for an architect's office. Daylight infuses the space from the perimeter and above. A new raised floor provides system distribution flexibility to support the movement of desks and equipment, enabling project teams to rapidly reconfigure. Nearly everything is nomadic. Desks, tables, files, chairs, even partition walls, are on wheels. Making and the products of making are everywhere.

ShopBot
shopbottools.com

SHIP SHAPE

The lobby stair was designed with and fabricated by A. Zahner Co. It is a single run from the entry-level lobby to the upper-level studio. The only structure in this stair is metal plate. The side plates are creased to create a graceful angled flare at the lower landing. The alternating triangular stringers between treads both allow view through and tie the stair together with a structural lattice. The joints at the bottom and top of the stair are reminiscent of a ship gangplank. The full-scale prototype of two treads and one riser remains in our office collection.

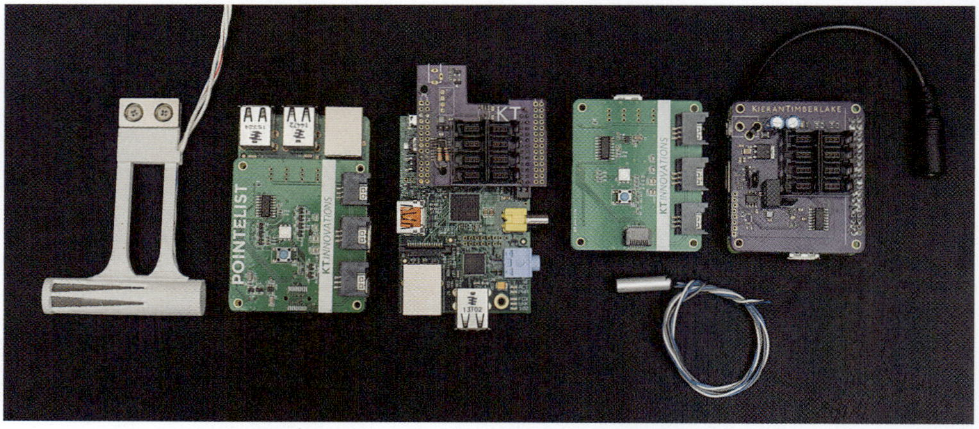

SENSING

Architecture is never really finished. It can always learn and get better. As part of the fit out of Ortlieb's, we installed a wireless sensor network at dozens of locations to monitor temperature and humidity. A weather station was installed on the roof to provide specific microclimatic data. During our first summer, we operated the building using only natural ventilation and fans. Temperature and humidity conditions were mapped across that summer, and staff surveys recorded individual perceptions of comfort. We did our best to moderate conditions with night flushes, opening and closing windows, personal fans, and large shop fans.

Ultimately, too many people were too uncomfortable, so we added air conditioning. With our automated systems and sensor data, we can be very targeted about when and how we use it.

GLAZING SURFACE TEMPERATURE
ROOF SURFACE TEMPERATURE
SLAB TEMPERATURE
STEEL SURFACE TEMPERATURE
TILE SURFACE TEMPERATURE

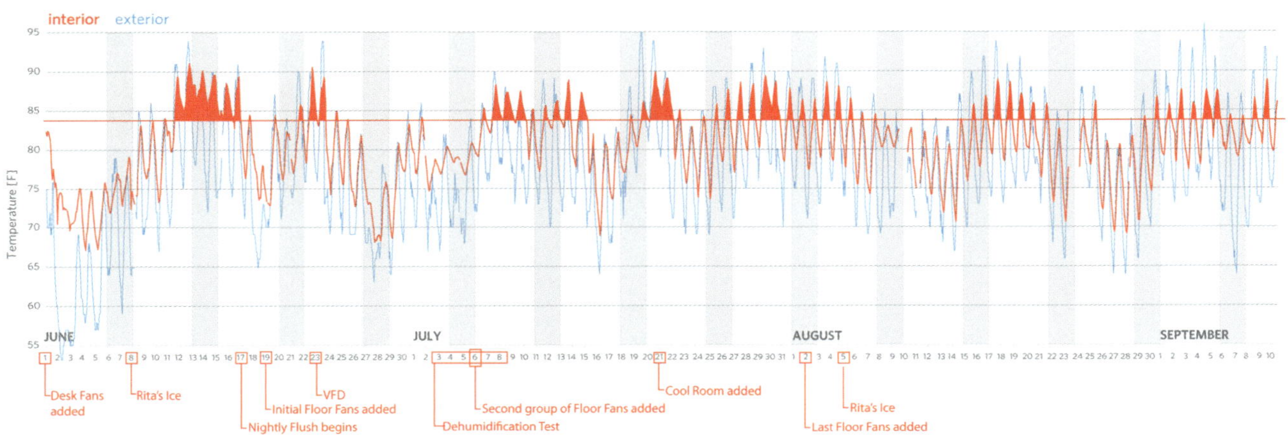
interior
exterior
Temperature [F]
95
90
85
80
75
70
65
60
55
JUNE
JULY
AUGUST
SEPTEMBER
Desk Fans added
Rita's Ice
VFD
Initial Floor Fans added
Nightly Flush begins
Second group of Floor Fans added
Dehumidification Test
Cool Room added
Rita's Ice
Last Floor Fans added

STRONG FEELINGS

Good things often come from failure. The tool we developed to correlate temperature and humidity with how individuals were feeling and where they were working is now a web-based survey app called Roast that allows those who manage buildings to optimize temperature with regard to occupant comfort. Using this tool, we continue to drive our energy use profile down year by year with new initiatives and building management practices. Our ultimate goal is an energy use index of zero by 2030.

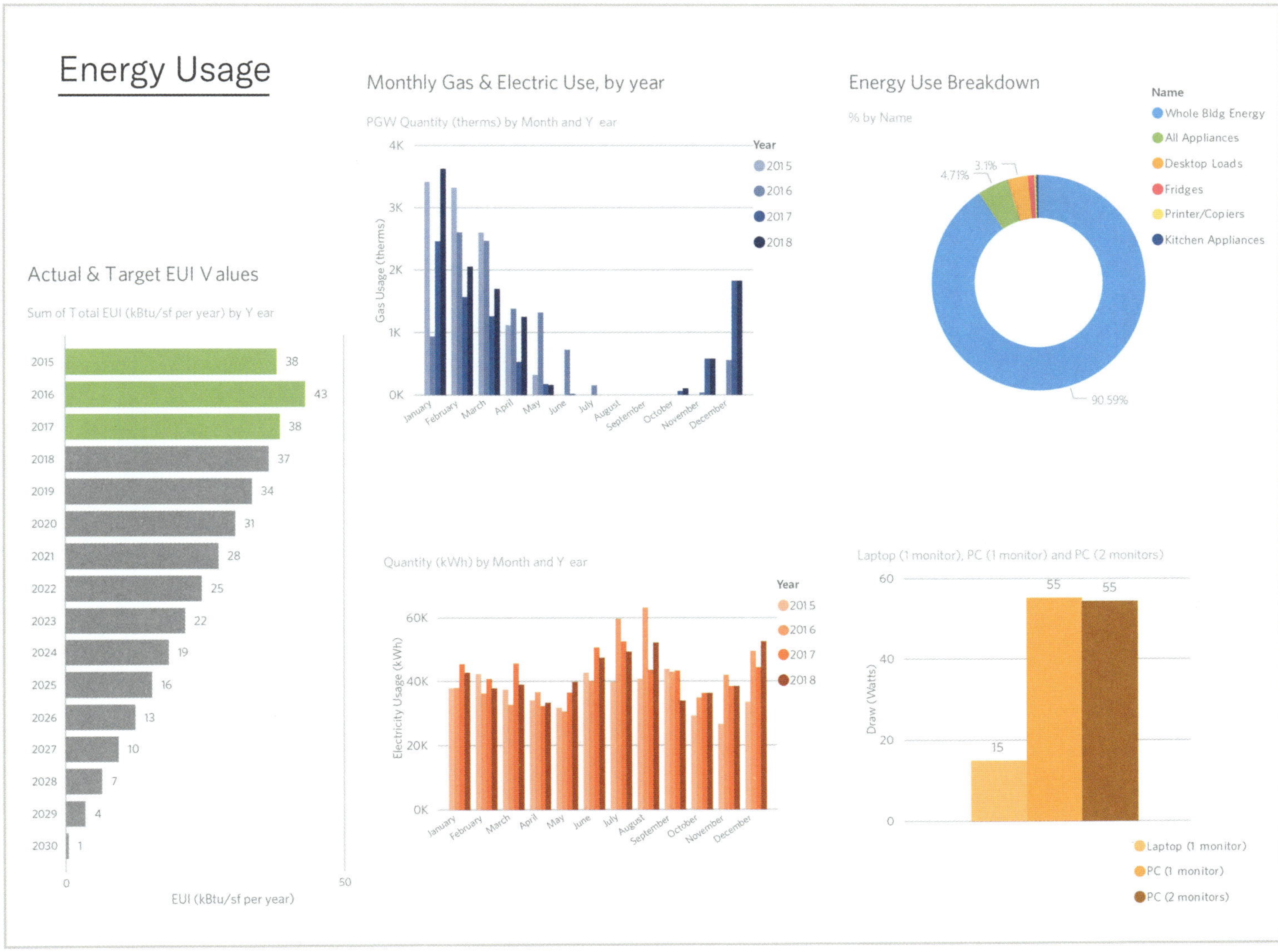
Energy Usage
Actual & Target EUI Values
Sum of Total EUI (kBtu/sf per year) by Year
2015 38
2016 43
2017 38
2018 37
2019 34
2020 31
2021 28
2022 25
2023 22
2024 19
2025 16
2026 13
2027 10
2028 7
2029 4
2030 1
0
50
EUI (kBtu/sf per year)
Monthly Gas & Electric Use, by year
PGW Quantity (therms) by Month and Year
4K
3K
2K
1K
0K
Gas Usage (therms)
Year
2015
2016
2017
2018
January February March April May June July August September October November December
Quantity (kWh) by Month and Year
60K
40K
20K
0K
Electricity Usage (kWh)
Energy Use Breakdown
% by Name
Name
Whole Bldg Energy
All Appliances
Desktop Loads
Fridges
Printer/Copiers
Kitchen Appliances
4.71%
3.1%
90.59%
Laptop (1 monitor), PC (1 monitor) and PC (2 monitors)
60
40
20
0
Draw (Watts)
15
55
55
Laptop (1 monitor)
PC (1 monitor)
PC (2 monitors)

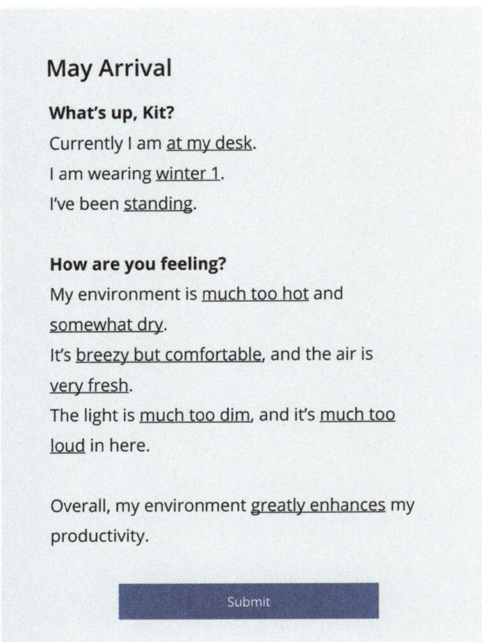
May Arrival
What's up, Kit?
Currently I am at my desk.
I am wearing winter 1.
I've been standing.
How are you feeling?
My environment is much too hot and somewhat dry.
It's breezy but comfortable, and the air is very fresh.
The light is much too dim, and it's much too loud in here.
Overall, my environment greatly enhances my productivity.
Submit

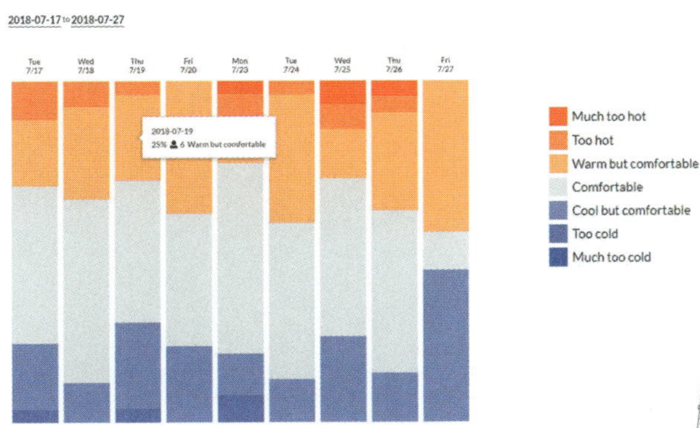
2018-07-17 to 2018-07-27
Tue 7/17
Wed 7/18
Thu 7/19
Fri 7/20
Mon 7/23
Tue 7/24
Wed 7/25
Thu 7/26
Fri 7/27
Much too hot
Too hot
Warm but comfortable
Comfortable
Cool but comfortable
Too cold
Much too cold

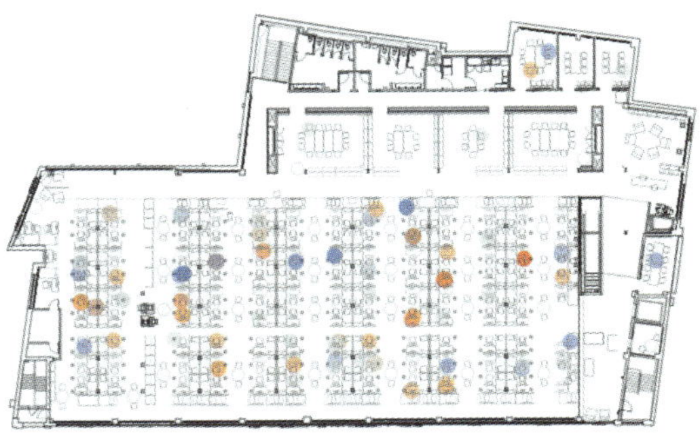

Green St
ONE WAY
NO TURN
CONGREGAT ON ROD
LOVE PEACE AND PURSUE IT

ALOM

Rodeph Shalom Renovation and Addition

Congregation Rodeph Shalom

Philadelphia, Pennsylvania

Founded in 1795, Rodeph Shalom is the oldest Ashkenazic congregation in the Western Hemisphere. It had many homes before settling into its current building on North Broad Street. Located north of Philadelphia's City Hall, the 1928 synagogue was designed by the Philadelphia architecture firm Simon & Simon and is listed on the National Register of Historic Places.

As the city expanded through the latter half of the nineteenth century and the first decades of the twentieth century, North Broad Street became home to many cultural and religious institutions. With block after block of row homes to the east and west of Broad, this was a thriving neighborhood of immigrants drawn to the city by its manufacturing base. After World War II, however, an exodus to suburbia began. The population base supporting the institutional corridor along the length of North Broad Street declined, and along with it, the institutions themselves. The adjoining Central Presbyterian Church was demolished in 1952 and turned into a used car lot. Row homes behind were abandoned and demolished. But through it all, Rodeph Shalom remained. It is today a significant anchor and contributor to the rebirth of the North Broad Street corridor.

All religious institutions evolve to meet the needs of their congregations. While core rituals conducted in the historic sanctuary remain, other obligations have expanded with the growing congregation. The physical changes sought by the congregation enable the programmatic evolution of Rodeph Shalom toward a more fully accessible institution. In the broadest sense of the term, accessibility here includes not only the ethical and legal requirements to remove physical barriers to entry, but also the presentation of the congregation as one that faces out as well as in. The intent is to preserve the inward focus of the sanctuary while simultaneously presenting an invitation that extends beyond worship to include community gatherings, education, social outreach, and display of Jewish art. While postwar urban renewal saw the unfortunate demolition of significant structures around the synagogue, it is that adjoining land that today enables Rodeph Shalom to expand and adjust its facilities to these evolving aspirations.

The original historic synagogue is an outstanding example of Byzantine Revival architecture. The exterior is limestone-clad with terracotta ornamentation atop the cornices. Three monumental, mosaic-covered arches announce the entry on North Broad Street. An ornamented attic story crowns the volume of the sanctuary as it steps back from the perimeter of the main volume. Significantly for the massing of the addition, five tall windows along both the north and south flanks admit light to the sanctuary. The main floor within has a lobby along the Broad Street frontage that provides access to the sanctuary. The existing education and meeting spaces to the rear, however, had no direct connection from Broad Street. They were largely conceived as a separate building, with the entry located along a side street. The only internal connection from the main lobby to the education and meeting spaces at the rear was down a stair and across a basement service corridor. Physical accessibility and connectivity were challenges everywhere.

Despite these weaknesses in the original building design, much in the 1928 synagogue was moving and wonderful. The urban presentation to the city along Broad Street and the spatial qualities and ornamentation of the entry lobby and sanctuary resonated for all. These spaces embody respect and memory for the congregation. The core design insight here was to in no way change this existing procession from the city to the historic sanctuary. Rather, we sought to extend the Broad Street lobby by adding a second front along the open south side of the site. The new additions along the south side of the historic building parallel the old in an artful conversation across time. We acknowledge, respect, and defer to the originating structure while altering and extending its function, use, and image.

This dialogue between old and new is first and foremost about connections both lateral and vertical. The front lobby now connects at grade from Broad Street through an expanded gallery to a new accessible entry. This entry provides a gracious events lobby and vertical connections through an elevator and stairs to all four levels of the building and to the basement auditorium. Along this south passage, new rooms extend the synagogue program. Along the North Broad Street frontage, a community room transforms the presentation of the congregation to the city. Like the historic synagogue, the street front base of the community room is limestone clad, but behind and within this wall, a channel glass-clad volume emerges as a luminous beacon to the city. The corners of the room open with chamfered glass bays to glancing views, engaging inside and out in new ways. Adjacent to the community room is a walled courtyard, an outdoor room that is about the same size as the community room and extends the gallery space to the outside for events. This open courtyard defers to the main sanctuary, allowing the five arched stained-glass windows to continue to admit southern light into the main sanctuary. Beyond these windows, a library and new south entry create gracious space for arrival and lingering before and after services and events. The addition here steps up two levels to provide additional education space, with the whole of the complex connected by a new elevator and stair tower that together punctuate this spatial give and take between old and new.

Continuity and change—both necessary to existence—here engage in an appreciative yet assertive conversation. Through a deeply respectful approach that extends rather than mimics, old and new are each made more artful and rich. What is old is given new life, and what is new is imbued with nearly a century of memory.

ILLUMINATED

This small addition is simultaneously a deferential and assertive partner to the much larger structure. The Byzantine Revival synagogue has tall, multi-story limestone piers flanking its three elaborate portals. It is a heavy and relatively opaque presence to the city. The addition extends the material but not the form or masonry construction techniques of the synagogue. Its glass lantern above is an analogue to the synagogue attic story, achieved not through ornamentation but through illumination of the community room within.

CONGREGATION R
אוהב שלום ורודף שלום
LOVE PEACE AND PURSUE IT

PRECINCT

The addition is an open, layered screen to the south—part landscape, part architecture. A row of trees borders the street and sets up the new precinct. A new drive and walk reorients entry, with a flanking tiled portico. The glass-walled community room is pushed up to Broad Street as a symbol of light and welcome. An outdoor walled court allows the full height of the five Byzantine arched windows and flanking piers to display themselves. The new lobby, stair, and elevator pull away from the historic structure and align themselves astride a later addition, opening views to the synagogue beyond.

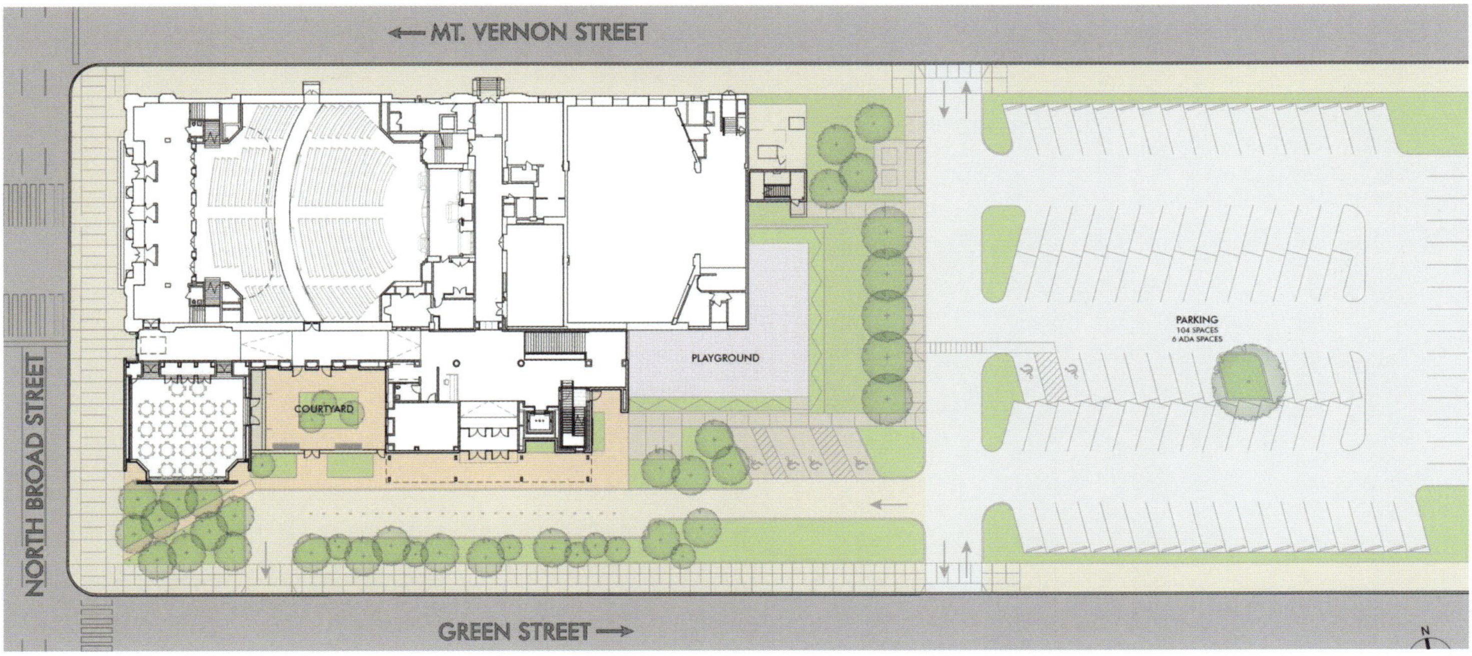
MT. VERNON STREET
NORTH BROAD STREET
GREEN STREET
COURTYARD
PLAYGROUND
PARKING
104 SPACES
6 ADA SPACES
N

WELCOME

The incisive moment in the addition is the provision of new entry. Neither the historic main Broad Street entry nor the north-facing Mt. Vernon Street entry was accessible. Neither communicated welcome. Further, the Broad Street entry opens to a very small lobby that gives direct access only to the synagogue, not the school. The new tiled portico opens to a parallel interior hall that gives light, view, and access to the community room, Jewish art gallery, rabbi's office, event lobby, elevator, and stair.

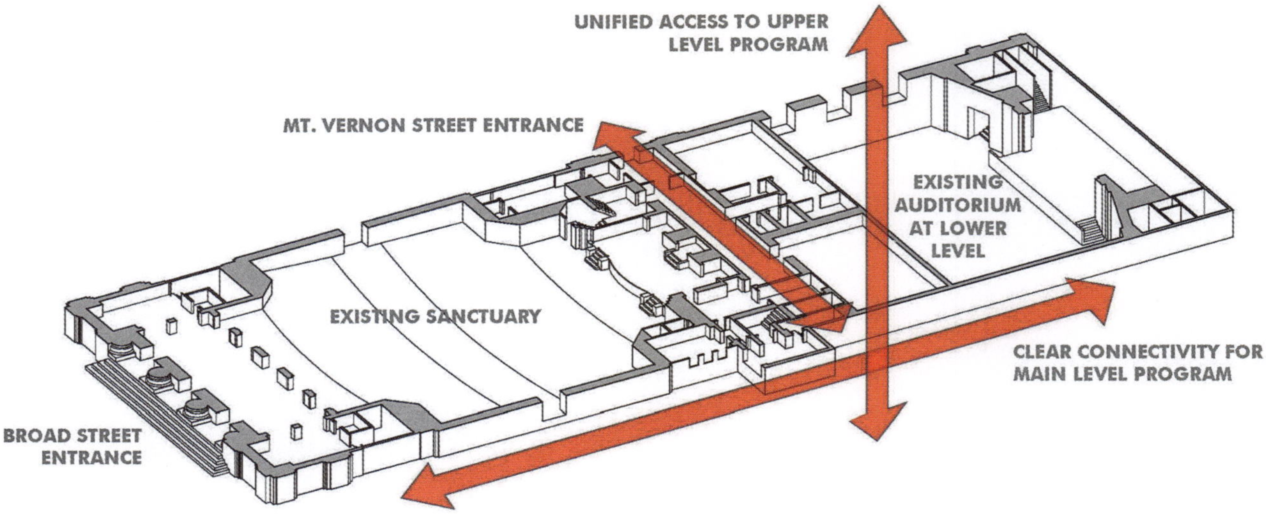

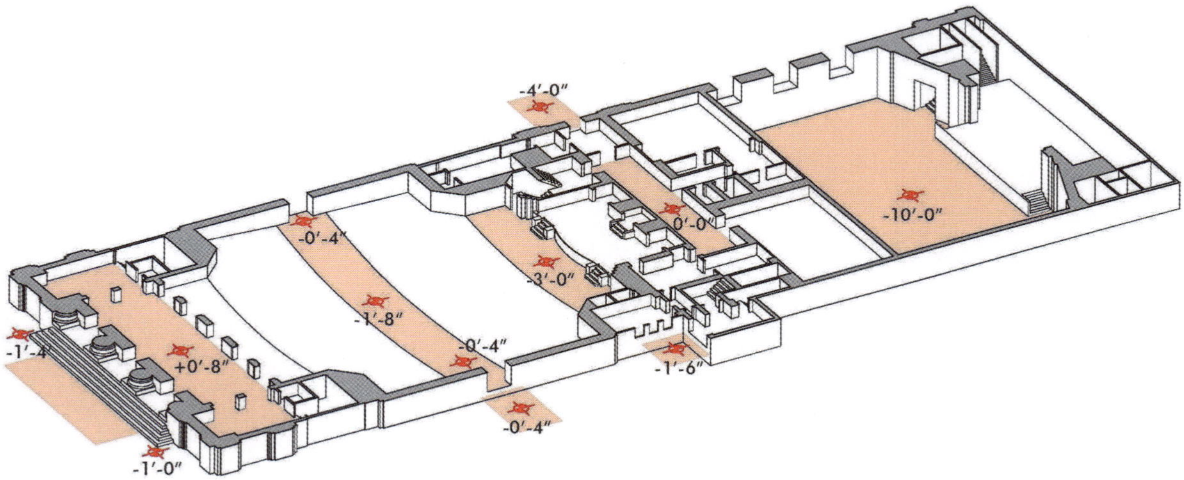

MOVEMENT

The addition unlocks the full potential of the historic structure and the later additions to the rear. Alternating circulation and major spaces were layered from the Broad Street frontage through to the school at the rear. The basement was the only lateral internal connection between spaces. The addition of a new lobby and hallway to the south, coupled with the new stair and elevator, re-centers the whole of the complex. All paths and passages, be they horizontal or vertical, lead to the new community, event, and casual meeting spaces for the congregation.

DESERT PALETTE

The fundamental aesthetic conversation between old and new is in the inversion of the wall-to-glass ratio. Whereas the historic synagogue is largely wall, with dramatic light admitted to the interior through relatively small stain glass windows, the addition is the opposite. The play of materials carries this conversation between architectural histories further, including the new exterior tile portico and the mosaic tile interiors of the historic synagogue, and new and old ornamental metals at gates and entry portals.

The colors here are evocative of the desert, including the Jerusalem stone used for floors of the new lobby and galleries. The trees are Jerusalem Cyprus.

DECK
DECK
C-2

High Horse Ranch
Private Residence

Willits, California

Procession and place give sequence, order, and form to this Northern California home with two guest cabins. The three structures are simple and almost temple-like, but the architecture begins long before one even senses them. Their positions, orientation, and sequence of arrival are orchestrated within the hilltop setting.

Passage begins to the southeast, well below the house and cabins. A gravel drive cuts gently across the steep slope as it ascends. From this vantage along the slopes of the valley below, the main house and the cabins have yet to appear. The steep incline of the site is covered in thick forests with an occasional meadow clearing. Together the slope and forest conspire to conceal the architecture, offering only occasional reveals. The drive gradually encircles the hill above in a long arc, ending in a clearing behind and below the main house. The slope of the site conceals parking in this clearing from view within the houses and cabins. The rest of the ascent is by foot, first up to the house, then out in opposing directions to the cabins.

The ridge siting for the main house is a natural clearing in the forest. It is entered from the back, at the end of a crescent footpath, alongside weathered steel walls. A cantilevered roof overhangs these walls, signaling entry. Steps ascend from the entry path to a limestone plinth that extends the interior out beneath the welcoming overhang above the front door. A full-height window slot visually extends the arrival path through the bedroom wing, across a sliver view alongside the gallery and out to the east. The entry door is to the right, through the solid back walls. A pair of thin walls are here joined together as a thickened service core. A powder room, coat closet, kitchen equipment, and pantry occupy this core along the north edge of the great room.

To the south of the master bedroom and study wing, this core is hollowed out to become a gallery. The solidity and thickness of these walls render the north-south views more potent by establishing a focused threshold as one passes through the entry vestibule, across the living room to expansive views down to the Redwood Valley below, a headwater of the Russian River to the south. Pivoting left, toward the bedroom wing, yet another transverse view focuses one across the study, through a pair of doors into a vista of the small canyon behind.

As seen from within the landscape procession sequence, the house itself is something of a compass, orienting viewers, focusing their gaze, and offering contrasting views simultaneously across architecture and landscape: narrow and intimate, foreground to far ground, lower valley to upper canyon, open meadow to closed forest.

The living space is set upon a shallow limestone platform in the found clearing atop the hill. This platform in the clearing extends the boundaries of the house, drawing the living areas out beneath the expansive southern overhang. It almost feels as though this stone viewing platform was inevitable and straddled the crown of the hill before the house was even an idea. The main room is a large sheltering roof that cantilevers to the south atop five slender columns anchored in the stone platform below. They in turn support five exposed roof beams that frame back to the solid service core.

Operable clerestory windows atop the service core admit north light and open to draw air across the interior. The rhythmic north-south graining of space and furnishings draws outside in and inside out, with the great room filtering the passage of air, light, and view. The great room is elemental and simple. It has the feel of an ancient, trabeated temple atop an elevated stone platform, translated into wood with pivoting glass walls as columns.

The two guest cabins are both pragmatic and poetic. While their occupants are dependent on the main house for meals and community, the cabins offer privacy and solitude. Each has a sleeping space with a bath, study desk, covered porch, and fire pit. They embrace and celebrate the daily ritual of sleep, sheltered above, with a fire for warmth. They are as elemental as primitive huts, equally secure from and integrated with nature. Each is very much its own place, solitary in the steeply sloping forested landscape. At the same time, the cabins are satellites that extend the procession of the main house outward. The whole is not a compound of dwelling units but instead more like a planet with a pair of moons, each cabin visible from the main dwelling but at some remove. It is the procession across the site that links the whole.

Writing a book about how to change the way we conceive, design, fabricate, and build architecture is one thing. Building true to that book is another, the work of a lifetime. The owners of this home—a former tech CEO turned artist and a former doctor turned musician—had read our book *Refabricating Architecture*. They had also seen our prior efforts to bring the book to life at Loblolly House on the Eastern Shore of Maryland and at Cellophane House at The Museum of Modern Art. They challenged us to perfect the thesis of that book using off-site manufacturing strategies on this remote, hilly site in the Mendocino Forest. Touching the fragile hilltop site lightly was important. Rooting the home to this steeply sloping land, even while fabricating most of it three hours down the road in San Jose, was the primary design challenge.

Prior to our involvement, the owners had observed the site across the days, seasons, and years. It taught them how to live lightly on the land, moving gently along the slopes, within the forests and clearings, deleting little and altering less. They listened carefully, and so did we. The place told us where to add the simple paths, platforms, and shelters within which the owners and their guests now dwell. It told us where to be expansive and where to be intimate, where to view the land from afar, and where to see nature up close. Rather than imposing upon the landscape, the architecture of High Horse Ranch arises from within this beautiful, rugged place.

SOLITUDE

Before beginning design, the owners lightly renovated an old garage and lived on the site. They set up lawn chairs, watching the property at different times of the day and year. When they came to us, they had a well-formed idea about where they wished to place the house, in a hilltop clearing between two valleys. The procession up to the house was orchestrated from these early observations. It culminates in a surprise opening to the spectacular long valley view.

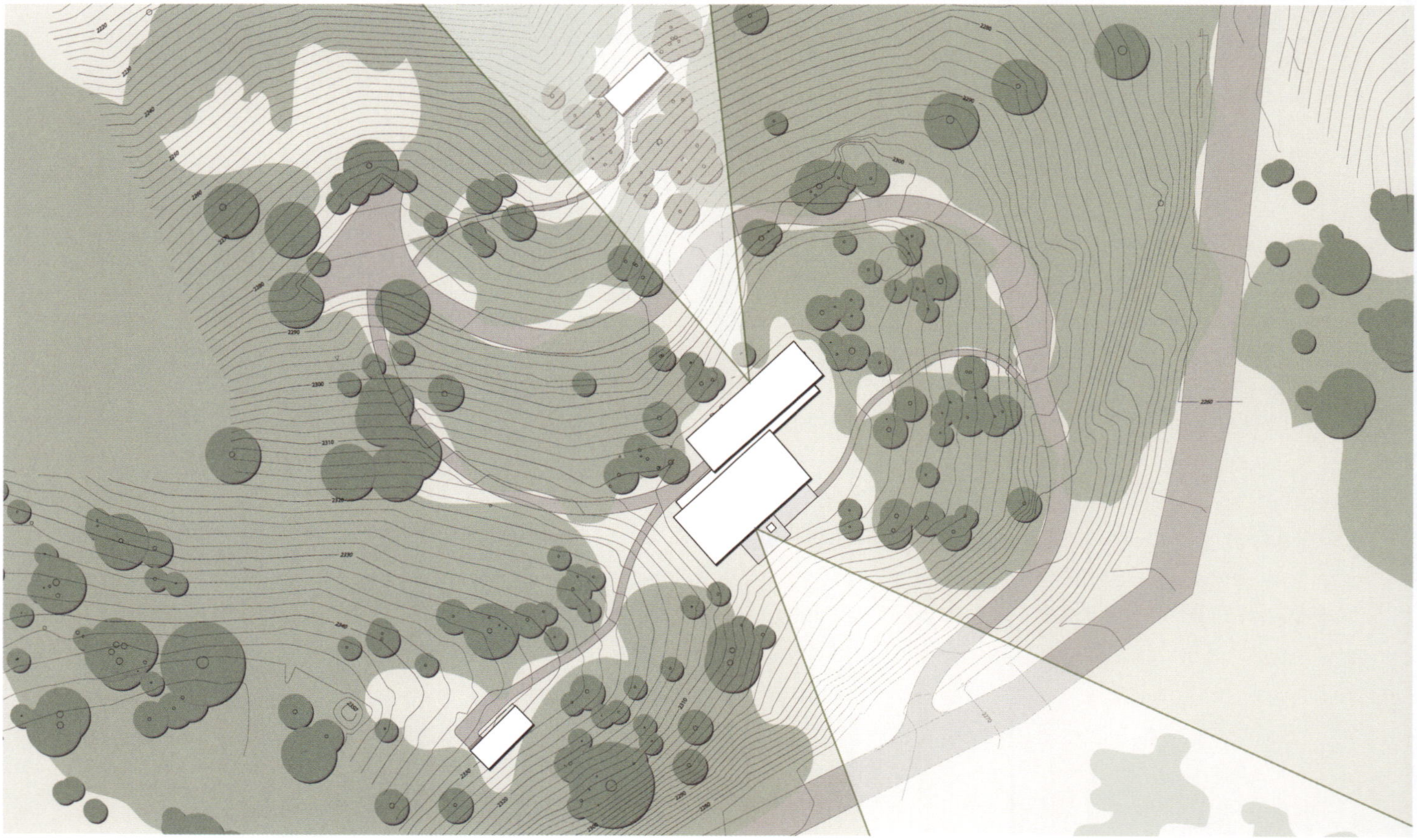

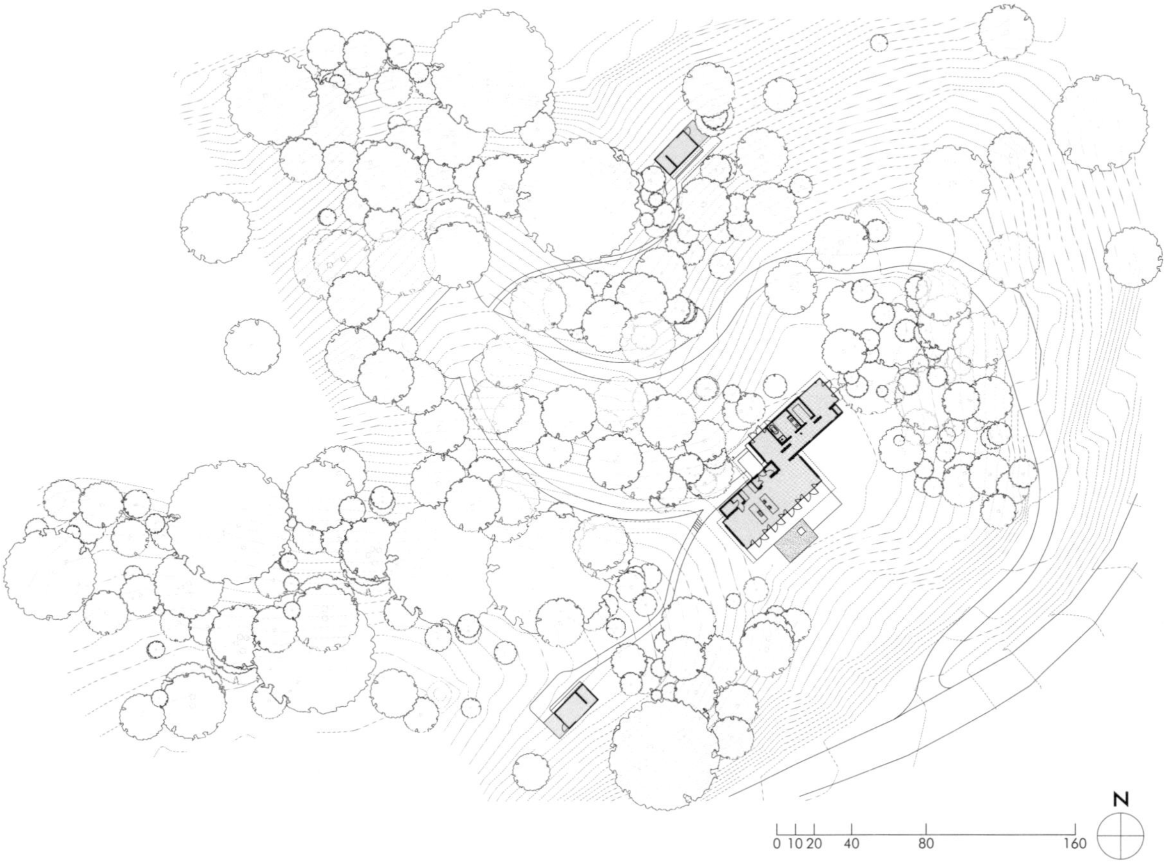

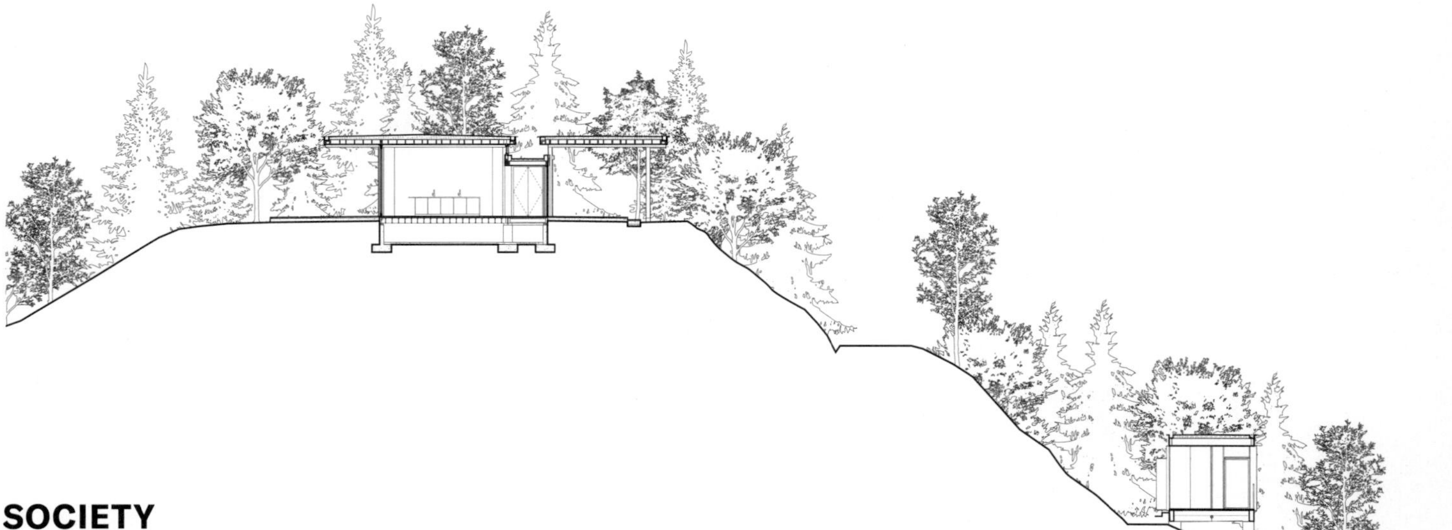

SOCIETY

The ranch is conceived as a social enterprise, a place for hosting guests. The owners had a narrative about this from the outset. Guests would live in their own private cabins in the woods, with the main house as a gathering place for the communal rituals of daily life: coffee, meals, drinks, and socializing. The cabins are a short walk from the main house, each set upon an elevated treehouse-like platform in the woods, with a porch entry, single bedroom, and bath. The wall opposite the bed is floor-to-ceiling glass.

OUT OF SITE

Off-site fabrication was an interest from the start, with the owner drawn to us by our manifesto publication, *Refabricating Architecture*, as well as Loblolly and Cellophane houses. Predictability, control, and precision were shared aspirations. The alternating wet and dry seasons also suggested factory fabrication in the wet season and site erection during the dry season. In the end, the off-site production schedule did not align perfectly with the seasons. Modules were shipped with fewer finishes than desired in order to take advantage of dry weather.

PRECISION

ASSEMBLY

A small foundation and crawlspace is the site platform and plinth for the house. The architectural space plan and the modularity of the offsite assembly strategy were developed in tandem. A narrow service core with bathroom, kitchen, mechanical space, and hallway was built as a fully enclosed module. It sits between the public and private wings of the house and is a conceptual and structural anchor for these spaces.

The great room is composed of several roof and column panels, complete with overhangs. Its long expanse of operable glass wall is stabilized by the service core modules.

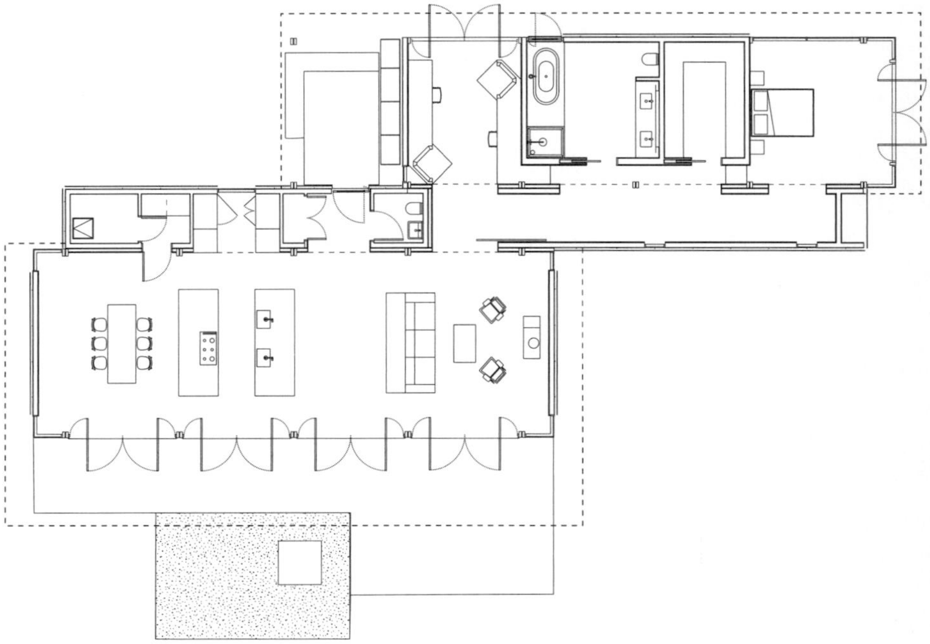

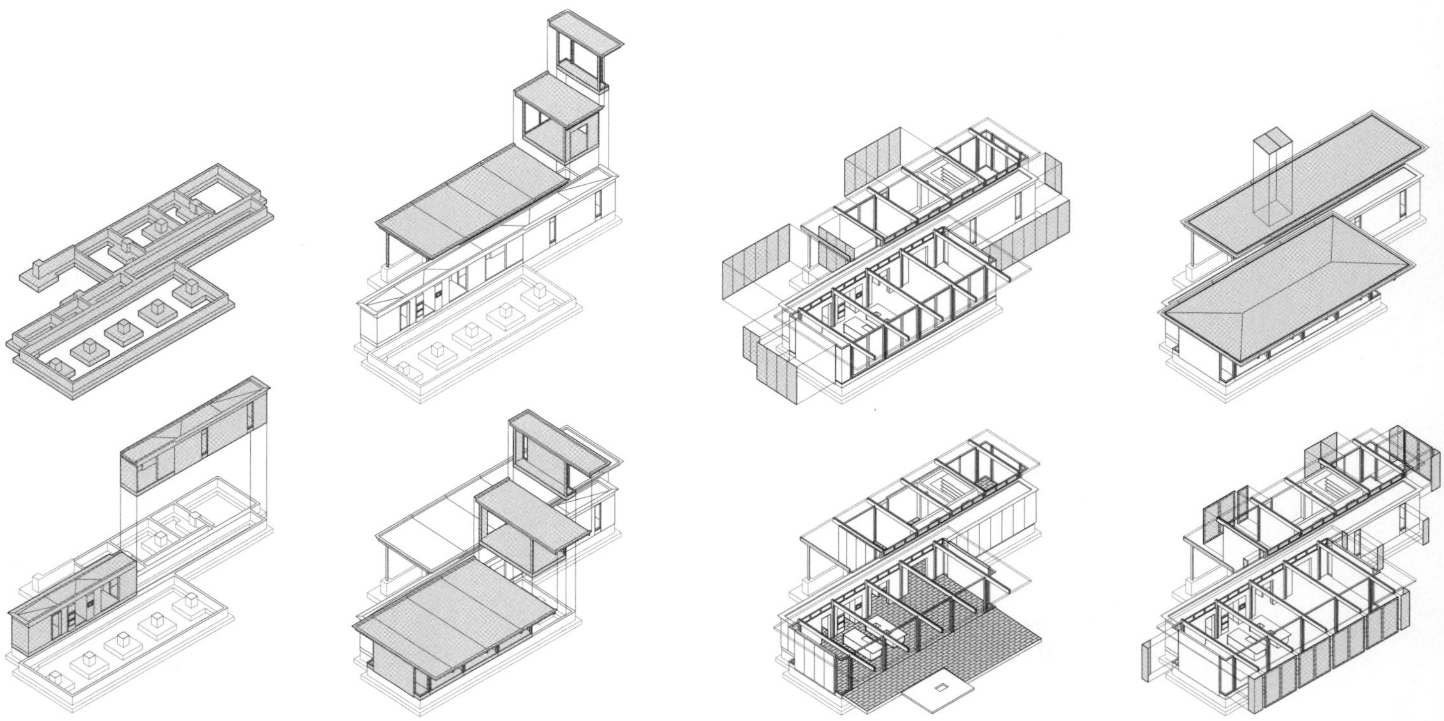

L-6

ELEMENTAL

The interior materials are almost entirely wood atop a stone floor. The ceilings are naturally finished, while the walls are painted white as clean surfaces for art. There is no drywall anywhere.

The Corten steel expanded mesh exterior walls draw from the colors and tones of the landscape, specifically the maroon bark of the Pacific madrone trees that peel and reveal shiny fragments of smooth purple and green bark below. The openings in the expanded metal mesh pick up the soft dappled light that filters through the adjoining forest understory.

Pendleton West
Wellesley College
Wellesley, Massachusetts

Wellesley College was founded in 1870. In a 1902 letter to President Caroline Hazard, Frederick Law Olmsted used a few extraordinarily precise words to describe his acropolis-like vision for the College's Norumbega Hill: "The plateaus, however, are somewhat larger [than the rounded glacial hummocks characteristic of the campus] and are made up of two fairly distinct parts, the upper flat and the escarpment so that a dividing line of construction which follows the edge of the flat simply recognizes a natural division and emphasizes it." It would be thirty more years before Founders Hall, Green Hall, and Pendleton Hall, all fine collegiate Gothic structures, realized the core of this vision of origin, defining a new Academic Quadrangle with structures along the escarpment. Each structure negotiates the hill town-like climb from the surrounding valleys to the plateau beyond.

In 1958, Paul Rudolph completed the remaining two walls of this Quadrangle with his L-shaped Jewett Center for the Arts. Rafael Moneo's 1993 Davis Art Center extends Rudolph's entry to the Academic Quadrangle further west. The adjacent Pendleton Hall, a 1934 design by Charles Klauder, was built for chemistry and had never been comprehensively renewed when the arts moved in during the 1970s. With this project, Wellesley wanted to both update Pendleton and consolidate Pendleton and Jewett to give prominence to the arts and create a new front door on the Academic Quadrangle.

If you stare at the south wall of Pendleton Hall from the Quad, the tall ceilings and generous window-to-wall ratio reveal the bones of an early twentieth-century loft waiting to happen. The central act of renewal here was demolition of the double-loaded corridor, stair, elevator shaft, and finishes to reveal the concrete structure and open plan. Envisioned anew as an arts loft housing painting, drawing, sculpture, graphic design, printmaking, and architecture, the efficiency of Pendleton increased to allow the full program—including new digital arts space—to fit within the existing volume. As an added benefit, the blending of paths through the newly opened program spaces expose art-making and cultivate cross-disciplinary work.

The small 10,000-square-foot addition we designed is both a workhorse and a work of art that connects Jewett and Pendleton in order to fuse the arts together. It also provides a new front door and presence for the arts—transforming Pendleton Hall with a new code-compliant stair and elevator at four levels, and making the Academic Quadrangle fully accessible for the first time. New music rehearsal spaces were best hosted in the new structure, where sound isolation, spatial volume, and acoustical performance could be carefully constructed.

A thoughtful approach was likewise needed to negotiate the interplay between landscape and architecture. Wellesley is a campus of hills and valleys. Meadows line the vales while buildings and quadrangles sit astride and atop the hills. A green veil of trees everywhere anchors the slopes of the hills, a magical inhabitable scrim between natural and built worlds through which paths meander to ascend the steep slopes. This veil had all but disappeared to the west of the addition. The landscape design of Michael Van Valkenburgh reinstates the veil, extending it across the sloping landscape to the west.

The addition takes root in the Norumbega hillside and negotiates three full building levels between the north entry and the Academic Quadrangle to the south. It is in large part a poured-in-place retaining wall at its first two floors. It made sense in such a small building to simply continue the concrete structure up to the third level of the rehearsal hall.

Like Olmsted, we were very much moved by the extraordinary natural textures of the site—especially the adjoining veil of trees—and wanted to incorporate them into the material of the addition. We began to think of the addition as a hand-crafted wooden building inside and out, evidencing the process of making. The concrete formwork at the exterior and within internal passages and stairs would be imprinted with the memory of wood from the formwork. We sought varied imprints using randomly generated patterns of width, length, depth, and finish. At poured-in-place retaining walls, horizontal sediment-like striations were used. At the upper volume of the rehearsal hall, precast concrete panels enclose the building. The formwork here is vertical, but with more variation in width and depth, giving rise to an appearance inspired by the bark of the nearby trees.

There is no material better at showing the method of construction, negotiating a myriad of site conditions, and embracing natural phenomena than concrete. The density of the concrete also goes a long way toward deadening vibration and slowing the transfer of heat. In the rehearsal spaces, a vertical white oak wood liner, with spaces between the boards, allows for the passage of sound to an absorbing liner within, tuning the space to the desired proportions of sound absorption and reflection.

In a larger sense, this new structure is also tuned to its historic surroundings. Campuses begin with order, but incremental evolution across time introduces disorder. Paul Rudolph's introduction of Jewett Hall at Wellesley created a monumental entry to the Academic Quadrangle from the west. It aligned with the great tower of Green Hall, the tallest structure at Wellesley. Over the ensuing years, however, the development of the campus shifted to the northwest with a new Campus Center, parking structure, and athletic facilities. What for Rudolph functioned as a decidedly tertiary, narrow stair to the Academic Quad had become the principal entry. As we reflected upon these altered circumstances, reparation became an obligation of the project, to rebalance the campus plan with a major new entry, now defined by the addition.

We see our work here as part of a rich and respectful intergenerational dialogue across several histories: the 1902 Olmsted Plan, Charles Klauder's 1934 Pendleton Hall, Paul Rudolph's 1958 Jewett Art Center, and Rafael Moneo's 1993 Davis Art Museum. Our addition is Pendleton's fourth pavilion, extending the rhythm of the three original pavilions that project down-slope to the north along the perimeter of Norumbega Hill. The proportion of its massing draws the large block of the Davis Museum into the overall composition along Campus Drive. The north terrace and the passageway wrapping the base recall the artful way in which Green Hall engages the slopes of Norumbega Hill with intimately scaled passages and terraced landscapes of pause. The west portal and stairs up to the Academic Quad engage Jewett with a new entry portal, setting up a delightful side-by-side pairing of the original 1956 brick-and-concrete stair with the expanded stair.

Passages guide us at Wellesley: across a campus; up, over, and around a remarkable topography; through a verdant landscape; and into an architectural conversation experienced across the history of the college. With new passageways through and between the Academic Quad and arts buildings, Pendleton West and Jewett Arts Center serve a new generation of students in a building that celebrates a truly unique campus as well as the traditions of making within its walls.

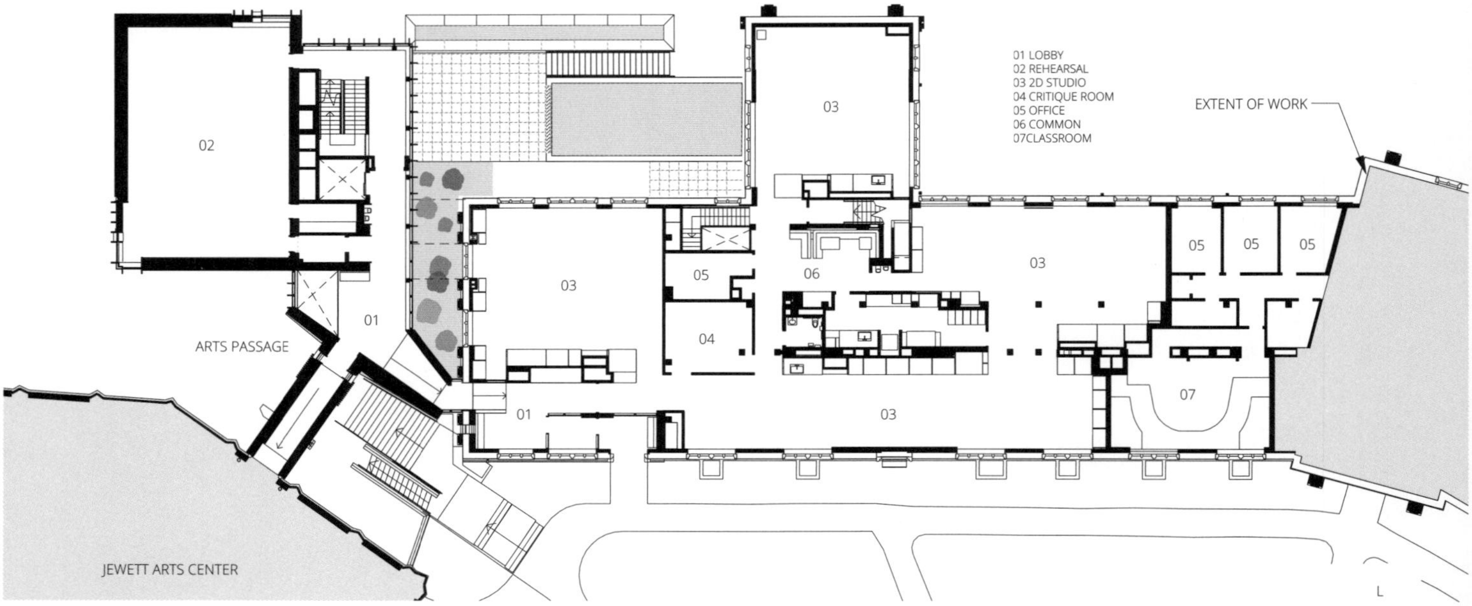

Addition and Renovation

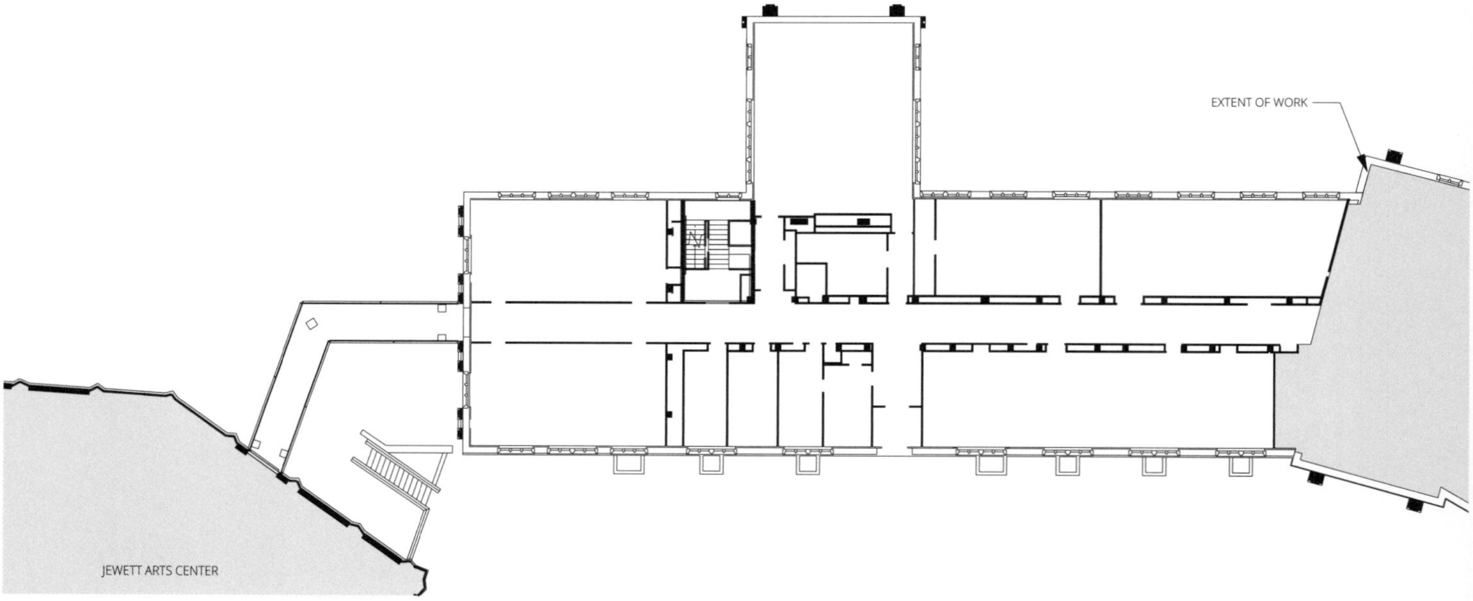

Existing

IMPRESSIONS

The small addition is half-building and half-landscape passage. It is a sieve that gathers, embraces, and focuses campus walks arriving from all directions—one slipping past and another wrapping the corner of the addition as it ascends beneath the overhang of the rehearsal hall above.

The low-raking western sun captures shadows on the vertical board-formed precast concrete. It casts an ephemeral, bark-like presence across the facade in harmony with the adjacent mature conifers. The whole is a poem in wood as it moves from tree, to milled window walls, to the memory of wood impressed into concrete.

FOUND LANDSCAPE

Frederick Law Olmsted described a vision for a new Academic Quadrangle atop a plateau at the center of the picturesque hills and valleys of the Wellesley campus. It was a vision that integrated a found landscape of escarpment with an architecture that formed itself across several decades.

This small addition and renovation fuses building and nature into a new tapestry at an important intersection between historic buildings. Green roofs atop new and old lace walkways, connectors, and passages to a new courtyard defined by Pendleton and its addition.

WHOLE GRAINS

Architecture here forms itself about landscape, not the other way around. We began with the tree, and wood milled from it, as the dominant material inside and out. We placed great emphasis on handcraft and sought form that left evidence of the process of making that would one day occur within and about the new and renovated architecture.

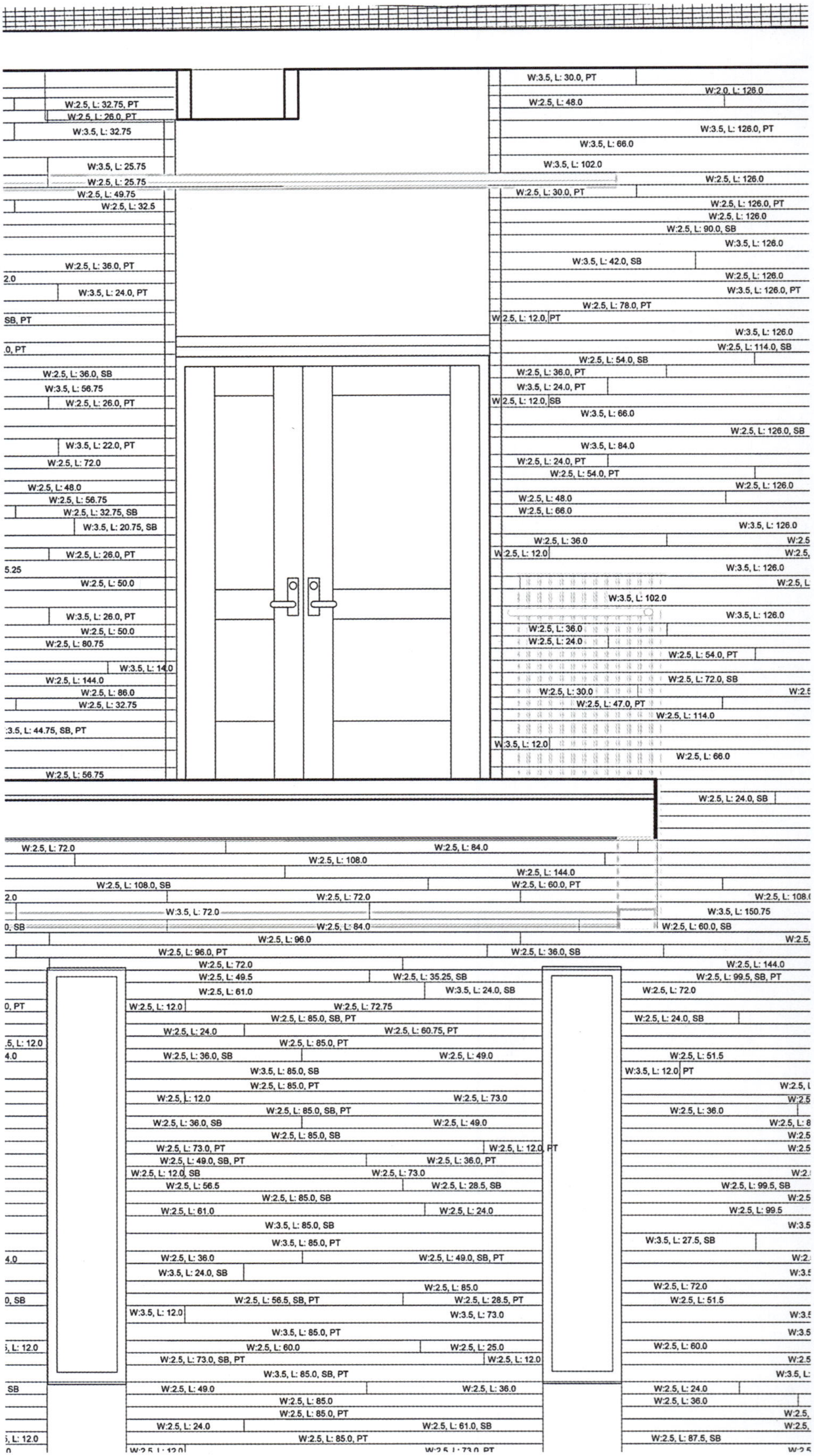

SEEKING IMPERFECTION

Randomness, or at least the appearance of randomness, is a characteristic of nature that is difficult to attain in the work of humans. Our minds tend toward order even when we seek the opposite. The builders did not want this daunting task, and we did not trust ourselves. So we scripted varying lengths, widths, and finishes of board formwork, using computation to generate randomness at this passageway wall. Even the computer struggled. We adjusted the outcomes by hand and eye to eliminate excessive clustering. It was worth the effort. Concrete is more artful and forgiving when it is deliberately imperfect. That is what it wants to be, especially when it is formed on-site.

1-800-UR-RENTS
United Rentals
1284296
United Rentals
KEEP
CLEAR
United Rentals

ATTUNED

The addition is a wooden building. Exterior and interior concrete surfaces reflect the grain and character of the wood within which they are molded. At the interior of the rehearsal hall, milled and finished white oak boards line the surfaces. We were inspired here by the sounding box of the piano, with its strings and felt linings. The walls of the room represent an inversion of the positives (strings) and negatives (spaces between the strings) of the piano.

The acoustician modeled precise ratios of solid reflective material and soft absorptive material to tune the room to a range of vocal and instrumental performance. The red felt liner behind absorbs sound, while the white oak boards atop reflect sound. Doors in the walls can be opened to add absorption and to provide access to concealed building systems.

Engineering Research Center
Brown University

Providence, Rhode Island

New research space was only the originating obligation at Brown. But that was no surprise—wonderful architecture always expands beyond its origins, drawing in realm after realm of endeavor and aspiration for community and place.

Engineering at Brown was a department within a Liberal Arts university, not a school in its own right, until 2010. As a department, it grew in three separate physical increments over several decades. Prince Laboratory, built in 1962, is a two-story flexible loft structure for engineering fabrication. Barus & Holley Hall, which followed in 1965, is a mid-rise structure housing both Physics and Engineering. It is an internally focused plan, with a windowless corridor on all the upper floors. Lastly, a single-story teaching facility, Giancarlo Engineering Laboratories, was added in 2001 between Prince and Barus & Holley. Each structure had a separate entry and circulation, with at best tangential connections.

Early planning studies suggested a fourth building with yet another bridge connection back to Barus & Holley, further compounding the problem. The collection of buildings needed to become a School of Engineering. We began with questions: How might the new Engineering Research Center draw the disparate assembly of earlier structures into a school? Could it become a front door and a living room for the school in addition to providing research laboratories? We created options. Ultimately, the university, the School of Engineering, and the design team settled on a vision for the Engineering Research Center as a connective network that fused the three existing structures together.

This was the critical moment of vision that transformed the idea of a School of Engineering into a physical presence. Architecture here takes an idea that exists first in name and organizational structure and renders it far more potent by giving it architectural form. Through the agency of this vision, an L-shaped addition extends across both Barus & Holley and Giancarlo, joining them to Prince Laboratory. Most importantly, this addition is a frontispiece—a facade in the very best and deepest sense of the word—that provides factual as well as visual unity for the School of Engineering, rendering it a true community and offering circulation between previously disconnected buildings. Passage from the courtyard through the facade enters a living room, like the great room of a house writ large. It has a place to eat. It is bounded at the front door by a teaching classroom and passage to Prince Lab. On the opposite side, a bleacher/stair ascends to a large seminar room that connects to Barus & Holley and the new laboratories above. This same stair also descends to the nanotechnology and biotechnology cleanrooms and the imaging suite in the new Engineering Research Center, offering open and continuous vertical connectivity. The School of Engineering now has a physical place of its own, allowing it to become a coherent and compelling whole.

How might we go even further—beyond architecture—in the use of physical form to give substance to this growing school bound together by research and learning across several disciplines? In the Renaissance and Enlightenment worlds of Humanism, the realms of art and engineering were linked, and often experienced and depicted as different ways of seeing the same universe. Today they are largely viewed as worlds apart. An opportunity arose through the university's Public Art Program to bring an artist into the architecture while the project was still in development and construction. Spencer Finch joined us. He interpreted and extended the architecture through his work entitled *The Garden in the Brain*. Instead of installing a single piece, he developed a serial work of tessellations, underlying geometric patterns, that use architectural materials to convey the fundamental structure of the world as engineers know it. The art of tessellation is everywhere in the architecture, as it is in life: in the paving at the front door, in the glass fritting of the teaching laboratory, in wood and tile floors, in bathroom tiles, and lining the wall of the cleanroom. Art is here a community builder just as surely as architecture. Like the building itself, which fuses disparate structures into a new whole, this work of art must be discovered through daily exposure and exploration, seeking the patterning in the everyday.

Within the laboratories, collaboration and the constancy of change are the generators of design. They are built to serve different types of research, not the customized needs of individual researchers. The resulting laboratories are large and loft-like, with multiple principal investigators occupying bench space in accordance with shifting needs and funding. The design and organization of exposed and readily accessible mechanical and electrical systems become central expressions of the architecture here. Office space is similarly pooled in adjoining open plan spaces, with flexible furnishings and without fixed partitions. These spaces are readily adapted, assigned, and reassigned as demand and collaborations shift.

While laboratories often work best with maximum wall space and limited incursion of daylight, we sought to maximize daylight and view in the collaborative work and conference spaces. As at Brockman Hall for Physics at Rice University, each building elevation is individually tuned to solar orientation—maximizing daylight, minimizing glare, and managing solar gain based upon season.

Vertical glass fiber reinforced concrete fins are the constant unifying and rhythmic element of the facades. Their depth varies in accordance with solar exposure: deep for shading to the south and west, vestigial at the north. Across the west facade atop the courtyard portico, a corridor shields collaborative work areas from solar exposure. This allows the fins here to be less deep, affording expansive western views to the historic campus. Lateral expanded metal screens provide additional solar shading to the south and project ever-changing patterns of shade and shadow on the fins. Environmental performance here becomes a compelling and ever-changing aesthetic event.

Expanding our aspirations for connection and community ever outward, we intended not only that the laboratories aggregate to form a School of Engineering, but that they do so as part of the larger university. Science and engineering expansions have largely occurred in the past fifty years, accelerating in the past few decades. At older universities, the available space has often been peripheral to the historic campus. At Brown, this expansion occurred to the east of the nineteenth-century campus. Nonetheless, the original organizing axis of the campus remains potent at Brown and in Providence, extending across several blocks to the east toward the School of Engineering.

We wondered how the new Brown Engineering Research Center might extend the wholeness of the campus plan, fusing and connecting landscape and architecture across a centuries-long conversation of expansion. The places of memory at Brown are first and foremost outdoor rooms: campus greens along the central campus axis. The use of the architecture to form just such an outdoor room, an Engineering Quadrangle, extends campus history in a compelling way. Given the smaller scale and the integrated curriculum of study at Brown, it is especially appropriate that Engineering be integrated with the Liberal Arts and Sciences through the campus plan. The paths at the new Engineering Quad line the perimeter, giving primacy to the green itself. A street-level entry through a sheltering porch at Brook Street connects the architecture to the city grid. A welcoming orange glow emanates from a cleanroom window and signifies purpose and invitation. An open portico lines the eastern edge of the Engineering Quad, connecting the interior living room with the Quad, the campus, and the city beyond.

Architecture is most resonant when it expands its reach. If we begin and end with shelter and purpose, we have only building, useful but not sufficient. The more we give agency to the building as a citizen, the more potent it becomes.

PATTERN SEEKING

In his inspirational book, *A Beautiful Question: Finding Nature's Deep Design*, the Nobel Prize-winning theoretical physicist Frank Wilczek describes all mathematics and science throughout history as a quest to uncover and reveal the underlying structure of the natural world. Here at Brown, the artist Spencer Finch engages the architecture of engineering in a quest for this underlying beauty. In his *Garden in the Brain*, Finch explores "nature's deep design" through tessellations in several locations throughout the building. Art and engineering exist here not as separate worlds, but as a single continuum with each contributing equally in our quest to understand.

STEMMING

All architecture has obligations beyond the program and use it shelters. A campus becomes a unified whole only through cumulative acts of design that extend an overarching vision. The architecture of the Engineering Research Center gives form and place to a new campus green. It extends the originating vision of the Brown campus as an outdoor room atop a Providence hill and further embraces the obligations of the campus as a citizen of the city. The east-facing bay window along Brook Street is a lantern that shelters an urban "porch" and front yard that are equally of the campus and in the city.

UNCOMMON

Building facades share vertical rhythms of window mullions and shading fins, but each is tuned to orientation. Variations in the depths of the vertical fins depending upon exposure to eastern and western sun, along with glass fritting and use of horizontal expanded metal panels at the south, all work in tandem to minimize glare and unwanted solar gain.

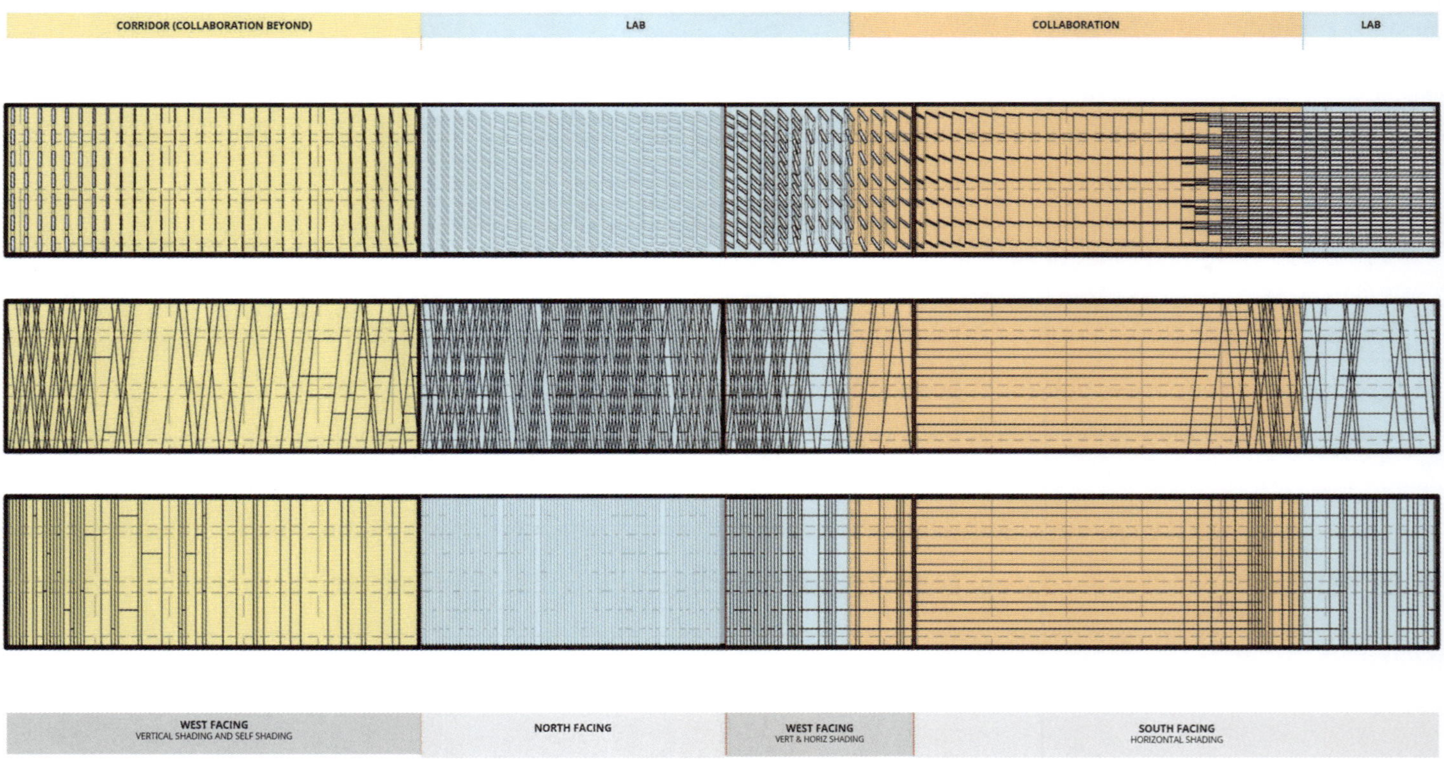

Level 2

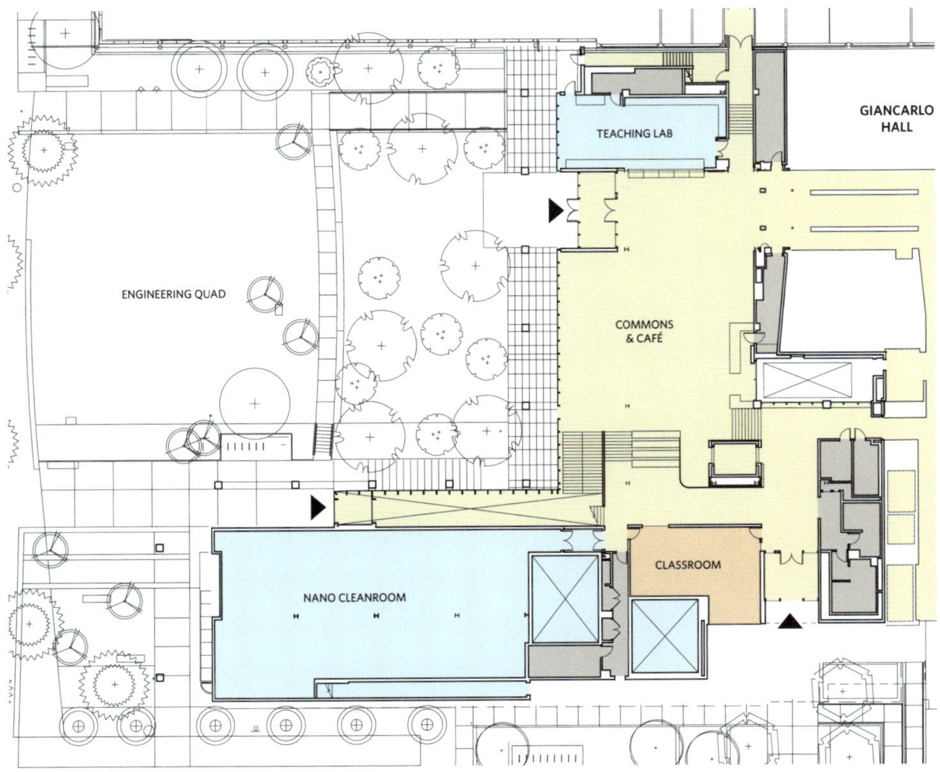

Level 1

EXPOSURE

Programs are located based in part on orientation to the sun. Collaborative office workspaces that thrive in daylight, with views, are located to the south and west. Laboratories that require little daylight and view are positioned to the north and east.

The single most important place in the building was not even in the original program brief. Arrival is from all directions into the Commons, creating a crossroads and giving a center to a School of Engineering that never had one. It draws research out of the laboratory into a broader community.

TEST FIN

Extensive prototyping throughout the design process afforded us deep aesthetic and technical control of the exterior walls. Initial prototyping to test concept and materials was built in our shop and displayed outside to experience in daylight. A subsequent visual prototype was erected at the site, again with further testing of material choice. The beauty of the ever-shifting geometric patterns of light and shade cast by the expanded metal on the glass fiber-reinforced concrete fins was a wonderful surprise. A final performance mock-up was erected and tested in Florida.

TESSELLATED

The architecture casts its own tessellations of light and shade across the days and seasons. These are accompanied by the geometric tessellations of Spencer Finch's *Garden in the Brain*. Just as these patterns exist everywhere in engineering and in nature, so too are Finch's tessellations arrayed everywhere in the architecture. They await discovery throughout the building.

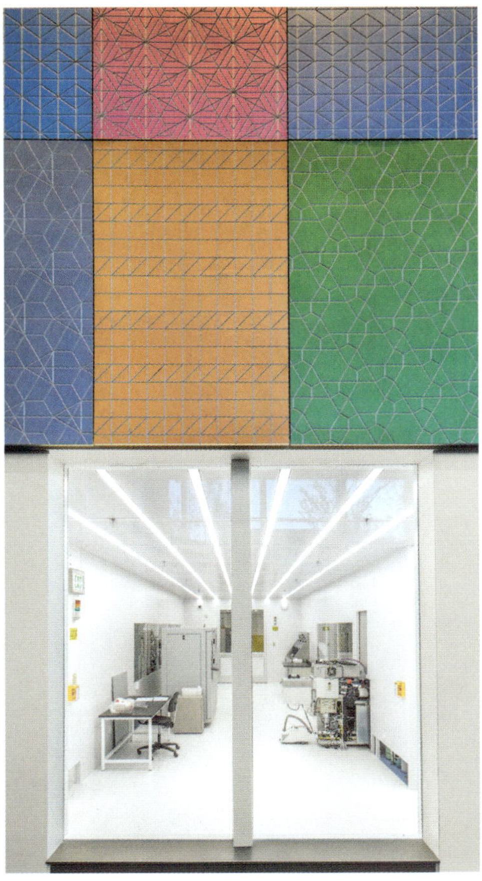

RADIANT

Facilities to advance research and teaching are the driving core of this building program. Laboratories range across several engineering disciplines, including advanced microelectronic and bio clean rooms and an imaging suite. The mechanical services in these rooms require an entire floor above that is of equal size to the space occupied by the research equipment below.

A "marigold glass" window filters out infrared and ultraviolet radiation. This magical window has an allure all its own. It is an eye to the inner workings of a world that previously lay hidden to passersby, rendering it part of the campus and city.

345

HAT HOUSE IN WHICH IT
AL, AND PROCEED TO R
GREE TO PASS THE BILL
SHALL LIKEWISE BE RECO
OLD AND SILVER COIN A
CONSENT OF THE CONGR
STATE ON IM
THE CONSENT
INTO ANY A

ALL HAVE ORIGINATED,
ONSIDER IT. IF AFTER S
SHALL BE SENT, TOGETH
SIDERED, AND IF APPROV
ENDER IN PAYMENT OF D
TION OF CONTRACTS OR
S, LAY ANY IMPOSTS OR
EXECUTING IT'S INSPECT
ORTS OR EXPORTS, SHAL
BE SUBJECT TO THE RE
CONGRESS, LAY ANY DU
REEMENT OR COMPACT W
NVADED, OR IN SUCH IMM
SHALL BE VESTED I

US Embassy in London
US Department of State

London, United Kingdom

Embassy design over the past decades has been dominated by circumstance. In response to attacks on American embassies across the world, a Standard Embassy Design was developed by the State Department in the 1990s to protect Americans working overseas. This Standard Design was set forth in volumes of written and drawn prescriptive requirements. While it is appropriately derived from security threats, these prescriptions result in a largely defensive architecture disconnected from place and people. All architecture embodies meaning and can be read. The Standard Embassy Design projects a defensive vision of our nation that removes, excludes, and obscures.

The architecture of our embassies can and must be better than this. Without form, architecture becomes circumstance. Without circumstance, all that remains is form. The art of architecture fuses the two. An embassy's form must move us, and its circumstances must secure us. We do not have to choose.

The occasion to build a new embassy in London provided the impetus to elevate prior approaches through a design competition. Our objective from the outset of the competition and throughout the development of the design never wavered. We sought a new embassy that in both form and circumstance would become an inspiring environment for diplomacy and an elegant diplomat for the environment.

Our goal was to symbolize and project the core values of our nation and our relationship with the United Kingdom: solidarity, stability, respect, transparency. We sought an architecture that was deeply wedded to its place. An architecture that welcomed and formed itself about all circumstance, including security. After the design competition, the Department of State adopted a Design Excellence program to replace Standard Embassy Design. Under this program, which has since been retired, several new embassies have followed the lead established in London with architecture that is both secure and aspirational.

We began with form. Had we begun with the thousands of circumstances referenced in the volumes of design standards and requirements, we would have never arrived at an elemental architecture. But symbols matter. The cube conveys solidity and strength, qualities of both the United States and its relationship with the United Kingdom. It is a received form—elemental, Platonic—that transcends circumstance and time. It also accommodates the myriad visual massing and security requirements of the site.

The site is centered south of the Thames, within the Nine Elms section of London. The backbone of this developing district is defined by four parallel infrastructural strands and boundaries: the Thames and Nine Elms Lane along the northern edge, a Network Rail viaduct at the south border, and a new green pedestrian way lacing through the center. Standing proudly atop a shallow earthen dome, the embassy engages the ground with a monumental thirty-foot-high colonnade at the base of the cube. The open columns refer all the way back to the Athenian origins of democracy. While security concerns are paramount where the building meets the ground, the architecture can and must simultaneously project openness and welcome. The columns that engage the glass cube with the ground, coupled with the secure core wall beyond, accomplish both.

The landscape plan further fuses the embassy to its site. The passages along Nine Elms Lane and the greenway curve around the site perimeter, spiraling inward through the entry pavilions. The crescent-shaped pond perimeter begins this spiraling movement, extending it to the main entry pavilion. From here, a low wall and bench continue this gently spiraling geometry to the north toward and through the consular entry. Form and circumstance are one here. The pond and wall seat give substance to security, but they are first welcoming urban landscape. Choosing one over the other is not architecture. Architecture chooses both.

Woven within the cubic volume are three distinct programs: consular services, agency offices, and building services to support staff. Each engages the spiraling perimeter with a security pavilion. The main entry proceeds into a towering lobby. The core wall of the embassy is here dominated by the Great Seal of the United States and the names of every ambassador to the Court of St. James. The lobby opens onto a terrace that overlooks the pond and landscape toward the Thames. An expansive glass stair opens down to a gallery and meeting halls, with a vast mural by the American artist Mark Bradford stretching across the length and height of the core wall.

Proceeding in the opposite direction from the lobby, one enters the office core. Circulation throughout the office floors continues the spiraling landscape forms of the site upward through a sequence of two-story gardens that ascend through the upper levels of offices. Each of these gardens evokes a region of the United States and connects two floors together with an open stair, inviting spiraling movement upward from floor to floor through the interior gardens. The use of these gardens and their connecting stairs allows staff to move openly between floors, encountering colleagues along the way. Open-plan, highly flexible workspaces and demountable offices are interspersed between the gardens.

The consular entry sweeps into the embassy off the plaza that engages the pedestrian greenway. The great arc of the perimeter site wall and path spirals up to and through the base of the cube, drawing those seeking consular services to the interior. Consular services are separated at the first two levels into citizen and non-citizen. Both lobbies and waiting areas extend as daylight-filled halls along the entire north flank of the embassy. They afford expansive views across the pond in the foreground to the Thames and the city beyond. Sculpted ceilings reinforce the opening of these halls toward the river from the individual transaction stations that line the internal core.

The agenda for the new embassy to become a diplomat for the environment is equally lofty. LEED Platinum and BREEAM Outstanding ratings are the aspiration for this building. However, security requirements obviate many passive strategies that most high-performance buildings rely upon. The result is a building that begins with a substantial energy deficit. Dozens of alternative strategies were developed to evolve the embassy beyond these deficits to the highest levels of performance. The elegant high-performance design of the building skin is central to these results. This skin has inner and outer layers. Each embodies several functionalities. The inner glass envelope is blast resistive, highly insulated, and thermally broken. The outer layer is a polymer skin stretched across staggered aluminum frames. This polymer skin both protects the south, east, and west facades from unwanted solar gain and reduces glare in the workplace, allowing daylight to project deeply into the interior.

The geometry of the building skin is also a magical receptor for light. Light dances in ever-shifting patterns and colors across the curvature of the hourglass-shaped frames. The time of day, weather, and season of the year all play the facades. In the fog, the building skin takes on the grey of the day while rendering it silver. As the sun sets, it transforms the embassy with a golden hue, coming alive in a swiftly shifting texture of last light—first golden, then orange. The stable cubic geometry of the inner envelope and the volume within is the perfect foil to magnify and animate the light of day in all its transformative glory. These are the lasting memories the new embassy provides. Under continual transformation, its elegant, elemental form is a receptor designed to surprise and delight.

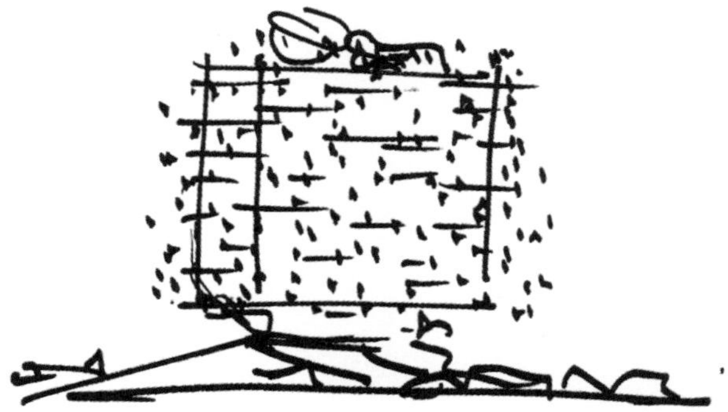

CUBED

Sometimes it is the most constrained design problem that yields the swiftest insight into a compelling and elegant solution. There were literally thousands of constraints enumerated in the dozens of design manuals that were given to the four competition teams. Within weeks of beginning, we settled upon a transparent cubic massing elevated upon an earthen mound. An outer envelope shades the cube.

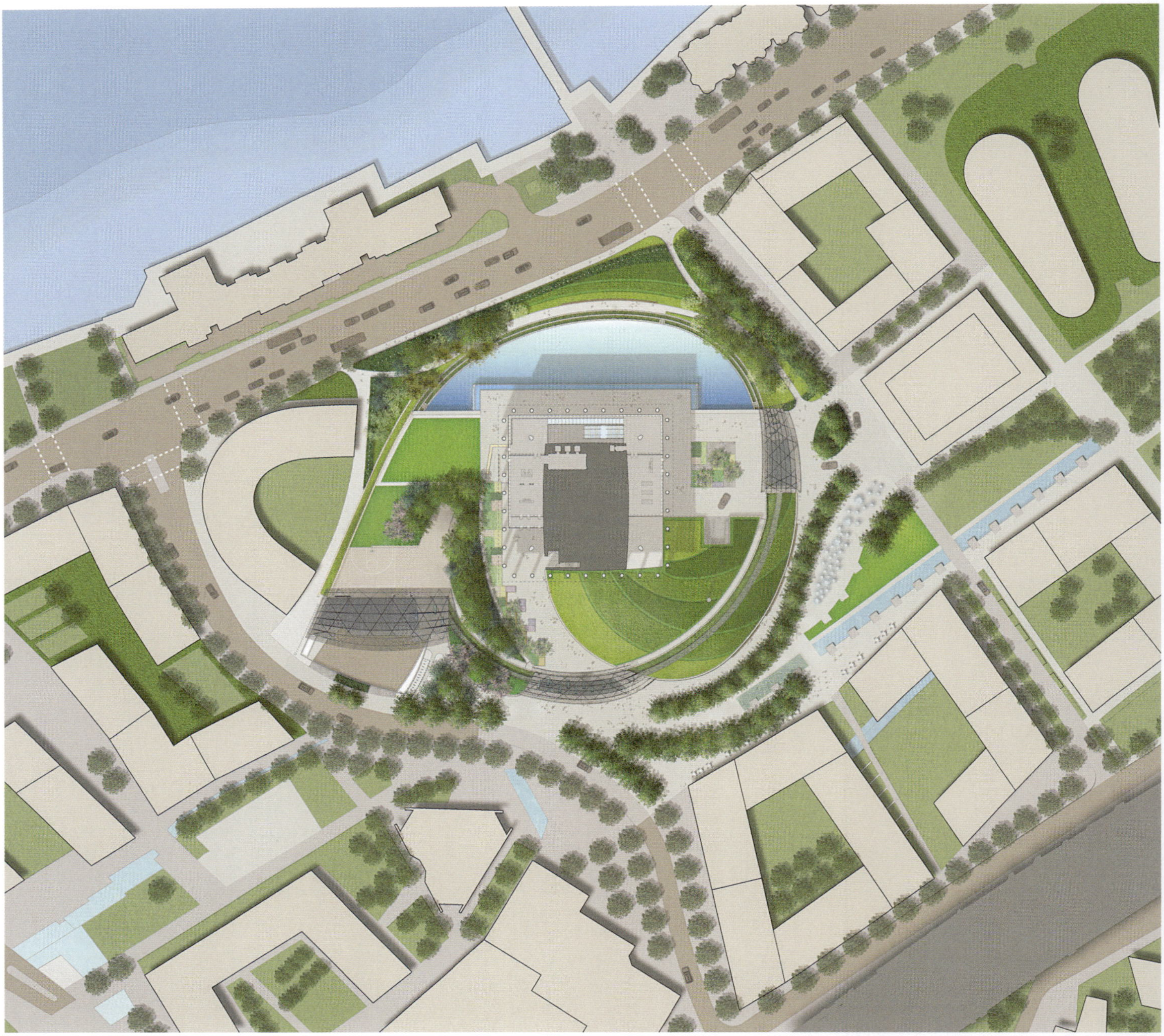

URBANISM

The site is along the south bank of the Thames, midway between Vauxhall and Battersea Bridges. Previously home to an array of single-story warehouses, the Nine Elms development district is anchored and centered by the new embassy. A pedestrian greenway parallel to the river gives order to the urbanism of the rapidly evolving district. The greenway encircles the embassy at grade and spirals up, into, around, and through the cube with several aerial gardens. The landscape is integral to the architecture and urbanism, giving life to the architecture and moments of respite to the city.

Embassy gardens

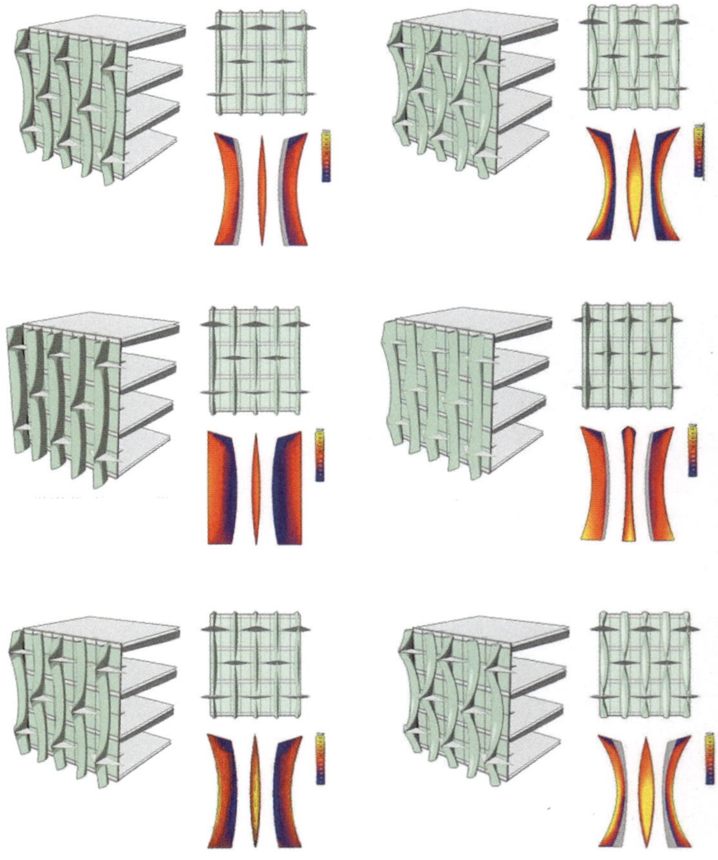

LUCIDITY

The glass envelope is composed of multiple layers of structurally laminated glass to either side of a sealed airspace. Glass types were evaluated for clarity and transparency, coupled with thermal performance and glare reduction. Configuration of the outer envelope was assessed for several qualities through study of alternative geometries. Visual data outputs on the forms themselves were especially useful as we sought to optimize performance and beauty.

VOLUME

The building's form emerged from integration, not addition. Landscape grounds form to place. It both welcomes visitors and secures occupants. Structure rises from deep within the ground and creates the skeletal form through which all the dozens of building systems course. A high-performance glass envelope encloses the frame, protecting occupants and providing daylight and view. A scrim of ETFE wraps an aluminum frame, protecting the interior from glare and unwanted solar gain. Aerial gardens spiral up from the ground, connecting floor levels.

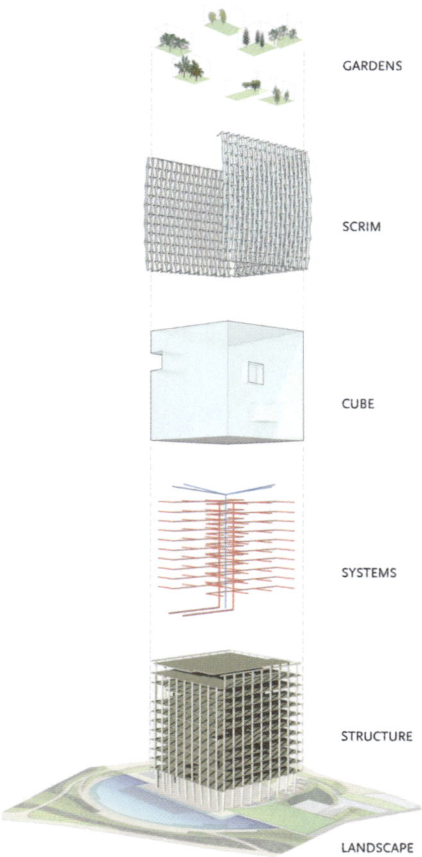

GARDENS

Gardens are everywhere at the embassy, inside and out. They encircle the exterior, drawing the new development district within its orbit. A pathway along Nine Elms Lane invites the passerby to walk along the curving arc of the pond, between the embassy and the Thames. That walk emerges at a new plaza, with a curving bench facing the central greenway. Several two-story gardens connect floors within the embassy and encourage meandering vertical passage though work areas outside of the central elevator and stair core. Each interior garden is designed to anchor a meeting and conference area, with plantings that evoke American landscapes.

MULTIFUNCTION

Space planning in embassies was previously based on fixed-in-place offices and partitions. Floors here are designed with rapid reconfiguration, visibility, and access to daylight as central principles. Demountable glass-enclosed offices and work areas line the core. Open-plan work stations reside in the zone between these offices and the perimeter, with daylight flooding the full depth of the interior. The main elevator and stair lobby opens to exterior views to the south. Hallways around the core always end with views to the exterior, providing orientation. In addition to conference rooms at the interior gardens, casual meeting areas are arrayed throughout the offices.

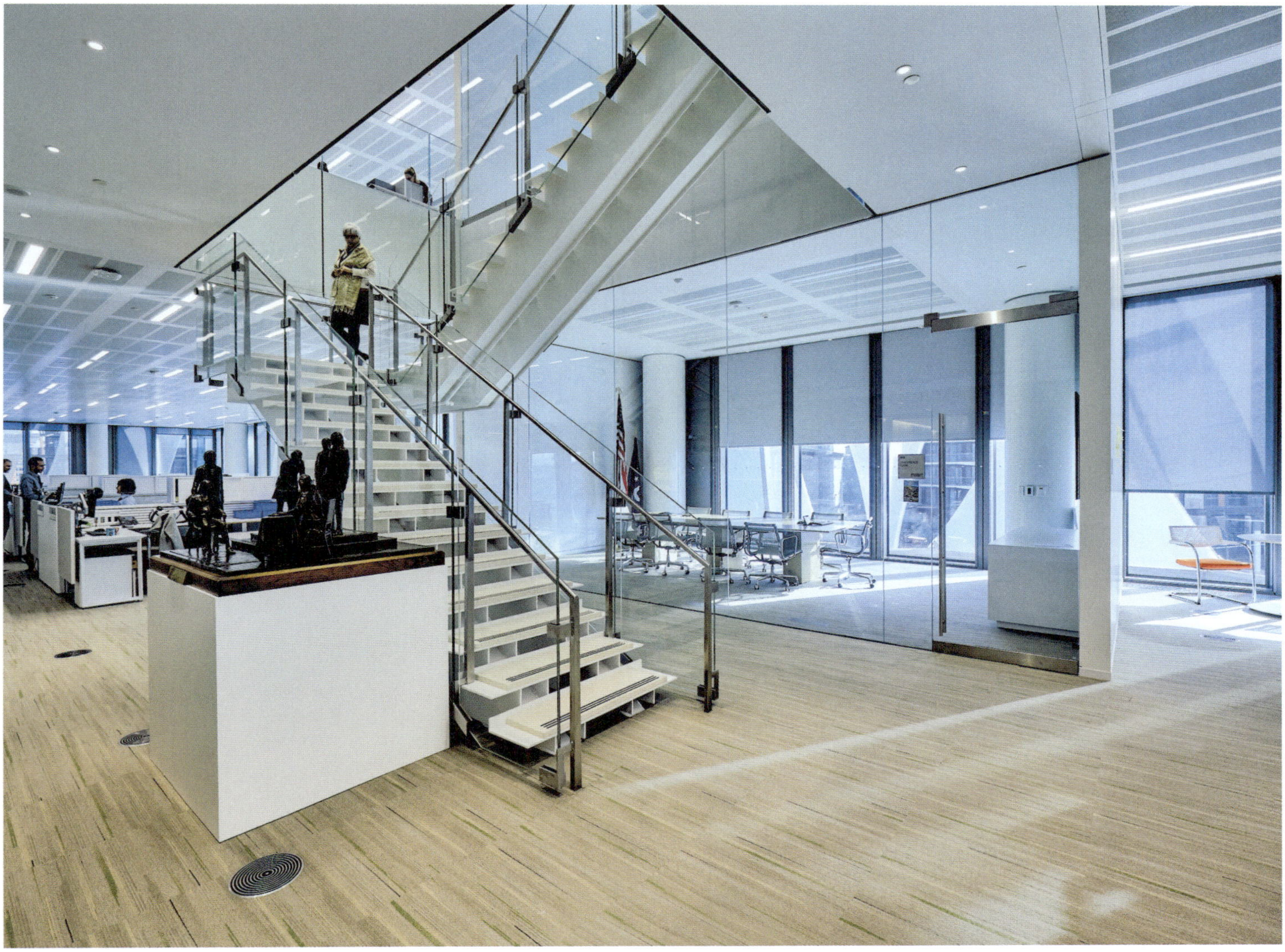

ARTFUL

Art is central to the cultural message embassies can convey. The US Department of State's Art in Embassies program has long promoted the cultural exchange that is part of the American mission overseas. In many instances, art has been added to long-finished buildings. Here, art was integral to the design, with the ground level of the architectural core envisioned as a canvas, inside and out. The cultural dialogue begins at the exterior where the American artist Sean Scully's *Golden Frieze* creates painterly fields of color with tiny mosaic tiles. In the entry lobby, British artist Rachel Whiteread's *Flat Pack House* unfolds across the two-story space. Just around the corner, facing the Thames River, the American artist Mark Bradford's monumental painting titled *We the People* grounds the architectural core.

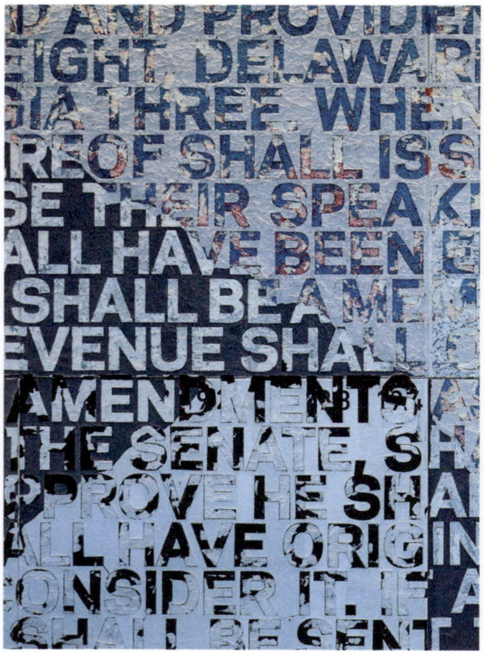

Image Credits

Drawings and photographs in this book are from KieranTimberlake's collection, except as noted below.

Cellophane House
Photographs by Peter Aaron/OTTO: pages 10, 15; Christopher Leaman, 21; Michael Moran/OTTO, page 21; Universal Services Associates, Inc.: page 14; Albert Vecerka/Esto: pages 17–19

Brockman Hall for Physics
Photographs by Peter Aaron/OTTO: pages 22, 29 (middle right, bottom left), 30, 33 (bottom left), 34 (top right); Paul Hester: page 29 (top right, middle left), 32 (top right); Formwork drawing for columns at Brockman Hall by Frederick Langford: page 33; Michael Moran/OTTO: pages 27, 28, 29 (top, bottom right), 34 (bottom left); Red Wing Aerials: page 26; Rice University: pages 34–35

Morse and Ezra Stiles Colleges
Photographs courtesy Manuscripts and Archives, Yale University Library: Eero Saarinen with model of Morse and Ezra Stiles Colleges circa 1958: page 36; Aerial view of courtyards at Samuel F. B. Morse and Ezra Stiles Colleges, Yale University: page 42, Morse or Stiles College interior: page 46 (top left), Costantino Nivola sculptures at Morse and Stiles Colleges: page 47 (bottom); Site Plan drawing by OLIN: page 44 (top); Photographs by Peter Aaron/OTTO: pages 44 (bottom left), 45, 47 (middle), 49; Richard Barnes: pages 46 (top right, bottom right), 47 (top), 48

Charles David Keeling Apartments
Photographs by David Harrison: pages 55, 56, 62; Tim Griffith: pages 50, 57, 63

Quaker Meeting House and Arts Center
Photograph courtesy Library of Congress, Prints & Photographs Division, HABS, HABS PA, 6687-13: Race Street Friends Meeting House, Philadelphia, 1999: page 69; Michael Moran/OTTO: pages 64, 72 (top), 73–77

Center City Building
Photographs by Peter Aaron: pages 78, 82, 84, 85, 86 (top, bottom); UNCC Wade Bruton: pages 86 (middle right), 87; Sharon Dowell Art, LLC: page 86 (middle left); Hannah Barnhardt: page 87 (middle right)

Edgar N. Putman Event Pavilion
Photographs by Michael Moran/OTTO: pages 88, 93, 95; Halkin Mason Photography: pages 96–97; Rusty Kennedy/AP: page 99

Dilworth Park
Photographs courtesy Center City District: Aerial view of Dilworth Plaza: page 106 (bottom); Ice Skaters in Dilworth Park: page 112 (bottom left); Courtesy City of Philadelphia: Section Through the Engine House of the Center Square Water Works: page 104 (bottom right), View of City Hall from the northwest, 1938: page 105; Courtesy of the Free Library of Philadelphia: Philadelphia, PA.: Dutch edition of the first plan for Philadelphia, devised by William Penn and Thomas Holme in 1682 and printed in Amsterdam in 1684: page 104 (bottom left); Courtesy of the Pennsylvania Academy of the Fine Arts, Philadelphia, Pennsylvania: John Lewis Krimmel-Fourth of July in Centre Square: page 104 (top); Courtesy Historical Society of Pennsylvania: Views of Construction of New City Building stereograph, c.1875: page 110 (top), Fourth of July Celebration in Center Square watercolor, 1819: page 112 (top); Photographs by James Ewing/OTTO: pages 100, 107–109, 111 (top); Public assembly in Dilworth Park, Courtesy OLIN: page 113

Pound Ridge House
Topographic drawing courtesy of Reed Hilderbrand: page 114; Photographs by Peter Aaron/OTTO: pages 124–125

Consortium for Building Energy Innovation
Photographs by Michael Moran: pages 128, 134, 136 (top right, bottom right), 139–141; Imagery ©2019 Google, Map data ©2019 Google: page 130; Stocktrek Images, Inc./Alamy Stock Photo: page 133

River House Renewal
Photographs by Michael Moran: pages 142, 148, 149, 151, 152, 153, 155, 156 (top); Peter Vanderwarker: page 154 (top)

Ortlieb's Bottling house
Photographs by Michael Moran: pages 158, 164–165; Courtesy Ortlieb Brewing Company: pages 162, 164–165; Christopher Leaman: pages 164–165, 168–169; Jason Fulford: pages 164; Zahner/Tex Jernigan: pages 166–167

Congregation Rodeph Shalom Renovation and Addition
Photographs by James Ewing/OTTO: pages 172, 176, 177, 179, 180 (top, middle), 181, 183, 184 (top), 185; Graydon Wood, courtesy of Rodeph Shalom: page 184 (bottom)

High Horse Ranch
Photographs by Kyle Jeffers: pages 186, 191, 194, 195, 197; Tim Griffith: pages 190, 193, 198–199; Madrone tree photograph by Tom Dempsey/Photoseek.com: page 198; Madrone bark photo by Brian Michelsen/Creative Commons: page 199

Pendleton West
Photographs by Kimberly Maroon: page 200; Michael Moran/OTTO: pages 205, 206, 207, 210, 212, 213; Landscape drawing by Michael Van Valkenburgh: page 206

Engineering Research Center
Photographs by Peter Aaron/OTTO: pages 218-221, 225 (bottom), 227; Warren Jagger: pages 214, 225 (middle, top), 226 (top); Special thanks to Spencer Finch for the *Garden in the Brain* artworks depicted in these photographs

US Embassy in London
Photographs by Richard Bryant: pages 239 (center), 243 (bottom); KieranTimberlake/Matthew Krissel: pages 228, 233, 235, 237, 239–242, 243 (top); Aerial photograph of Nine Elms courtesy Studio amd: page 234; Aerial photo of London Embassy courtesy Jason Hawkes: page 238 (bottom); Construction photo courtesy Bureau of Overseas Buildings Operations: page 238 (top); Special thanks to artists Rachel Whiteread, *Flat Pack House*, Sean Scully, *Golden Frieze*, and Mark Bradford, *We the People* depicted in these photographs

Design by KieranTimberlake
Book Team: Stephen Kieran, James Timberlake, Carly Regn, Dan Preston, Andrea Calabretta, Elizabeth Fite, and Carin Whitney

Additional Photo Credits
Photographs courtesy Chris Leaman: pages 6, 246
Slipcase: Peter Aaron/OTTO, Richard Bryant, Tim Griffith, Chris Leaman, Michael Moran/OTTO

Library of Congress Cataloging-in-Publication Data is available
ISBN: 978-1-58093-554-8

10 9 8 7 6 5 4 3 2 1
Printed in China

The Monacelli Press
6 West 18th Street
New York, New York 10011
www.monacellipress.com